THE POWER OF
BELIEFS

7 Beliefs that will change your life

Published by Brolga Publishing Pty Ltd
ABN 46 063 962 443
PO Box 12544
A'Beckett St
Melbourne, VIC, 8006
Australia

email: markzocchi@brolgapublishing.com.au

National Library of Australia Cataloguing-in-Publication entry
    Author: Schnabel, Rik
    Title: The power of beliefs : 7 beliefs that will change your life /
    ISBN: 9781922175434 (paperback)
    Subjects: Thought and thinking
              Self-consciousness (Awareness)
              Self-actualization (Psychology)
    Dewey Number: 153.42

Printed in Australia
Cover design & typesetting by Wanissa Somsuphangsri

BE PUBLISHED

Publish through a successful publisher. National Distribution, Dennis Jones & Associates
International Distribution to the United Kingdom, North America.
Sales Representation to South East Asia
Email: markzocchi@brolgapublishing.com.au

THE POWER OF
BELIEFS

7 Beliefs that will change your life

RIK SCHNABEL

YOU MADE THIS HAPPEN

If you wondered how this book came to be in your hands right now, at this very moment in time, look no further than your beliefs. Few things happen by chance.

You made this moment happen.

Possibly what lead you to pick up this book was something you saw on the cover or a word you read that triggered something, a memory perchance — or it somehow spoke to you at a much deeper level. How it called out to you or how you called it to you is not important.

My guess is that for you, there is something profound in this book, something life shifting. As is true in life, your next quest is to find your next step — the one that will show itself to you in the next corridor, in the next passage or in the next conversation. It is there for you to discover. You just have to open your mind a little and trust your intuition.

Can I make one simple suggestion before we progress further? Write on this page, the very date that you started reading this book because I assure you, you will remember this day with fond memories, because this is the start of something special. Don't ask how or why right now — it's not time to know these answers. Perhaps this is when you find out who you really are or who you really can be, your highest potential that has been with you all along. Today you found it.

Today's Date: ....

To discuss engaging Rik Schnabel for speaking events, workshops, training or one on one coaching.

Contact rebecca.spencer@lifebeyondlimits.com.au

or *Life Beyond Limits Pty Ltd*. on +613 8669 1121

www.LifeBeyondLimits.com.au

For more information about *Life Beyond Limits, Career and Life Mastery* program (CALM) —

visit: http://www.lifebeyondlimits.com.au/calm-i.html

CONTENTS

*Your **Beliefs** become your Thoughts*
Your Thoughts become your Words
Your Words become Actions
Your Actions become your Habits
Your Habits become your Values
*Your Values become your **Destiny**.*

— Mahatma Gandhi.

DEDICATION

For those who have made the conscious choice to evolve, this book is for you. If you desire to make your mark on the world, your beliefs will determine your results — choose them wisely.

I also dedicate this book to the courageous ones, the great ones, the smart ones and the unique ones who whole-heartedly committed to their evolutionary beliefs.

ACKNOWLEDGEMENTS

To my family and my dearest friends who believed in me and encouraged me to voice this work — thank you, thank you, thank you. In the beginning it wasn't easy, as my message seemed too left of field. Thanks to your encouragement, my message is fast becoming mainstream and it is helping to change the way the world thinks. The world is awakening.

This body of work is representative of much of what we do with the help of our company, *Life Beyond Limits*. Your faith in us helped us to keep going when the odds were against us. For this we thank you. You know who you are.

On a personal level, a massive and eternal thank you must go to my earth angel and my gorgeous wife Rebecca for your support, coaching, and life shifting intuitive guidance. I know I can become totally focused and as such a right pain in the butt, particularly when I'm writing or preparing for my talks, trainings and seminars. Thank you for your understanding, eternal patience and taking the time to read my incessant drafts and redrafts. We've grown so much over the years and for all that you are and have become, I love you. You are my life partner. To my heart's delight, my daughters Zoe and Sienna, you are the reason your mother and I do what we do. We want you both to learn from our mistakes, our insights and become the best you can be. We hope this knowledge will be our empowering legacy, our gift to you and your world.

Thank you to my dear friend and our brilliant audio man at *SoundStage*, Warren French. I appreciate our inspirational conversations and your dedication to record our talks, events and deliver our audio products via www.DigitalWisdom.eu, these allow our message to reach those beyond our physical reach. Thank you for your patience as my passion to share this content has us often go over the allotted time at our events. To Warren's wife Cheryl, his daughter Erica and sons Allan and Patrick, thank you for letting him play with us.

To our *Life Beyond Limits Career and Life Mastery* students and our *Life Team*, our extended family, who have courageously allowed us to train and advance you. Those teachings allowed me to further develop these concepts and insights — thank you, I am eternally grateful.

I would also like to thank my good friends and neighbours on the Sapphire Coast, Di Marshall and John Stewart, for reading through my first draft and offering me your wonderful thoughts and beliefs. Thanks to Nikki Barrett for editing the first chapter. Thank you to Julie Capaldo, Senior Editor at Brolga Publishing for her helpful editing and easy to follow proof markings and Wanissa Somsuphangsri for your putting all the pieces together to make this book happen. So many people will have been drawn to this book because of the cover which I love so much, so very special thanks to Wanissa Somsuphangsri for your brilliant design work – thank you! Thanks of course, must always go to my publisher Mark Zocchi for publishing my books and for his continual belief in my message.

Finally and most importantly, a huge thank you must go to you for following your guidance to purchase this book. I can only trust that my words were well chosen and help you to create a *Life Beyond Limits*. I look forward to hearing about your courageous adventures and your evolvement.

INTRODUCTION — BELIEF, FAITH AND TRUST

Beliefs cause wars and they can bring about peace. They will make us cry just as easily as they will incite us to laugh. In fact, our beliefs determine everything we can do and everything we cannot. The beliefs of our presidents, our prime ministers and leaders determine the state of our nations, their beliefs hold enormous power, as do ours. Yet little time, if any at all, is invested in determining our beliefs or changing them. This book will give you the tools and the insights you need to move your career and your life forward. You will know your beliefs more intimately and you will also discover how you can change them.

Beliefs are invisible programs running in the back of our minds that controls when we think, how we think and what we think. While some people are aware that these programs are influencing their decisions and shaping their lives, most don't have a clue how to change them. Unchecked, they can self-sabotage careers and businesses. They can degenerate health and destroy relationships or they can become our greatest ally. This book gives you the critical missing piece. It is "*Version 5.0*" thinking and it comes with a whole new set of beliefs that will powerfully and positively impact every area of your life.

It's no surprise that the large majority of our beliefs come from our parents. We're unconscious of most of our beliefs that run our invisible programs on autopilot. They influence our lives profoundly and often subtlety. Some beliefs serve us well and some do not serve us at all. If we possess one or more of the *seven viral beliefs* (outlined in Chapters 12 to 18), they will negate our dreams and desires. In the following pages you will learn to understand your beliefs and in the final chapters you will learn how to change them.

Looking backwards, just one generation ago, to our parents — the Version of software that was installed into their brains may have served them well, but does their thinking, their belief system serve you? If our parents' brains had a Version of software installed, what Version would that be? *Version 1.0* or *Version 2.0* perhaps? The more compelling question is: Would *you* be happy to install your parents' software directly into your brain? Would it serve you today? Would you thrive or just survive in today's world?

Please understand that it is NOT my intention to criticise our parents but to ask the question: *Would you accept your parent's thinking into your brain, without question?* Maybe you already have? I certainly did and it caused me four decades of hardships and conflict.

When I was a child, matters of the world were very different to my parent's pre-World War II world. My quest through this book is to expand your thinking and perhaps even offer you a mindware upgrade.

If your business, your career, your relationships, your health or your life are not where you want them to be right now, then look no further than your beliefs. A mindware upgrade might be exactly what is needed.

Is it time to review our education system? While our traditional educationalists teach us to *learn* and *remember*, we are seldom taught how to install a Version of thinking that is current and will have us thrive in this changing world. We are not taught *how* to think. More so, we are not taught to think like successful adults, entrepreneurs, business people and leaders. Could it be old thinking to simply put more data into our heads without upgrading the software? Perhaps we're jamming too much into an archaic hard drive filled with age-old viruses? What if it's a software upgrade that's really needed? A new way of thinking might be exactly what is required? It was Einstein who said: "We cannot solve our problems with the same *level of thinking* that created them." Einstein was definitely onto something seriously transformational.

I believe that many of the problems in the world today can be solved — if we can just upgrade our mindsets. In this so-called advanced age, so many people are still locked in by the boundary conditions of their forefathers' thinking. They may have aspirational level ten dreams though unfortunately they possess level nine or less thinking.

The aspirations of tomorrow and the problems of today cannot be solved with the Version of software we used in the seventies, the eighties or even the nineties for that matter. That software is redundant today. The world is vastly different. Our world operates at much faster speeds and is more complex than it ever was. The masses need an upgrade merely to cope.

Between surfing and writing, I am a teacher and a trainer of the neural sciences, an accredited trainer of Neuro-Linguistic Programming (NLP) and Life Coaching. On writing this introduction and according to my *Coaching and Training Log*, I've clocked up 7,408 coaching hours and 8,676 training hours. In this time of working as a brain untrainer with thousands of people around the world, I have come to realise some golden gems that I hope will liberate you from the *seven viral beliefs* that imprison us. These seven beliefs choke us and moderate our efforts to create our greatest aspirations. They are responsible for stopping us from growing our businesses, denying us the opportunity to express our love, negating our life's dreams and suppressing our passions. We have words for the outcomes of these *seven viral beliefs* — they are; *self-sabotage, blame, guilt, anger, sadness* and *fear*. Why do I call these beliefs *viral*? Because like a virus, they permeate our operating system, they harm most everything we do; they block our potential and stifle our ability to function effectively. Helping you to get beyond the negating results of these *seven viral beliefs* is what inspired me to write this book.

My aim is to get you to breakthrough, to go beyond your limits and discover what greatness can come from you. Should this book help you to realise your dreams, that would be worth every hour I invested in writing it. It would be the ultimate gift to us both.

When you get beyond your limits, it's almost magical and certainly empowering. Ten years ago, I founded our company *Life Beyond Limits* and I cannot even find the words to share with you the joy that I get from watching people remove these seven debilitating beliefs. As I witness this miracle in a person, it often appears like I am observing two completely different people. The joy of this experience is what led me to start our training institution and our coaching company. Though I often ask myself, what are we *really* doing as a service to the wider community — I believe it's all about upgrading people's belief systems to give them the *belief, faith* and *trust* in themselves to realise their dreams. Helping them to become more conscious and make better *conscious* decisions is where it all begins. So let us begin this transformational journey together.

1

ARE YOUR BELIEFS
REALLY YOURS?

The tiniest of tiniest fleas can jump up to 33 centimetres (13 inches) high. While that might not be much of an achievement by your standards, it's approximately 200 times their own height. Imagine if you could do that? By comparison, it would be like a 182 centimetre (six foot) human jumping a 90-story building! An amazing feat by anyone's standards.

When we speak about our highest potential, what is truly possible for us — for you and for me? I believe few know what that actually is. This is largely due to the *seven viral beliefs* working quietly in the background of our thinking. These blind us to our unlimited potential and have conditioned us to thinking we're less when, we know at some level, we're actually more. I will reserve those *seven viral beliefs* until later in this book as the lead up to these beliefs is far more important right now and you need to learn a little more about how you have come to this very moment before we advance your future. So how did we learn to limit ourselves?

YOUR BELIEFS TELL YOU HOW HIGH YOU CAN JUMP

Over the years there have been numerous experiments involving fleas and their amazing ability to jump *and* to become conditioned. One such experiment involved placing a bunch of fleas into a jar. The moment the fleas' feet touched the bottom of the jar, they immediately and automatically jumped out of the jar. Again they were placed in the jar but this time a lid was quickly placed on top. After three days the lid was removed and the fleas no longer jumped out of the jar. In only three days they were conditioned to jump just short of the lid. Profoundly, the fleas would never jump out of the jar again. They were trained for life! More so, because the fleas' offspring modelled their parent's behaviour, the next generation would also not be able to jump out of the jar.[1]

As humans, there is no jar. There is no lid. There is just an invisible cap called *limiting beliefs*. *Limiting beliefs* are at the core of what restricts our potential and is the glue that keeps us stuck in conditioned patterns. Chances are these limiting patterns will be invisibly driven by one if not all of the *seven viral beliefs*.

I THOUGHT, MY THOUGHTS WERE MY OWN

What I am about to share with you might sound crazy — it certainly does to me, now! For most of my life I truly believed that my thoughts were my own. It wasn't until I turned 40 that I came to realise that my voice was my parent's voice. I was running off *their* belief systems — I was conditioned to *their* limitations and so I was recreating *their* life. At moments of crisis, I heard their words, "There, there, it will all be okay," and it never was.

There was an invisible rudder that navigated me without my knowledge and a lid sat on top of me called 'limitation'. In that moment of realisation, I knew that if I wanted the life I dreamed for myself, I needed to upgrade my mind's software to a more advanced Version.

I used to get so angry; at some level I knew I could be more. The visions I held for my life were frustratingly unachievable. I soon came to realise that my aspirations were *level ten* dreams though my thinking was running off *level three* or less, software. It was a recipe for failure, after failure, after failure, after failure. I was seriously banging my head against a wall. My frustrations led me to search for answers. I then entered a new doorway into the realm of psychology, neuro-linguistic programming and metaphysics. I quickly realised that our beliefs provide the very reasons that most of us never get what we want. It's the same reason that fleas reduce how high they can jump and in so doing, reduce their potential — no wonder they bite! They're just as frustrated as we are!

My parents who I love unconditionally and am eternally grateful to, were post war immigrants, trying to make a go of it in their newly found home in Australia. They had it tough hitting up against their lid. Their mindsets served them well during the war, where they had to literally do almost anything to survive. World War II ended May 1945. I was born 16 years later in my parents' new home in Australia and their post-depression and post-war belief systems were still running them. Their "I don't have enough…" beliefs had them hording and storing jars, containers, food, materials in a three-bedroom home on a quarter acre block in suburban Victoria, Australia.

Our home became a storage facility with wall-to-wall cupboards. Our small backyard was cluttered and looked like a Denpasar market. Stacks on stacks, wall-to-wall. If it wasn't for my siblings and me, I'm sure my dad would have built more storage underground and perhaps even an air-raid shelter, just in case. Even though the war was over, the threat was still nestled deeply in their neurology. It revealed itself through their words that they learned during wartime, their actions and how they lived. Their "war language" told me that they I had to "fight to survive" and to "not trust anyone." They also told me "life was cruel" and that I would have to "work hard just to pay the bills." Though for me, I wanted a more prosperous life, nevertheless my parents' impoverished beliefs would not allow for prosperity. When times change, our thinking needs to change too.

The world today has greatly changed from post-World War II thinking and while we once believed that *bigger is better*, today our greener thinking has turned us around completely — some now believe that *less is more* and we need to be more globally responsible with our ambitions. What once took a whole floor of computers can now be done on our smart phones. The thinking that engineered the technology revolution came from a whole new level of thought, and an upgraded belief system. So how did we evolve and how do we evolve our thinking?

SOME PEOPLE'S THINKING IS A CAVE, WHILE OTHERS IS A CASTLE

Some wonder why their life is exactly as it is right now. What caused it to be so? Quietly working in the background of every thought and behind every action lives an invisible series of beliefs. They'll drive us to success or into a brick wall if we're not careful! If we're not happy about the road we're on, then perhaps it's time to change the driver. The driver is our beliefs. Change the beliefs and we change our life! As Gandhi rightly stated, "Our beliefs become our destiny!"

Akin to a religion, what we *believe* about people determines how we interact with them. What we *believe* about money predicates how much or how little we make. What we *believe* about our value as a person determines how much money we get to keep. What we *believe* about how attractive we are determines how we approach others and whom we choose as our partners. As Robert Anton Wilson said, "What the believer believes, the prover proves." What we *believe* we can or can't do is right, unless of course we change our beliefs. Beliefs are the keystones of our lives and form the very architecture of our thinking. Some people's thinking is a cave, while other's is a castle.

So where is all this heading? In short, to wherever you want it to go. If you want the life you are living now then you're likely heading in the right direction, you're doing fine. But if you want to create the life of your unrealised dreams, then get off the road you are on. It is time to upgrade your thinking to a whole new level of beliefs. By the time you have finished this book, you are going to be much wiser about the science and psychology of dream creation. More so, you will have a bigger and better picture of how your inner world impacts your outer world. This book's aim is to put you back in the driver seat of your life.

To get the most from this book and its research, I'm going to ask you to be courageous as self-realisation can sometimes be a little challenging, perhaps even seem harsh. Realising that a series of beliefs can be the very cause of pain in our lives, can for some, be too big a pill to swallow, particularly as we realise that our thoughts are not even our own. I have found that this can cause us to become a bit angry, for some, very angry. Particularly as we recognise that the large majority of our beliefs were accepted into our reality without us even realising.

WE'VE BEEN PROGRAMMED TO THINK THE WAY WE DO

Have we been programmed to think the way we do? *Yes* is the answer and *relentlessly* is the frequency. For most of us, we are creating what our parents want — after all, most of our beliefs are actually theirs. The list of *belief builders* may as well start at the beginning of our lives, with our parents or carers. Sometimes those carers included the TV. So the list of influencers can extend to advertisers, the characters in your favourite television show, the media as a whole, and extend to governments and authority figures. This is our wake-up call, no one is to blame, not even you. Though in awakening, we now finally have the chance to learn from our beliefs and choose new ones.

Those children, who have grown to become a parent will upon hearing themselves, realise that their beliefs, sound like their mum or dad's beliefs. Some for the first time realise how much of their parents' beliefs have been accepted as their own. If we provided a life education for parents, or even children for that matter, could we change the very course of history? Had we coached Klara and Alois Hitler, Adolf's parents, would we have averted World War II? If Mark Chapman's father, David had changed the beliefs that lead to the physical abuse of his son — would John Lennon still be alive penning songs?

Our beliefs are the most powerful filters in our thinking. Our beliefs create biases, convictions and determine everything we do. Our beliefs are our thoughts in motion and therefore influence our emotions. How good or bad we feel are outcomes of our beliefs. One bad flight might have us believing that air travel is dangerous and may have us choosing never to fly again and so limiting our adventurous spirit. Just like one long and painful labour may have us avoiding sex, or our partner perhaps.

The dictionary defines *belief* as *confidence, faith* and *trust*. I suggest that these three words determine everything we do! In order to do anything, we need to firstly believe it can be done, or we would not even attempt it.

CHANGE IS NOT BAD — IT'S JUST DIFFERENT

The vital role that our beliefs play in our lives cannot be understated. Some people upon reading this book will do an about face on many of their beliefs. They are the courageous ones who will become the liberated ones. Though change at first typically feels foreign and some people when they experience this new feeling called *change*, will call it *bad*. It's not *bad* — it's just *different*. This however makes sense why the elephant that is at first chained and then tied with rope, knows its boundaries and will not test or break the rope. So too for the long serving prisoner, rehabilitation can feel harder than committing another crime to return to the jailhouse. Crazy as it may sound, this is the power of our beliefs. Regardless of what they are, we will mostly defend our beliefs, even if they *don't* serve us. And if they don't serve us then our beLIEfs are lies! I personally found it ironic that the word "lie" is found in the middle of "belief."

The dictionary also suggests that beliefs are, *Confidence in the existence or truth of something*. Though I'm guessing that you once believed in Santa, do you still believe in him? Do you still have confidence in him being real? Chances are, as an adult, you no longer believe. So beliefs once thought to be true can become no longer true for us.

ARE BELIEFS TRUTHS OR LIES?

Beliefs are two things at once. They are truths and they are lies. They are truths because we of course *believe* our beliefs. We'll defend them regardless of whether they serve us or not. As Richard Bach, author of "Jonathon Livingston Seagull" wrote, "If you argue for your limitations you get to keep them." History has proved that we'll argue for our beliefs, even to the death, Adolf Hitler and Saddam Hussein are just two that spring to mind.

The truth of the matter is that our beliefs are certainly powerful and fateful, though once changed, they become by comparison, lies. Or were they lies in the very first instance? What you are about to discover is that some of your most fundamental beliefs that really do determine the course of your life are actually fabrications. In coaching we call the process of fabrications and justifications "installations." Page-by-page you will come to realise that many of your beliefs we're installed into your brain by something or someone other than you. The challenge is working out which beliefs are the *lies* and not serving you, which ones are *true* and which ones would you like to become true.

If thoughts hold the power to influence our actions, then beliefs are the nucleus of that power. When we are truly unleashed, when our beliefs are well designed to deliver our maximum potential, how much power do we really have? And to what extent do our beliefs have influence over this power?

What if you completely removed all the limiting beliefs from your neurology? What if you removed all the useless conditioning that placed a lid on you? What can you truly do? What will you do? The late astronomer Carl Sagan had a wonderful formula for measuring the truthfulness of any belief. He said, "Extraordinary claims demand extraordinary evidence."

I am going to make an extraordinary claim right here and now. By the end of this book, you will be able to identify the beliefs that create your problems and remove them. In doing so, many of your problems will dissolve. Adopt the beliefs of the super successful and you too can be super successful. It can be that easy. My question is, *Why do so many people make it so hard?*

2

THE EVOLUTION OF BELIEFS

There's an old saying, "Knowledge is power" but is it true? Within our vernacular there are many sayings such as this one, which are so easily accepted into our belief systems. Particularly when we continue to hear them stated by so-called *educated* people and more-so when those people hold status and authority. You would imagine that Charles H. Duell, the *Commissioner* of the US Office of Patents was such an authority. Back in 1899 he said, "Everything that can be invented has been invented." According to the US Office of Patents there has been 7,951,655 Utility Patents issued alone from 1900 to 2013[1]. He sure got that wrong.

Even a software genius and once the world's richest man for over a decade would have all the knowledge and credibility necessary to make the following prediction. Bill Gates, Co-Founder and Chairman of *Microsoft Corporation*® once said, "640K ought to be enough for anyone," and Lord Kelvin, president of the Royal Society in 1895 was quoted as saying, "Heavier-than air flying machines are impossible."

Intelligent people are just as capable of speaking through their limiting beliefs as their non-intelligent counterparts. Eventually we see their limitations, particularly when we have hindsight as our sage. So is it true that *knowledge is power*? Knowing you've got cancer is not what I would call *power*. Knowing your business is about to collapse is hardly power. Discovering that your partner just cheated on you will instead feel disempowering. Although, with powerful beliefs and enduring focus, you can soon discover how to solve all of these problems and *that* is truly powerful.

KNOWLEDGE IS NOT POWER — POWERFUL BELIEFS ARE

We can be the *Trivial Pursuit*® whiz — we can know lots of things about a lot of stuff, but it doesn't mean we're powerful. An IQ like Einstein's of 160 plus and a bunch of crappy beliefs coupled with the need for power might just be the makings of a dictator, a scam artist or perhaps a modern day Al Capone! Knowledge is not necessarily power — powerful beliefs are power.

Today the large majority of the western world can access endless knowledge, yet collectively, we're still not empowered. So knowledge alone is not the answer — knowledge can be useful but it does NOT necessarily give us power.

It seems that no matter how hard we try, no matter how much knowledge we pack into our skulls, some people will never get what they want from life. They'll resolve this frustrating situation by saying, "It wasn't meant to be" or "It is obviously not my destiny" or perhaps they conclude, "I don't deserve success." Their beliefs will stop them from ever trying again. Knowledge is helpful, though empowering beliefs are true power. Though today it seems that the large majority believe that climbing to the top of the mountain of knowledge is the pinnacle. This belief has us setting our sights to know it all, when we are much better served by realising that the purpose of knowledge is to evolve.

OUR OVER THINKING IS CREATING 'LOGICAL ERRORS'

In this abundant universe, we can have whatever we want as long as we're prepared to invest in empowering beliefs and remove those limiting beliefs that get in our way. Otherwise, we'll rationalise our non-results away and our failures will all make sense — they logically and typically do. This is what I call a *logical error*. Due to intellect having such a high value in our societies, we aim to think through our problems without addressing the very beliefs that have caused them to be. It will have us over think almost everything.

I have come to discover that the reasons at the core of this *logical error* are found in the *seven viral beliefs*. Later in the book I'll detail those seven beliefs that typically have us getting in our own way. Though these beliefs are a result of the specific Version of *neurological software* that actually runs our thinking and determines our beliefs. It's not that our thinking *per se* is at fault; it's the fault of the software that runs the very thinking itself. To simplify this and enhance your understanding, I'm calling this model of thought, 'The Evolution of Beliefs'. It will explain why it is important to our evolution to upgrade our neural networks to get what we want from our lives and remove our frustrations.

21ST CENTURY SUCCESS IS LIMITED WITH VERSION 4.0 OR BELOW — THE WORLD HAS CHANGED

This model is easy to understand by thinking of our brain in the same way in which we think of a computer, it answers the aforementioned conundrum of why people don't get what they want, simply. For example, can you imagine creating the sophisticated spreadsheets, word files, *YouTube®* videos and artwork that we can so easily produce with our computers today, using the old DOS programs of yesteryear? It's just not possible — not for me anyway. Yet that's precisely what many frustrated individuals are trying to do, when they aim to create success in a *Version 5.0* world with *Version 4.0* or less thinking.

Let's run another analogy. If we possessed Sir Richard Branson's Version of thinking with its associated beliefs, then chances are we would be able to create our own Version of *Virgin®*, if that took our fancy. Of course we may have to allow those beliefs to draw to them the necessary skills and connections too. The point that I am making here, is what stops others from becoming a billionaire is NOT present in Richard Branson's Version of beliefs — wealth is so much easier. As the late Jim Rohn once said, "If someone hands you a million dollars, best you become a millionaire or you won't get to keep the money." Our manifestations are merely a result of our current belief systems. This will make much more sense as we unpack *The Evolution of Beliefs*. Though we're not there yet, because there is a bigger and more important question that must be answered first.

IS OUR THINKING A VIRUS OR DID WE INSTALL IT?

If our brain *is* like a computer and the software determines what it can and cannot do, then the critical question is: *From whom did we get this Version of software?* Was it a virus or did we install it knowingly? As I touched on this in the previous chapter, you'll know that the answer is — whomever we were exposed to *mostly* from birth to age ten.

As children, our brains are like little computers taking WiFi downloads from our parents and carers, without firewalls or virus protection. It seems that for most of us, our beliefs are not really our own, but derived from our parent's Version of beliefs. To think of us as little *belief system magnets* would be an accurate summation of our childhood.

It makes sense and is widely accepted today that both nature (meaning our genes) and nurture (the environment we grow up in) are known to significantly affect traits like our height and weight, our intelligent quotient (IQ), and our chance of developing behavioural problems or autism. For too long, scientists have been aiming to discover which has the greater impact upon who we become — *nature* or *nurture*? I believe we're asking the wrong question but we're looking in the right area. Instead of asking *what* has the greatest influence, I would be asking from *where* and *whom*?

Dr Oliver Davis, who led the Wellcome Trust-funded study, published in the *Molecular Psychiatry* journal said, "There are any number of environments that vary geographically in the UK, from social environments like health care or education provision to physical environments like altitude, the weather or pollution. The message that these maps really drive home is that your genes are not your destiny. There are plenty of things that can affect how your particular human genome expresses itself, and one of those things is where you grow up."[2] Most modern families intuitively know this and as a result are choosing to live further away from their parents.

"Family members want intimacy at a distance," says Deborah Carr, professor of sociology at Rutgers University. "They want love and support from their kin, but they also want to maintain their independence and autonomy. Often, that means buying a home in another neighbourhood. While some parents want grandparents to be a part of their children's lives (and to help out with their care)," Carr says, "Some parents of young children might worry that their parents will try to impose outdated ideas (beliefs) about child rearing and discipline."[3]

OUR PARENTS INFLUENCE OUR BELIEFS, WHICH DETERMINES OUR LANGUAGE AND SO SHAPES HOW WE THINK AND VIEW THE WORLD

The lives we are living today are largely a result of our parents' beliefs and the actual language that was expressed repetitively derives from those very beliefs. Those words and concepts held by our parents instil and enforce our beliefs. In other words, our learned words circulate through our neurology to become us. Prior to hearing "We can't afford that," we might not have had any idea of our parents' financial situation. If we keep hearing that phrase, it will form our beliefs around money.

To examine the opposite, what would happen if we took an impoverished child and placed them into the household of a rich family? What would happen for example, if a Somalian child were adopted into the family of billionaire Donald Trump? Knowing the power of beliefs, it is highly likely that that child would grow up to mirror the Trump genes rather than that of its parents. The Somalian child's likelihood of creating wealth would be very high. Our parents influence our beliefs, which determines our language and so shapes how we view the world — and of course how we view the world is how the world *is* according to us.

Scientists believe that our formative language is acquired most easily during the first ten years of life. During these years, the circuits in children's brains become wired by the words they acquire. A child's repeated exposure to words builds the word's meaning and helps their brain build the neural connections that become the child's operating platform, their software to run the analogy.[4]

VERSION 1.0 SURVIVALIST THINKING —
OUR FIRST BELIEF SYSTEM

We know that our *environment* and our *parents* formed our foundational belief systems. We also know that these influence our prejudices, our judgements and colour our world. So we can safely assume that our parents' beliefs came from their parents, and so the chain of beliefs may have formed from the earliest of times.

We could safely assume that when dinosaurs ruled the earth (the environment), the mothers and fathers (the parents) of the time had their prime focus on their clan's survival (relative beliefs). It could also be assumed that due to their environment, their prevailing belief system would have them favouring *safety* over becoming dinosaur dinner, *death*. Perhaps their language at the time was a thesaurus full of sounds or words describing *safety* or how fast to *run*! Prehistoric thinking, due to the very nature of the *life or death* environment was most likely *fear-based* and to make this book's journey simple, let's call this *Version 1.0 — Survivalist Thinking*.

The Evolution of Beliefs

AVOID

FAVOUR

DEATH

160,000 YEARS AGO – NEANDERTHAL MAN
**SURVIVALIST
V1.0**

SAFETY

Copyright 2013 – Rik Schnabel

Now before we go any further, I'm about to categorise each level of belief *Version 1.0, 2.0, 3.0, 4.0* and *5.0* to help you gain an insight into, *The Evolution of Beliefs.* The perfectionists and historians might argue that I've missed a Version or that a specific Version of beliefs may have happened slightly earlier or later. Understand that the intention is to help you to know how beliefs have evolved — dates are not critical, while sequence is.

If we can progress one step further and place a stake in the ground by assuming that *Survivalist Thinking* — is our earliest cluster of beliefs, it's our *Version 1.0* belief system and houses our very first neural software download. *Survivalist Thinking* is a batch of beliefs that favours *safety* over *death.* Even today in the 21st century, working with people to help them to shift their beliefs, I have found that *Survivalist Thinking* remains in the modern brain. These beliefs exist in an older part of our brain that houses the *amygdala.* While our amygdala decodes emotions it also stores fear memories and determines possible threats. In threat, it signals our *hypothalamus* that activates the vital 'fight or flight' response via 'norepinephrine' (noradrenaline) and the hormone 'epinephrine' (adrenaline).

ANY DECISION MADE IN FEAR IS USUALLY THE WRONG DECISION

While we know it is important to remain alive, it is not always the best decision to play everything safe. Keeping safe usually means we don't try anything new and hence, we do not progress. Today's world is moving much faster than it ever did and we need to keep up. If we don't get beyond our fear responses we won't just get left behind, we'll be left for dead! Any decision made in fear is usually the wrong decision.

For most people, living in a rapidly changing world is firing off our neurology within the *amygdala* like a fireworks display. Our *Survivalist Thinking* is alert to any form of threat. Therefore losing one's job or relationship is neurologically overplayed as a threat to life itself. Equally, when a person does anything that is different from the normal patterns of life, such as visiting a new country or going on holidays, these can cause high levels of anxiety that is a by-product of that old 'fear of death' response. Taking a holiday (doing something different) doesn't necessarily mean we'll die — however our unconscious *Survivalist* belief system is not logical and seldom makes sense. To understand human behaviour sometimes means we must go beyond logic.

SURVIVALIST UPGRADES TO *VERSION 2.0* HIERARCHIC THINKING

As humanity evolved from clans and into civilisations and hierarchies, I believe we progressed to *Version 2.0* beliefs. This new Version now included a reward and penalty function. Someone, perhaps an authority of some higher order decides whether or not we get the prize or the pain. *Version 2.0* is *Hierarchic* as it suggests that one is above the other in privilege. *Hierarchic* thinking requires a whole new system of beliefs that allow us to acquiesce to rules and rulers. On a global scale, once our world became civilised and we created order, the rulers and the ruled appeared. Our thinking needed to evolve in order for a system of class to work. We couldn't have our people running like a *pot á feu'* like savages at every threat — we needed order. We had to have them follow the systems that were created by the rulers.

If *Survivalist, Version 1.0* thinking goes back to Neanderthal man, then *Hierarchic Version 2.0* thinking goes back before the first legal system was created in the year 1176, before the Roman Empire. Conceivably it began at the writing of the 'Ten Commandments' given to Moses. The moment that laws and systems were created, the moment one ruled many is when *Hierarchic* beliefs were formed in our ever-evolving brain. We had to adjust our thinking and beliefs so we could rule or be ruled.

The Evolution of Beliefs

AVOID

FAVOUR

DENIAL

CIRCA 2000 BC
**HIERARCHIC
V2.0**

REWARD

Copyright 2013 – Rik Schnabel

Hierarchic thinking actualised the very structure on which ancient societies were born and predetermined their quality of life. If we go back to early Roman times, during the Iron Age, a person's quality of life depended in many ways on their *rank* within the social structure. Two Romans living at the same time, in the same city could have very different lives. If they were rich for example, life was good. The rich lived in beautiful homes with luxurious furnishings, often in the hills outside of Rome, away from the noise and pungent smells. They were surrounded by servants and slaves to cater to their every desire and whim. They ate well, lived well and held exclusive banquets, serving their guests the exotic dishes of the day.

Poorer Romans, however, could only dream of such a life. Their lives were harsh and today their treatment would be seen as cruel. They lived in the rancid city in shabby, squalid houses that could collapse or burn at any moment. If times were really hard, they might abandon their newborn babies into the streets, hoping that someone else would take them in as a servant or a slave. The wealthy people's social standing was above the poor and while the poor were slaves to the system, the poorest were slaves to all.[5]

Even in England just 200 years ago, during the 1800s, history witnessed many developments in policing and punishment. The response to increasing levels of crime led to a strict punitive set of laws being set against crimes of the time. Most of the new laws introduced during that period were concerned with the defence of property, which some commentators have interpreted as a form of class suppression of the poor by the rich. 'The Bloody Code' as it was later called, saw crimes being punished by severe penalties. During the early 1800s more than 200 types of crime could lead to death by execution! In just 100 years, 3,524 people were hung in England and Wales, 1,353 less than half for murder.[6]

Version 2.0 thinking or *Hierarchic* gave us the ability to create structures, rules and rulers, laws and lawlessness, systems, governance and kingdoms. *Version 2.0 thinking* introduced structural thinking, ownership and rank. If you put *Version 1.0* and 2.0 together, we get the basic structure of most military organisations — they're typically systems with a hierarchic structure of rank, stringent rules and is concerned with a country's safety. In summary, the military system *avoids death*, and *favours safety* and its system *rewards* conformist and excellent behaviour with rank and *punishes* rebellious and non-excellent behaviour with *denial* of rank and segregation. In other words, it is a *Hierarchic* system of thinking motivated by *Survivalist* beliefs.

The military model helps us explain *The Evolution of Beliefs* where our beliefs typically have us moving away from something

(Avoid) in preference to (Favour) something else.

Suffice to say, our collective history is ingrained in the oldest parts of our brain. We intrinsically know that the world reacts to most things we do with either *pain* in the form of: segregation, incarceration, penalty or criticism or with *pleasure* in the form of: praise, acceptance, extra privileges or acclaim. This of course depends on where we are within the hierarchy.

Rulers are seldom ruled by the same set of laws that they themselves set. Even today, some rulers' corrupt behaviours have featured in the news, politicians, police, company leaders, corporate bosses and even parents to name a few who have acted like they were above the law either overtly or from behind closed doors.

The beliefs that came from *Version 2.0 thinking* perhaps served the rulers well during the industrial revolution when management styles were not much more than retributive and primeval. During these times, and sadly even today, if employees and children for that matter, don't do what they are told, pain is applied. It may not always be a physical pain, as psychological pressure is also applied in the form of denial of privileges, being ostracised or losing one's job to verbal threats which today we call *verbal abuse* or *bullying*. These are just some of the examples that an employer and parent might utilise to get their way. Though we now know that if we continue to use punishment, we will either suppress talent or experience a surge of suppressed emotion in the form of rebellion.

THE 1960S WELCOMES
A NEW VERSION OF THINKING

Now while *rebellion* came in many forms and at many times

throughout our history, collectively, in the western world, there was a dramatic surge of rebellion in the sixties. A new generation was born and rebellion gushed *en masse*. This new generation accepted a new software upgrade, with a unique difference. Typically, communally we can upgrade as a shift in consciousness or the result of a significant emotional event. The Vietnam War was such an event. It was cataclysmically enough to warrant a new download. It seemed that the values of a whole generation hit a fork in the road, neither *Version 1.0* nor *Version 2.0 thinking* possessed the attributes to deal with the emotional upwelling that was stirring.

Once upon a time *Version 1.0* and *2.0 thinking* had us, like the good little puppies that we were, just doing what our *owners* and *rulers* told us to do. If we were told to go to war we did. The Vietnam War was different. It was the first war of the television era. The TV viewing public got much closer to this war than any before it. But to add salt to an already open wound, the US, the UK and the Australian governments utilised a system called 'The Draft' to bolster recruits for the war effort. The Draft was a system of conscription that threatened lower class registrants and middle class registrants alike. Enter the next download, *Version 3.0 thinking, Rebellion*. While with *Version 1.0* we were ruled by fear of death and *Version 2.0 thinking* had us fearing denial so we did what we were told and adhered to laws, rules and rewards. This new *Version 3.0 thinking* was revolutionary in the true sense of the word. A stake was planted firmly in the ground that said we would no longer do what we were told; we would no longer follow rules that we could not and would not believe in. Without *Version 3.0 Rebellion*, we would have put our lives on the line for a cause unquestioningly.

A Shift from *Hierarchic* to *Version 3.0 Rebellion*

Version 3.0 thinking provided the world with *Rebellion*, the opportunity to voice our opinions, avoid rules and control and favour freedom. It gave us our first collective opportunity to flex our free will. It granted us self-imposed rights for the first time in our history and it extended our vocabulary to the word *NO!* Though this didn't come without resistance and without a price. This new belief system had us picketing, chanting and challenging many of the current belief systems of a hierarchic world filled with rulers and the ruled.

The Evolution of Beliefs

AVOID   FAVOUR

RULES &
CONTROL

CIRCA 1960
**REBELLION
V3.0**
Copyright 2013 – Rik Schnabel

FREEDOM &
EQUALITY

Rebellion brought to the world's attention a highly articulate man — his name, Martin Luther King Jr who then surfed this new wave and unleashed the 'African-American Civil Rights Movement'. He didn't use fear, nor punishment or reward, he used something much more powerful, a rebellious vision — he had *a dream*!

Around the time of Martin Luther King Jr's address to 25,000 people, another man whose mission was *freedom* and the abolition of *apartheid* in South Africa was being imprisoned and removed from view. It would be 27 years later, on February 11, 1990 that Nelson Mandela would be released to reveal his Version of *Rebellion*. In the meantime, a rebellious folk singer Robert Allen Zimmerman wrote protest songs under the name of Bob Dylan. He penned that, "The times are a'changing…" as our thinking revelled in this new upgrade.

This new *Version 3.0 Rebellion* was powerful and affronted the norms of the time. It delivered a whole new level of questioning that lead women to make a statement of independence and equality. Prior to the 'Feminist Movement', women were only known as mothers or housewives and some burned their bras as a symbol of liberation. It was about equality and it came with a mindfulness that was refreshing. Both women and men were changing. It would become the age of movements. The civil rights movement, the student movement, the anti-Vietnam War movement, the women's movement, the gay rights movement, and the environmental movement followed. Each, to varying degrees, changed government policy and perhaps more importantly, changed how almost every person in the western world lives today. *Rebellion* was rife! *Version 3.0* thinking was alive and thriving. It was like a virus that spread quickly through music, through people stepping up onto a soap box, and through the world's fastest growing broadcast medium, namely TV. We could now view the world from the safety of our living rooms.

Supporters of these historical movements questioned traditional practices. They questioned how people were treated. They challenged the current belief system; they began asking "why?" In the US, people were asking, "*Why* did black and white children attend separate schools?" In the western world there was social unrest and even more questions, "*Why* were women prevented from holding certain jobs?" In the warring worlds, they asked "*Why* could a person be drafted at 18 but was not able to vote until 21?" This questioning inspired people to begin organising movements to fight against injustice and for equal rights for all people.

In addition, they did not use traditional methods of political activity. Instead of voting for a political candidate and then hoping that the elected official would make good their policies, these protesters believed in a more direct democracy. They took direct action, immediate action: public marches, picketing, sit-ins, rallies, petition drives, and teach-ins, all to win converts to their causes and change public policies at the local, state and federal levels. They contributed their time, energy, and passion with the hope of making a better and more just society for all.[7]

Version 3.0 gave stage to a new generation of zealots, demonstrators, protestors, passionate thinkers; these emerging leaders became our courageous, highly vocal, public communicators. Some musicians were so revolutionary, that history delivered them to iconic status. A quantum evolution was forming as artists, poets and musicians such as Bob Dylan, The Beatles, Donovan, Crosby, Stills Nash & Young, Woody Guthrie, Pete Seeger, Joan Baez and Buffy Sainte-Marie among others who somehow tapped into a new software upgrade and *Rebellion* took a quantum leap right across the globe.

While the musicians' platforms became their music, other courageous public communicators challenged almost everything and anything, in their own creative way. A new wave was incipient and its growth hormone was *creativity*.

Anti-consumerist and artist, Andy Warhol challenged the art world itself and mass consumption using oil paints, acrylic paints, silkscreen ink, metals, chemicals, and photographs. During the Vietnam War, in 1969, John Lennon and Yoko Ono used their fame and held two week-long *Bed-Ins for Peace* in Amsterdam and Montreal, which became their non-violent signature, their way of protesting against wars and promoting peace. The idea is derived from a sit-in, in which a group of protesters remains seated in front of an establishment until they are evicted, arrested, or their demands are met.[8]

Perhaps it was the experimentation with hallucinogenic drugs, perhaps it was something existential, the result was that this new generation rose *beyond* their parents' old beliefs and some got out of their heads altogether and leaped beyond *Version 3.0* thinking completely.

The common thread from *Version 1.0* to *Version 3.0 thinking* was *logic*. It was logical to fear being eaten by a dinosaur. It was logical to fear being beaten by the stick. It was even logical to become courageous and no longer fear authority, to take a stand against a war mongering government and presidency. Though a new wave of thinking, perhaps spurred on by *Rebellion*, realised that solutions sometimes required much more than *logic* could solve. *Version 4.0 thinking* took the world into hyperspace — it was beyond the current thinking, it was beyond this world.

The new US President, John F. Kennedy took office in January 1961 and in his inaugural speech, he said, "The world is very different now. For man holds in his mortal hands the power to abolish all forms of human poverty and all forms of human life. And yet the same revolutionary beliefs for which our forebears fought are still at issue around the globe…"[9] This new president also said America would be the first to land on the moon. This required a whole new level of thinking. *Version 4.0* delivered *Lateral Thinking* to the *Rebellion* and gave us a surge of creativity and an inspired voice.

VERSION 4.0 LATERAL THINKING LIBERATED US BEYOND LOGIC

'Lateral Thinking,' a phrase coined by Edward de Bono in 1967 seemed to be a logical transition into a brave new and illogical world. *Lateral Thinking* avoided the older and more traditional thinking and favoured adventurous thinking. This new belief system upgrade said: "Out with the old and in with the new." It meant of course that we could always get what we wanted by using the old ways, but now we could also think laterally, creatively. And create we did!

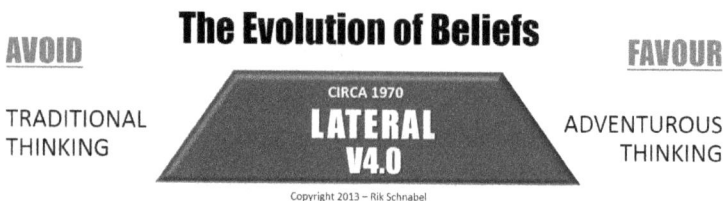

The Evolution of Beliefs

AVOID

TRADITIONAL
THINKING

CIRCA 1970
**LATERAL
V4.0**

FAVOUR

ADVENTUROUS
THINKING

Copyright 2013 – Rik Schnabel

The creative sprint from *Version 3.0 Rebellion* to *Version 4.0 Lateral* changed the world so vastly that today it looks nothing like it did in the 1960s or the 1970s! While we had already transformed travel with the invention of the automobile and airplanes and harnessed the atom, communications were upgraded with the advent of the telephone; innovation was quantum with the advent of the personal computer and the Internet. These things were unthinkable in 1900, but by the year 2000 they were commonplace.

If we thought we couldn't keep up then, consider how fast our world has moved in the last ten years! This *Lateral Thinking* meant anything could rule! Thinking laterally with the power of technology moved us forward at breakneck speeds. Some say it was good, some say it was great and others rejected it altogether — at first. *Lateral Thinking* was limitless and today we can do almost anything, technologically speaking. We can purchase most things that we used to travel to purchase, now using our computers and our phones. People no longer write letters. They *Tweet, Blog, Vlog* and to make life interesting they

Poke, Like and *Unlike* at the push of a button. *Great* became *Gr8* thanks to texting messages through the ether and a new belief system that valued *speed* over *literacy*.

Once upon a time we procured our favourite musical artist's album and we would all sit around the record player listening to every song while we pawed over the album cover, while the record player's stylus almost pierced through to the B side. Today our music libraries are more personal and less tribal. We download single *iTunes®*, not albums and listen to them on our personal devices. There are so many WiFi signals moving through the air connecting things to things without connecting to things! There are almost as many pocket computers (otherwise known as phones) as people on this planet! The jobs that our kids are studying for might not even exist by the time they graduate and when they do there will be new entirely jobs in existence, perhaps completely new industries! The world today is changing so fast that adaptability and flexibility is key. These two traits will not be found in *Survivalist*. They won't be found in *Hierarchic* either, nor *Rebellion*. A new thinking needed to emerge together with a whole new set of beliefs. *Lateral thinking* was perfect, until it went berserk.

VERSION 4.0 THINKING HAS A VIRUS — IT IS OUT OF CONTROL

Though *Version 4.0*'s addition of *Lateral Thinking* seemed to create a great deal of opportunity for anyone who downloaded its promise, it wasn't perfect, something went wrong, terribly wrong. The software had a bug and it drove us crazy. We soon realised that *Lateral Thinking* took some mastering and often conflicted with some of the beliefs that were installed with

Versions 1.0 to *3.0*. How could we be *creative* and yet *toe the line*? How could we be *innovators* and be like *everyone else*? How could we take such creative risks and not risk our very survival? Was creativity about thinking outside the square or was it about winning and being the best or was it going beyond competition?

Lateral Thinking knew no bounds. Our hands were untied and the gloves were off. *Rebellion* saw an end to many of the rules and *Lateral Thinking* broke them and blew them away, it thrived by breaking rules. Anyone could create anything, anywhere, anyhow at any time. Enter the Internet and it looked like a world gone mad. Bricks and mortar businesses were challenged by online ventures. Shotgun marketing and broad appeal messages gave way to the advent of the niche. Slow processes gave way to streamlined, real time computer and Internet systems. The 'cloud' rained on paper-based data recording and tomorrow the landscape may change again. Nothing is permanent in this new world of change.

People became polarised and confused as they *tried* to use *Lateral Thinking* but that took time and some mastery. It also required a new level of intelligence and when it didn't work, they got frustrated and just wanted to revert back to the old ways. Misoneism became the new disease as the traditionalist feared change and prophesised that the new technologies of the *Lateral* world was a fad and would eventually fade. It did not of course and innovation and creativity meant the world seemed to move away from the traditionalists even faster. The speed and breadth of creativity had created its own raft of problems. There were more options and much more choice than we had ever become used to. An upgrade was urgently required.

Today the large majority are still thinking through *Version 1.0* to *4.0* in what has become a *Version 5.0* world — a much faster and a far more complex world than ever before. The old software and its beliefs that ran our lives up to now, no longer works in this world. Just surviving will get us nowhere. Using *Hierarchic* reward or punishment we risk being incarcerated. *Rebellion* might not even be able to burst through. We could always get *Lateral*, though being creative so often just adds to the clutter. We may just be ignored as insignificant, banal or worse.

This contemporary world is fast, ever changing and difficult to keep pace. The military's invention of the Internet fell into the hands of those programmed with *Version 4.0* thinking and ideas took off in every direction imaginable. As a result, we're now drowning in the sea of data called 'The Information Age'; some call it the 'Misinformation Age'. We are over-whelmed, over-worked and a virus called *Frustration* has been launched. We are now looking for a simple solution, but what is it?

THE INFORMATION AGE GIVES WAY TO THE FOCUS AND FILTERING AGE

Where we once had little choice, today we're spoiled for choices. Once upon a time in Australia, to get a phone connected you only chose between one or two companies at most. Today Australia along with the rest of the world are confused by multiple service providers, complex plans that cannot be compared for value and complex product options. The dominant resource has now become the Internet and it is becoming a busier and busier space. The *information age* is cluttered and we must now give way to the *focus and filtering age*! We need to get better at filtering through the rubbish, the scams, the untruths and focus on what we want instead. However, we're expected to do much more in this faster paced world. Stress is now the new normal.

There is no shortage of information, though there now seems to be a shortage of time — so we better get focused or we'll get confused or worse, lost.

Our world is moving at such a rapid pace that few can keep up with it. At the time of writing this sentence, 100 hours of video are uploaded to *YouTube®* every minute. In just *one second*, no that's not a typo — every *one* second there are over 10,000 photos uploaded to *Instagram®*; 300,000 *Tweets*; 500,000 *Google®* searches; 12 Million *Facebook®* likes; 35,000 new websites are created — all of this happens every single second, of every day of every year! And that's today — what of tomorrow? Some 20 years ago there were only 130 websites! According to Netcraft's March 2012 website survey, they discovered 644,275,754 active websites, 30 years ago there were none![10]

The creativity brought on by *Lateral Thinking* has made our world faster, more congested, although it has given us cheaper access to tools that were once well beyond our grasp. Even the criminally minded have access to tools that once cost thousands and are now free! Yes, we now live in a complex world and to make matters worse and complicate life further, the criminally minded *Lateral* thinkers also reign supreme. We get emails posing as credible companies to hack our computer systems, download costly viruses or empty our bank accounts.

With the click of a mouse, online hackers are also now able to search photos of our families posted all over the web on sites such as *Facebook®*, *Twitter®* and *Photobucket®*. New technology and global positioning satellite services (GPS), make it so simple to track down a person even from an email, and actually pinpoint their location and the places they frequent. Hackers can even map out the precise location where a child's bedroom is within a home. The *Lateral* age has reactivated some of our old fearful *Survivalist* programs. Once we we're scared to let our children play on the street, now we fear for their safety at home on the Internet!

The *Lateral Thinking* of the criminal element knows no boundaries. A cold caller, claiming to be a representative of *Microsoft®*, tells us that they are checking into a computer problem that stems from our device. They go on to suggest that an infection or virus has been detected. Of course there is no virus and they're not from *Microsoft®*. They tell us they can help and direct us to a website that then allows the scammers to take remote control of our computer. The cold caller will then spend some time on the computer trying to demonstrate where the *problems* are and in the process convinces us to pay a fee for a service that will fix a problem our computer never had.

Scammers, identity thieves and hackers have grown more sophisticated. Today, some cyber-criminals are selling or *giving away* software that supposedly fights viruses, spyware and malware. In fact, their *rogue software* often doesn't work but actually infects our computers with the dangerous programs it is supposed to protect against! [11]

THE NOUGHTIES BRING ON
THE AGE OF CONSCIOUS AWARENESS

It's no wonder that our *Version 4.0* brains cannot cope in this *Version 5.0* world plagued with overwhelm, disappointment, confusion, frustration, deceit and rage — all of which lead to much bigger problems. According to the *World Health Organisation*, globally there are more than 350 million people of all ages that suffer from depression. Every year, almost one million people die from suicide; a global mortality rate of 16 per

100,000 or one death every 40 seconds and growing.[12]

Life on earth is not getting easier; it's getting harder for those whose software is not up to date. So if that's not enough to contend with, we still have to deal with the foibles of our older Version thinkers who are still our rulers and leaders — we need to upgrade our thinking more than ever. It's time for *Version 5.0 Thinking.*

3
WAKING UP FROM A TRANCE

The Information Age brought about by *Lateral Thinking — Version 4.0* now has information swimming above our heads in the ether and moving faster than our minds can cope. There has never been a time in history when the need for a revival is more imminent. We need to wake up and fast! We must become conscious. I'm calling this period, 'The Age of Conscious Awareness'. Never before has it been more important to move beyond the clutter and the deceptions spurred on by the *Lateral* thinkers who continually feed *The Information Age*.

In order to see the deceptions, we must awaken; we must become consciously aware of our environment and how we interact within it. We must also become aware of our viral need for more — our collective consumption trance.

Our response to the decades of indoctrination and advertising hypnosis adjusted our beliefs to 'keep up with the Joneses' and consume like there was no tomorrow. We equally need to wake up to the lies about what is *really* in our mass-produced foods and what is contained in the products we buy. How are they manufactured, what do they contain and what by-products do they emit into our atmosphere and oceans? We are fed lies by our rulers and governance and our so-called unbiased media; the truth about our monetary and economic system and who controls and influences it? More importantly, we need the truth about who we really are and what we can really do without being fed the lies of who we're not. We've had enough and we're sick of the lies. In fact the lies are making us sick! It's time to upgrade to *Version 5.0 thinking*.

VERSION 5.0 CONSCIOUSNESS AWARENESS — THE PATH TO TRUTH

While we are bombarded with so much information and misinformation, more than ever we must get clear about what *we* want from life. It is so easy to become distracted in this age of clutter and confusion where we buy other people's values and never question our own. Once upon a time, we only made phone calls in the office, at home and from the odd phone booth when needed. Today we make them at home, in the office, in the street, on the golf course, in our bedrooms — some even take and make calls from the toilet. We have sacrificed our privacy and free time over technology at our fingertips. We have diminished our nutrition intake as we value speed and convenience over our health. What is wrong with this picture?

Our beliefs were once only infiltrated and saturated by mainstream media, now they're assaulted by what we read on *Facebook*® and *Twitter*® and a throng of articles all over the internet. The multitude of disaster stories we read in magazines, in the press, on TV and on the Internet fills not just our heads but also our very souls with tripe that we consume daily. If we don't wake up, we'll adopt the newshounds beliefs and sadly, many of us already have!

What we now have access to has grown our list of fears. The information age means that information is getting in and it's not all good. We no longer just fear pain and penalty, today we fear the number one killer, cancer, the 'Adenovirus

14 Infection' (Killer Cold Virus), 'FOMO' (Fear Of Missing Out), electromagnetic pulses wiping out our computer data, cyber warfare, some paedophile cyber stalker threatening the wellbeing of our children or some creative megalomaniac who invents a new weapon of mass destruction and is not afraid to use it.

The Evolution of Beliefs

AVOID

FAVOUR

CIRCA 2000

DECEPTION **CONSCIOUS AWARENESS** TRUTH
V5.0

Copyright 2013 – Rik Schnabel

The new upgrade that we all need is simple. Become *Conscious*. Consciously aware of what we consume and conscious of what we think and become as a result. If we don't become cognisant, someone else will choose to utilise our hypnotic stupor to get into our psyche. Chances are, they already have. Studies have shown that within seven seconds of your child sitting in front of the TV, they're hypnotised. We've all been hypnotised for decades. Even singing our favourite song holds the power to change our beliefs — some are good, like The Beatles "All you need is love" and some like Metallica's "I Am Evil" from their "Kill 'Em All" album, the chorus is a sad affirmation that perhaps has been sung by a villain or two, "Am I evil? Yes I am. Am I evil? I am man, yes I am…" It's time to wake up, don't you agree?

Now before I take this next step with you, let me share my intent. What it's NOT is to make you feel bad and it's NOT to make you look or feel stupid. It's

❊
The mind is everything.
What you think
you become.
– Buddha

NOT even to make you sound like you are unaware of what you're doing. The pure purpose of what I'm about to ask you is to wake you up a little — to unplug you for a moment from the marketing machine. I'll say this upfront. Please understand, there is nothing wrong with buying nice things for yourself, your partner, your kids, your family or anyone for that matter. But know why you're *really* buying. Become conscious of what's really driving your purchases and life will get a lot easier and clearer. Please read the next paragraph and answer the questions honestly — just to yourself.

Does it matter to you what brand of car you drive? Is it important that your car is the latest model? Does it have to have all the extras or will it have to be the premium model? Honestly — does it matter?

Is it important to you what brand names appear on the clothes you wear or the accessories you choose? Would you prefer to look like Angelina Jolie or Brad Pitt or some other A- listed movie star?

Are you proud of the cost of your jewellery or the size or cut of your gems?

Is the size or position of your house important to you or do you feel you've made it because of the neighbourhood you live in or where you enjoyed your last holiday?

If you answered *yes* to any of these questions then someone has gotten into your psyche. There is no doubt about it. Brands, prestige, V.I.P., expense, glamour, Ritz, glitz and gizmos — even the idea of a bargain are *words* that were cleverly formed by marketing gurus to ensure you empty your purse or wallet as often as possible. Marketers and advertisers have been messing with your beliefs for decades!

Marketers are also using our self-esteem be it low or high

to have us buy things we don't really need — all of the time. The only way we can undo the spell we're under is by waking up. I know this only too well because I've been all four parts to this 21st Century problem: I've been in Advertising; Marketing; Sales; and I am also a Consumer. In my former life I worked in advertising for 20 years. For the last ten of those years I ran an advertising agency. I know what we did in our TV and radio commercials, billboards, magazines, newspapers and packaging to get people to buy — and sadly, it worked! Believe me when I say it's a psychological science. Advertising is the ultimate art of persuasion *en masse*.

Marketing is also a well-researched science of buyer behaviour and to get people to buy is often just a process of connecting the right dots. Sales in my view are probably the most honest of the four as there is little anonymity to it. You're up close and personal and what's more, you will most likely meet your clients again, so from that standpoint integrity is important — for some. Whereas advertising, marketing and sales ideas are conjured in offices. Like snipers, they're way up on high in their ivory towers. Why do I also rank consumers as not being honest? Here's why and by the way, I count myself as being a consumer too.

WE'LL BUY SOMETHING WE CAN HARDLY AFFORD TO MAKE A STATEMENT TO PEOPLE WE HARDLY KNOW

Consumers are often buying for all the wrong reasons. They're not even being honest with themselves. We'll buy a car we can hardly afford to make a statement to people we hardly know. Of course we'll aim to impress our friends, family and colleagues too. We hope our new purchases will say: *We've made it*, or *we're doing just fine* — when we really haven't and we're really not.

We will buy brands as a means to make our way into a social clique or as a means to gain acceptance. We'll go into a supermarket and buy a so-called 'food' because the label says its "Fat-Free Yoghurt," when it's not and we know it. If we're conscious, then we know that's just not true, but we like to believe it anyway. "This one is easy to get wrong," says **Kim Snyder,** nutritionist for celebrities like Drew Barrymore and Channing Tatum and author of *"The Beauty Detox Solution."* After all, yogurt is always made of wholesome dairy and fresh fruit right? Wrong. "Yogurt can contain tons of sugar. Read the label and you'll see yogurt often contains high-fructose corn syrup, artificial flavourings and artificial colours. One small container of fat-free yogurt can have upwards of 28 to 31 grams (approx. 1 ounce) of sugar," says Snyder.[1]

The way to evolve above this consumerist insanity is to strengthen our self-esteem by realising that we are not our clothes, our brands, our jobs or where we live. The path to truth is through consciousness. In fact we had to become conscious to move us out of our *Version 1.0 Survivalist* thinking when we recognised that our avoidance beliefs delivered us from the fear of *death* to *favour* beliefs that gave us *safety*.

The Evolution of Beliefs

AVOID		FAVOUR
DECEPTION	**CONSCIOUS AWARENESS** 2000s V5.0	TRUTH
TRADITIONAL THINKING	**LATERAL** CIRCA 1970 V4.0	ADVENTUROUS THINKING
RULES & CONTROL	**REBELLION** CIRCA 1960 V3.0	FREEDOM
DENIAL	**HIERARCHICAL** CIRCA 2000 BC V2.0	REWARD
FEAR	**SURVIVAL** 160,000 YEARS AGO – NEANDERTHAL MAN V1.0	SECURITY

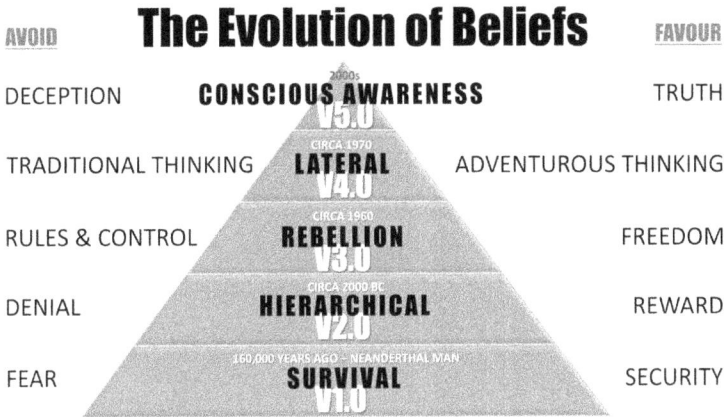

We then evolved into *Version 2.0 Hierarchical Thinking* where we *avoid* beliefs that *denied* us and *favour* beliefs that *reward* us. When we needed to, we took drastic action to break free of the *Hierarchy* and we moved to *Version 3.0 Rebellion Thinking*. Here we *avoid* beliefs based on *rules* and *control* and *favour* beliefs, which included ideas around *freedom* and *equality*. Though this thinking, while breakthrough, created more problems that required a whole new level of thinking.

Enter *Version 4.0 Lateral Thinking*. Here we *avoid* beliefs around *traditional thinking* and *favour* more *adventurous thinking*. This thinking spurred an innovative revolution and while many products transformed our lives and technology went into hyperspace, we spaced out. Now we have more choices than ever before. More distractions pulling at our senses to get our attention and much more clever ways to have us buy things we don't need. More so, ingesting foods and products that are simply not good for our mind, body or spirit.

It's time for a new upgrade into *Version 5.0 Conscious Awareness* that liberates us from and *avoids* beliefs that house *deception* and denies our true selves. We find ourselves searching for what is *really* good for us. *Conscious Awareness* liberates us to *favour truth*; our own *personal truth* and only we can know what that is. To get there, we must become conscious and make conscious decisions. In essence, we're saying: "I am not a product of my circumstances, I master my thinking, so therefore I create my life." Before we complete this chapter, let's summarise *The Evolution of Beliefs*:

1. *Version 1.0 Survivalist* beliefs move us from fear of *Death* to *Safety*
2. *Version 2.0 Hierarchic* beliefs move us from *Denial* to *Reward*
3. *Version 3.0 Rebellion* beliefs move us from *Rules and Control* to *Freedom and Equality*
4. *Version 4.0 Lateral* beliefs move us from *Traditional Thinking* to *Adventurous Thinking*
5. *Version 5.0 Conscious Awareness* beliefs move us from *Deception* to *Truth*

Moving to *Version 5.0 thinking* is not going to be everyone's cup of tea because it will require some work to remain conscious. And it is certain that some practice will be required to master this new upgrade. Though this is an upgrade of choice and not everyone will choose it. In my view, those who will decide to upgrade are those who truly wish to consciously create their lives, the courageous ones, and those who wish to become mentally fit. The rest will continue to fall under the spell of a world gone mad. Though how did it all begin?

4

INVISIBLE BELIEFS
THAT GUIDE YOU

Throughout our childhood we've installed thousands of
beliefs without consciously accepting them. Thousands
upon thousands of beliefs snuck into our minds by listening
to our parents' Version of thinking, among other influential
individuals. We've been fed a multitude of truths and many lies
by the media, marketing maestros, fathers, mothers and others
to sway everything from our purchasing habits, to our choice
to immunise, to choosing our life partners, right up to swaying
our vote!

According to *Freepress.net*, "There are many reasons the
scandal engulfing Rupert Murdoch's *News Corporation* has riveted
public attention around the world. It's a story that features all of
the classic elements: crimes, betrayal, abuse of power and even a
cover-up. But beneath Murdoch's public meltdown there resting
is a much larger beast, a bigger problem, and it's not confined
to England, where *News Corp* stands accused of hacking phones
and computers and bribing and misleading investigators. It's a
problem that creates a social cancer, one in which tarnishes our
view of the world, lowers our expectations and negates our
empowering beliefs. It's what happens when the media get too
powerful, too cosy with power — and government officials
become fearful of what that power can do to their election
hopes. As a result, governments fail to challenge the media and

its creators, the media magnates.

"More than any of the current crop of media moguls, Murdoch accrues political influence through his aggressive manipulation of News Corp's many media outlets. It's not just in the way Murdoch's media properties cover the news but how they use this coverage to give him favourable access to elected officials to promote News Corp's agenda. The company uses its media power to shape corporate-friendly policies and quash those that don't further its aims. News Corp also helps elect politicians with timely endorsements while punishing foes who get in its way with negative coverage and political threats.

"This relentless pursuit of power has worked in the United States, where neither the Federal Communications Commission nor Congress has mustered the courage to challenge runaway media consolidation or call Murdoch to account. Free Press has asked the FCC to assess the company's fitness to continue holding 27 television broadcast licenses in light of the widening scandal, and continues to urge Congress to conduct hearings into the allegations of News Corp's *rampant law breaking*.[1]

The biggest problem affronting our beliefs is the fact that Rupert Murdoch's media empire reaches a massive two thirds of the world's population. A much larger reach than any other media network. A little too much reach for one man with a *relentless pursuit of power* and the power to manipulate the populations' beliefs *en masse!*

All said, Rupert Murdoch isn't a bad man. His company News Corporation employs over 50,000 people around the world. His news is not bad and it's not good either. It just is. What we have to keep in mind is that Rupert has a belief system and a powerful media network that holds the power to change how wc think. We just need to be aware of that.

News by the way, isn't the only way to change an entire world's beliefs. Beliefs can be changed by breaking news or even by breaking water. Back in 1975 a dorsal fin broke the surface and in that one act, polarised our view of the sea. One movie changed how millions of people approached the ocean, if at all. Some could only hear the haunting music that conjures up a movie memory of a shark's dorsal fin breaking the surface. That movie of course was *Jaws*. What's more, people paid to have their belief in the ocean altered.

There is no other movie that has made a stronger impact on the United States then *Jaws*. Before *Jaws* came out, tens of thousands of people would flock every day to beaches across the United States. They would enjoy swimming carefree in the ocean, or in large lakes. Once *Jaws* came out, that all changed.

From coast to coast in the United States (and around the world), beaches started becoming bare. People who had either seen the movie, or watched the trailer could not even force themselves to go into the water. They were too scared that a giant shark would attack them.

Even in Michigan, beach populations plummeted in the years after *Jaws*. The State attempted to educate people on the fact that sharks cannot live in inland lakes, but they were not buying it. To this day, beach populations in Michigan have still not reached the levels that they were before the 1975 horror film. Over thirty-two years later, many are still affected by the scenes that they saw in *Jaws*. Whenever a shark attacks, or is even spotted, a dip in beach populations will be evident.

Universal Pictures, the company that brought us *Jaws*, conducted a survey that asked how many people would not go into the ocean to swim. It then asked: "What was the number one reason why people would not swim in the ocean." The answer: "Because I saw *Jaws*," had over 80% of the vote. The second reason was because the survey taker could not swim.

The music from *Jaws* has become one of the most recognized pieces of music in the world. The base line from that music can still send shivers up swimmers' backs after over three decades.[2]

The first shark attack I witnessed so dramatically and graphically in *Jaws* didn't scare me out of the water, though it changed my relationship with the ocean. I had to do some work around my fear as my love of the ocean was too important. These days I live near the ocean and go surfing every chance I get, thanks to changing my beliefs after witnessing *Jaws*. I have been on shark dives and I'll tell you right here and now, sharks are not easy to find. According to Mike Catalano, the head of the math education department at Dakota Wesleyan University in Mitchell, South Dakota, the chances of being attacked by a shark are 1 in 11.5 million.

For most, we already have many beliefs that do not serve us — too many for us to remember wilfully or even consciously. Although as we age, we are confronted by our unconscious beliefs, we recognise them as pain. We experience them when we struggle to find our place in the world and have no idea why our lives became that struggle. We become cognisant of our beliefs when we clumsily fumble to find love or when we strive to succeed or we aim to leave our mark on the world.

For some of us it became apparent that there were some *limiting* beliefs at the helm when we discovered at the end of the month that we were out of money *again*. For others their limiting beliefs arise when they just can't seem to get out of bed. There must be a reason for this lack of enthusiasm but they don't know why. They search for reasons and we know that when we look for reasons we soon find them.

If something's not right we'll keep looking until we find it. For most of us we became aware albeit *emotionally* of the beliefs that created a feeling in us that stopped us in our tracks. Some called that feeling *fear* as we concluded *the world is not safe* and therefore our belief extended to: *I am not safe*. Many of these neurological patterns were formed in our psychology a long time ago. Beliefs can so often be the unwelcomed invisible partner that whispers in our ears telling us that we cannot or will not achieve our dreams. So from where did these dream killers emerge?

IS THERE A *PARENT SCHOOL*?

As a parent, other than the prenatal classes I attended with my wife, I can't ever remember going to *Parent School* and learning how best to raise my children and become a *good* or *effective* parent. It's probably because most of us don't believe we need to be educated in this matter. After all, we too were children once and fully experienced the education and practical advice delivered by our parents. Our parent's didn't go to *Parent School* either! Wots more, there's nuffin wrong wif me mate! I woz raised good nuf!

Parenting can't be that hard — can it? So for many of us, we don't view parenting as a function that requires an education. We don't even view it as a problem. That's of course until it is a problem. Most of us raised our children in similar ways to that of our parents and for those who disagreed with their parent's ethos, often did the opposite. So the pendulum can swing from one extreme to another. Consider how much freedom you were given and how much you give your kids? How much love were you given and how much love do you give your children?

I came from working class parents and as a *latchkey kid* — I was given a great deal of independence. I walked to school on my own and at the end of school I walked home, opened up the door to my house and made myself something to eat. My father and mother came home much later. It's no surprise that as parents Rebecca and I are always aware of where our children are. We drive them to school each day though we know they could easily walk there on their own. The polarity is we now have to teach our children independence.

Most of us hope to God that our parenting nous is sufficient. Though for many, it's not — it's not obvious why, until much later in children's lives when as adults, they cannot make their lives match their dreams or they add drugs or alcohol to fill the holes in their lives. Those invisible beliefs are at work again, stirring up feelings of fear and inadequacy. If there's a problem, the root of the problem will most likely stem from the program that was installed in our early years and the way we were trained (raised), but it goes deeper still.

Enter mum and dad. Again, let me state this up front, this is NOT intended as a beat up of our parents, though we must understand at the outset that our parents raised us with perhaps *Version 2.0*, *3.0* or at best, *Version 4.0* thinking. The problem is that our current world requires *Version 5.0 thinking* to merely survive at this lightning fast pace, let alone create our dreams. It's time for some *truth*. *Our truth*, not our parent's truth or someone else's version of the truth that goads us into buying their beliefs or something they're selling.

The *Baby Boom* Parents born between 1946 and 1965, were raised by post war parents with *Version 2.0* and *3.0* thinking. When we take a moment to understand their truth, we'll find it grew from a seed of their environment and we'll quickly get a sense of their psychology. And as 80 percent of success is based on psychology we soon realise why we need to upgrade our brain to *Version 5.0 thinking* to accept and download a whole new raft of belief apps.

THE FIVE FEAR LANGUAGES

Due to the state of the world after World War II, the Baby Boomers learned how to skimp on spending. They mastered how to make their dollar stretch further and they did what they were told. When they got older and had more money, they spent up big, trying to make up for all they didn't have. In the main, they were not good money managers. Growing up, the hierarchical roles of the boss and the worker, the teacher and the student, the parent and the child were clear. The *rules* were not vague *guidelines*, they were laws set in stone and if subordinates did not abide by the rules, there were consequences. In some cases severe consequences and it usually meant pain of some sort.

If you've ever read Gary Chapman's insightful book — *The Five Love Languages*, the pain I'm talking about here is the exact opposite to Gary's *Five Love Languages*[3] — I would call them *Five Fear Languages* or *Punitive Language*. If you didn't do the right thing, and abide by the rules, one or more of the following five things would happen:

Gary Chapman's Five Love Languages (they're in the left column)

The 5 Love Languages	The 5 Fear Languages — Punitive Language
1. Words of Affirmation	1. Words of Abuse or no words at all
2. Quality Time	2. Hard Time
3. Receiving Gifts	3. Denial or Removal of Gifts
4. Acts of Service	4. Denial or Removal of Privileges — Acts of Avoidance
5. Physical Touch	5. Physical Pain — Segregation or Physical Abuse

As long ago as perhaps circa 2000 BC and much later, further reinforced during the industrial revolution — an idea was embraced and encouraged, *keep everyone in line.* The Baby Boomers were raised on this belief and today we call this idea *The Carrot and the Stick* and worse, it's still alive and well in parenting, in business, in sport, in social groups, in our educational system and in anyone's brain who as yet, still has not upgraded to *Version 5.0* thinking. It's time to wake up the corporate world, the advertisers, the marketers and the religious zealots — we're moving to a new refreshing truth, a revivalist *Version 5.0* thinking.

5

THE CARROT AND THE STICK
DOESN'T WORK

As a child of the pre-Baby Boomers, the *Silent Generation* — let me say that the *stick* was alive and well and whippy in my family and it hurt like hell. A strong belief of the *Silent Generation* was, 'Children should be seen and not heard'. As a child, if I spoke out or disagreed with my parents, their first line of defence was *#1 Words of Abuse*. I was given a good telling off, typically with a great deal of threat which usually advanced me to *#2* where I was given a *Hard Time* as everyone got involved, even my siblings (as it averted the negative attention from them).

If I persisted with my disagreement, the situation quickly degenerated to *#3 Denial or Removal of Gifts* and/or *#4 Denial or Removal of Privileges*. If I did it again my matriarchal family would send in the big gun — my mother. She would go straight to *#5 Physical Pain*.

Pain for me was the cane that my mother kept menacingly at the ready in a thin gap between the kitchen cupboards. The result? I didn't do it again. Now while that kept me quite, it worked for my parents, it didn't work for me. Eventually, in my teens, I shifted to *Version 3.0* thinking and rebelled. For this reason, the stick strategy for most will only suppress a person or worse, it will have them rebel. Thankfully, most of my early self-development training was focused on removing much of the psychological baggage I picked up as a child — phew! Thank God, that's over!

I also discovered that the carrot didn't work either. While it may have worked at first, eventually I became accustomed to the size of the reward. Soon enough, as the task became boring or harder to get myself motivated to complete the task, my expectations would grow to become even more ambitious. I expected more for doing less. The old rewards no longer seemed attractive enough.

Don't get me wrong, my parents were not bad and they weren't good either. They did the best they could with all the resources they had at the time. They have now both passed on and I still love them dearly. I cannot take away from my parents the great values they taught me, such as independence, persistence and a strong work ethic. These values led me to succeed in my career, much earlier than most. I've shifted many of those old debilitating beliefs and I've made peace with my past, and my parents. They were doing the best they could with the best software they had at the time, and the best they had was a brain installed with *Version 2.0* software — today it's redundant.

Further proof of *Version 2.0*'s redundancy can be found in Daniel Pink's book *Drive* — he suggests that, "Carrots and sticks can achieve precisely the opposite of their intended aims. Mechanisms designed to increase motivation can dampen it. Tactics aimed at boosting creativity can reduce it. Programs to promote good deeds can make them disappear. They can give us less of what we want — and more of what we don't want."[1] Pink also shares a well-cited study that reveals some paradigm shifting research.

"Psychologists Mark Lepper, David Greene and Robert

Nisbett discovered something which has become a classic in the field and among the most cited articles in the motivation literature. The three researchers watched a classroom of pre-schoolers for several days and identified the children who chose to spend their free playtime drawing. Then they fashioned an experiment to test the effect of rewarding an activity these children clearly enjoyed.

"The researchers divided the children into three groups. The first was the expected reward group. They showed each of these children a *Good Player Certificate* — adorned with a blue ribbon and featuring the child's name — and asked if the child wanted to draw in order to receive the award.

"The second group was the unexpected-award group. Researchers asked these children simply if they wanted to draw. If they decided to, when the session ended, the researchers handed each child one of the Good Player certificates. The third group was the no-award group. Researchers asked these children if they wanted to draw, but neither promised them a certificate at the beginning nor gave them one at the end.

"Two weeks later, back in the classroom, teachers set out paper and markers during the preschool's free play period while the researchers secretly observed the students. Children previously in the unexpected-award and no-award groups drew just as much, and with the same relish, as they had before the experiment. But the children in the first group — the ones who'd expected and then received an award — showed much less interest and spent much less time drawing."[2]

WHAT IF THE BELIEFS THAT AIM TO GROW OUR CORPORATIONS DO THE OPPOSITE?

So the beliefs we have come to accept about how to motivate people using the *carrot* or the *stick* are totally and completely wrong. Yet still today, many sales teams, management systems and companies around the globe are operating on no more than *Version 2.0* thinking and its associated beliefs. They're running off some outdated concept that might have worked for an earlier time — perhaps it worked long enough to see the research show that results improved. Once they got their research, which of course would have met their beliefs, they never researched their incentives or their management systems again. Though I bet that over time their results diminished and their teams burned and churned.

Version 2.0 thinking is hurting our corporate organisations. I recall many years ago working in a sales team that was entirely incentive-based. It also adopted a lot more of *Version 1.0* (Survivalist) and some *Version 2.0* thinking (Hierarchic). So it was comparable to the military in its aggressive tone and regiment — management embraced the *stick* mentality. And equally it was not unlike government in its hierarchy though commercialised with a high emphasis on incentives. You weren't paid an income; instead you earned a commission. If you didn't make your budget you got eight percent of your personal sales. If you made budget, you got ten percent of your sales. If you exceeded budget you got twelve percent of your sales. The complexities and confrontations arose when your budget was increased at a moment's notice. Typically right after you made or exceeded budget.

The sales director was the boss. The structure was painfully *hierarchic*. If you didn't *toe the line*, you had clients taken from your list and the real kick in the pants was when you made a sale, but the sales director chose not to approve the sale — for whatever reason he justified away. Not only was the burn and churn rife, so were the lawyers. I'd never worked in a company that had been taken to court so often — by its staff! It was highly competitive among the sales team, but only for short runs until another staff member would resign and choose to work for a competitor. It seemed from the outside professional but on the inside it was truly chaotic and caustic. Most of the sales staff utilised sniper-like tactics and usually fell onto their own bayonets. It was sad to watch. It's a little like listening to the Australian House of Representatives in action. Check out this hilarious YouTube®, http://bit.ly/OzPollies and witness some obvious *Version 2.0* thinking, and here's more, sadly from our current Prime Minister: http://bit.ly/OurPrimeMinistersViewofWomen

DO OUR LEADERS NEED TO UPGRADE TO *VERSION 5.0* THINKING?

While many of our corporate leaders would do well with a *Version 5.0* facelift, perhaps a shift in thinking should start with our leaders? Observe how so called political leaders, educated adults in Australia's political arena argue their points under the safety of parliament privilege. It takes only a small moment of listening to quickly realise that many heads of Government are still using *Version 1.0* or at best *Version 2.0* thinking. An easy way to know what *Version* someone possess, just observe how quickly they reach for the metaphorical stick when they don't know how to justify their point, argue their case or fix a problem! While there are no sticks apparent — listen to their words. They are often words that were used by primary school children and are often scathing and disrespectful.

If we truly want to see a better world, then an upgrade

should start with our leaders — though few leaders may think so. Many believe they've *arrived* and will not invest any further in their own self-development. I would love to see a leader who is truly congruent to a global cause that speaks with respect, authority and with *Version 5.0* thinking. Though here in Australia, many of our leaders today believe that intelligence, clever words and savvy politics is enough — *Sorry*.

If we want to see a harmonious world — we need to upgrade our thinking.

If we want world peace — we need to upgrade our thinking.

If we want to protect and conserve our environment — we need to upgrade our thinking.

If we want to sustain our planet's resources — we need to upgrade our thinking.

If we want our children to succeed — we need to upgrade *our* thinking.

If we want more responsible governance — we need to upgrade our thinking.

If we want to love and be loved — we need to upgrade our thinking.

If we truly want a world where everyone can enjoy life together as a much larger community, then we need a mindset upgrade to *Version 5.0* thinking *Conscious Awareness*. It is an opportunity to wake up to ourselves and our interrelationship with the world. We need to become conscious and open our hearts to become more caring when we interact with one another.

We know that our beliefs determine how we function and they stem from *Version 1.0* onwards. Our beliefs determine our lives, so who determines our beliefs? Let me share with you some ideas surrounding the concept of destiny and the associated beliefs, because I'm sure you get a sense that your brain is almost ready for its upgrade, you're in great shape — enjoy the rest of the download.

6

IS YOUR LIFE AN ACCIDENT?

Beliefs can incarcerate us or liberate us. One significant and eternal question is around a belief that I would call a major driver — do we have a destiny? Are we guided by some external force — God, Mohammad, Allah, Buddha or our Higher Selves perhaps?

My wealth mentor taught me that there is a natural flow to life, almost like a river that finds its easiest path. He told me that when you find your own personal flow, all would become easier. Though most of us are swimming as if our life depended upon it, swimming upstream against the current, when we could just go with the flow — and move downstream, in harmony with the river of life. For me, at first, this felt far too passive, but I soon got the lesson. I discovered that there are some powerful principles in the way that the world works and the way in which money works too. Not now, but later in the book I will share this with you in *Belief #4 — I don't have enough money* and it's likely to completely transform the way you think about money. But more about that later...

When our lives are not unfolding, as we would like it to, a blend of accidents and limiting beliefs are usually responsible. It is then that we are swimming against our natural flow and order of things. When we are in our natural flow, we are allowing our destiny — let's term it *a calling* perhaps. I found my calling by accident, literally. It all started when I was out of my natural flow, either way, I found myself in a complete mess one night. How did it all start? Who caused it? Was it me, someone else or some other force? All I know is that it had a lot to do with my beliefs at the time, it happened fast and came out of seemingly nowhere.

It began on a moonless night. I was driving along a country road that was leading me home, or so I thought. It was pitch-black and my car's illuminated speedometer needle was nudging 110 kph (69 mph) before something mysterious caused my car to jump and spin out of control. I never ever found out what happened to this day. But there I was in a car, out of control, spinning around wildly and my car's tyres were screeching across the rough texture of a bitumen road. It caused my heart to race; it was pounding into my throat. My headlights illuminated the darkness in circular flashes as I spun continuously out of control, my eyes blurred by speed and my mind was like spaghetti in a blender. Due to too many glasses of red wine I might add. Then, BANG!!!! I came to complete stop.

My passenger side door had collapsed in towards me in the driver seat. The left-hand-side pillar of my car was almost touching my left temple. It was over. My car was wrapped around a massive ghost gum tree. It was now hauntingly quiet except for the hissing steam escaping from my car's radiator. I took a big gasp of air as I realised I hadn't had a lungful for some time. The car was stopped. The engine was dead. I was in shock.

OUR LIVES BECOME PROTOTYPICAL OF THE VERSION OF THINKING THAT CREATED IT

Looking around my car, I could see the contents of my glove box strewn all around the inside, mostly on the floor. I felt the discomfort from my twisted dashboard that wrapped itself around my left side. I stared at the passenger's pillar that was bent inwards — it just kissed my head. I could see my passenger side rear taillight still glowing, reflected in my dangling external side mirror. The car was a distorted mess. It was a wreck. Not unlike my life at the time. Our *things* become a reflection of our *thoughts*. Our lives become prototypical of the version of thinking that created it.

For just a moment I wanted to believe that the whole thing was a dream. I turned the ignition key to "start," expecting the engine to reignite. It didn't. The last thing I saw before losing consciousness was what seemed to be a car's headlights shining from behind me and creating a spider web of light as it reflected into my broken windscreen.

In what seemed like seconds later, I found myself seated at the dinner table at my home. How I got there, still today I do not know. While I am certainly not proud of that time in my life, it serves to demonstrate the power of our beliefs. My beliefs created it.

MY BELIEFS CREATED MY DESTINY

This was my wake up call. In the months preceding my accident, I knew my actions were not aligned with my vision of my ideal life, nor were my beliefs. But I just kept hitting the snooze button saying to myself that I would deal with my problems later, tomorrow, another day. My final alarm was a car accident that was destined to happen to me in the Lesmurdie Hills of Western Australia. My beliefs created my destiny. While it was fuelled by the anger and the frustration of my company losing hundreds of thousands of dollars, it was also caused by alcohol.

It was not a great time of my life. My company looked like it was about to go belly up.

I believed that my company's misfortune was happening to all businesses during the recession of the 80s. Though that was not true — it was a lie I was telling myself. While it was my belief, that same belief was a lie to others. Everyone did not share the belief, as many multi-millionaires with *Version 4.0* thinking were created at this very same time in the very same pond. It wasn't nice, but then reality is sometimes far from nice. It wasn't pretty as the truth can be pretty ugly at times.

How do we come to end up in such predicaments? How have you come to end up here, in this very moment of time, reading this book? What caused *this* precise event to occur? Do you know? Was this book recommended to you or did you seek it out? Did it seek you out? Is it timely? Was it consciously created through strategic planning and design or was it an accident? Do you even believe in accidents? Or do you believe in destiny or both? Is your life the creation of your own design or are you moving along a destinal path of some sort? Your decisions determine what happens next. They become your beliefs, perhaps they're even part of your upgrade.

In my ten years of clinical work and through my extensive study into how our thinking works, I have come to believe (pardon the pun) that our beliefs are our life's drivers. I discovered that if you can change a person's beliefs, the issues would typically go with the beliefs that started them. Be our issues depression, anxiety, a phobia, financial hardship, poor health, anger, blame, sadness, guilt or fear; regardless of the issue, I believe that the one common denominator is that beliefs are at the core of the issue itself.

As I said in my previous book, *The Secrets to Creating a Life*

Beyond Limits, "…It is time to wake up from the deep sleep, the two-thousand year slumber that has entranced the multitudes of this planet into believing that they are less and limited. Incarcerated by fear, judgement and ridicule, the people of this planet are

> ❋
> *I am not a product of my circumstances. I am product of my decisions.*
> **– Stephen Covey**

discovering the keys to unlock the door of unlimited potential. There is no one master key, there are a series of steps that you can take and the first step is to wake up from the illusion of limitation. It is time to become fully conscious, to snap out of the haze of the busyness, to get beyond the stress and the pain that we have induced and endured for so long."[1] It all starts with our beliefs!

As we become aware of our beliefs, the drivers of our lives, then our *conscious awareness* grows. It is like one morning we awaken from a nightmare and start dreaming again, blissfully. With our new beliefs intact, we will look around to see a new world emerging. It will be the world of *your* creation. It isn't easy at first, as it seems that our old self resists the new way, no matter how glorious it may seem. It's not bad — it's just different. Nonetheless I must say that waking up requires a little more effort than staying in a trance and doing what you've always done. Though trust me, it's certainly worth it.

TAKE RESPONSIBILITY FOR YOUR LIFE. YOU ARE ITS CAUSE

Now that I review my car accident with the wisdom of time, it was predictable and at some level I knew it or something like it would come to shift me out of my stupor. I had been living so close to the edge of death that life had to wake me up to the beliefs that were driving my life down a predetermined road. The first step in any transformation is akin to the first step towards *unconscious incompetence* — *we don't know what we don't know*, so we must awaken. We must stop blaming other people, things or events for our lives being the way they are. If we want our lives to change, we need to take full responsibility for them and take account of the beliefs that predict our behaviour and so our lives.

Should you become as curious as a child again, courageous perhaps, you will discover that to transform your life, the very first step is to make a *decision* for a better life. It is only when we decide to improve or transform our lives that we will do the work. In the next chapter we'll explore the mechanics and structure of a transformation.

7

HOW TO ADD VALUE TO YOUR LIFE

On March 10 2000, the Internet bubble burst. The massive high tide on Internet stocks had receded and the business world lost its *belief* in this thing called 'The World Wide Web' and its promise to change the face of business and commerce. The faith in Internet stocks plummeted and its viability as a business was highly questionable. *Cisco's* stock declined by 86 percent, *Amazon's* stock value dropped from $107 per share to just $7. The business community expected Jeff Bezos's online bookstore to close the chapter on the Internet. For those who held the faith, Amazon's shares at time of writing are valued at $402.29 per share with a market capitalisation of $ 184.14 billion!

It was around the year 2000, around the time the world wide bubble POPPED! It was then that I got my most valuable business lesson. I call it my *Billion Dollar Degree* and I'll give you my lesson up front — trust me, it's worth billions! "Twenty percent of business success is due to mechanics and 80 percent is due to your psychology. Upgrade your psychology and you can adjust your mechanics to make anything succeed."

My *Billion Dollar Degree* all started from an idea that came to me almost in complete form, it came to me in a flash! I had just had the inside of my Mentone home painted and I added a feature wall of an inspirational colour to each room. I imagined that each time I looked into the colours I would become inspired. My belief seemed to work — no surprises there.

One evening I was walking through my lounge towards my study when I passed my favourite coloured wall. It was a massive wall of stunning turquoise, my favourite colour. Then BANG! It hit me! An idea that would not only change my financial fortune but would make tertiary education affordable for the entire world! I was so excited I couldn't sleep. I was still at my computer putting together the matrix of the idea at three am in the morning. I was excited and stimulated beyond measure.

At the time, real estate in Australia was becoming more and more expensive. People were saying that soon real estate would be out of reach of the youth of the day. Maybe it was this sort of conversation that stimulated the idea, I'm not sure. I can however recall thinking that one of the biggest costs in setting up a University or College was the acquisition of the real estate and the development costs. Unless you did it online! A web-based University means you don't need the real estate, you don't have to develop the land and you're not limited to where you build it! *And* you're not limited to seats in the lecture theatres or seats in the classes, plus you would save on wages too. Build it online and we could service any country at any time of the day! Bloody Brilliant! I just needed a few bright designers, developers and programmers and at the time, they were pumping them out of Universities all around the world. Tertiary educational content would be a little harder to obtain. But it just so happened that later that morning I would be meeting with a gentleman by the name of John Ledingham and taking him to the *Melbourne Grand Prix*. And guess what? John just so happened to own a College in the heart of Melbourne! His College of course owned tertiary educational content!

Before heading off to the *Grand Prix*, I called John and suggested we enjoy a coffee at the *Sheraton* near my office in Southbank. Over coffee I showed John the idea. His jaw dropped and he went weak at the knees. That day we agreed to become business partners in an online educational venture called *Intellect21*. Our first business plan included a financial plan that showed that with only a marginal percentage of the student market at the time, a figure of around 7,500 students our *Earnings Before Interest and Tax* (EBIT) would equate to $42 Million in our first year! By the way, the tertiary student population today is estimated at 20,802,305!

Within days we were in Indonesia pitching our idea when we were asked to meet a Vice Chancellor of a Universitas Terbuka that serviced over 175,000 distance education students! They had heard about our business and were highly enthusiastic about our mirrored visions. They wanted in and that would take our EBIT to almost $1 Billion! You could imagine what happened to our physiology and our psychology upon hearing *that* number. Now at $42 Million it's certainly a viable business, but at $1 Billion! Now that's a real game changer! Our physiology was up to it, but the question was — was our psychology up to it? Did we possess a billion dollar mindset and the self-esteem to make this work? Forgive me if I cut a very long story short...

LESS REALLY IS MORE; SOMETIMES WE NEED TO REMOVE TO ADD

How did it all turn out? One word — *tragically*. At the time, the size and scope of the business was well beyond us all. Universitas

Terbuka was not the only organisation to show interest in our venture. We had people from all over the world flying to our Melbourne office, so excited about *Intellect21* and wanting a slice of the action. Perhaps our business savvy at the time was not up to the task, as we were fumbling all over the place. Our business changed not only from day to day, but also from minute to minute and in truth we became scared of the enormity of this opportunity. While under our breath we probably all swore at each other for some of the dumb business decisions that we made. The truth was we made those decisions because our beliefs were not of the calibre required for an idea of this magnitude. We were running off *Version 4.0* thinking when we truly needed *Version 5.0*. We were certainly creative with our *Lateral Version 4.0* — but not *aware*. We needed to transform our psychology, but we didn't. My *Billion Dollar Degree* taught me a powerful lesson. It gave me the mechanics behind the development of a successful mindset. Let me share it with you.

The Path of Transformation

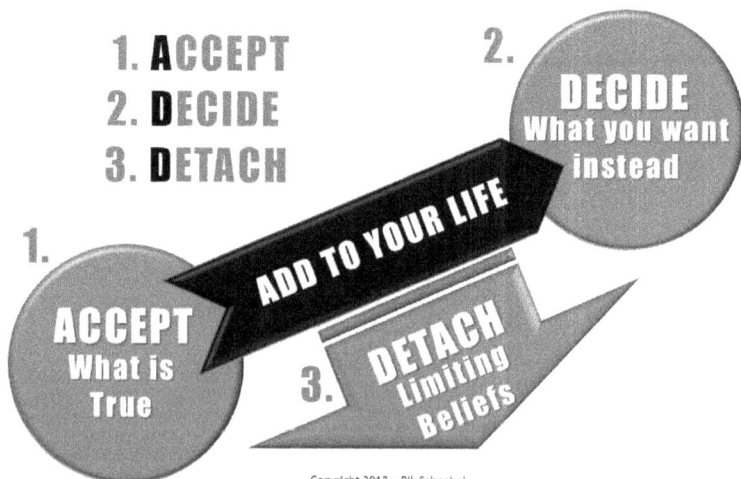

1. ACCEPT
2. DECIDE
3. DETACH

1. ACCEPT
What is True

2. DECIDE
What you want instead

3. DETACH
Limiting Beliefs

ADD TO YOUR LIFE

I have discovered that to truly transform we must add by subtracting. I call it *the* 'ADD formula'; Accept + Decide - Detach = Transformation. *ACCEPT* the situation as it really is, and if it's not desirable, then *DECIDE* what we want *instead* and *DETACH* from all that is making the situation worse than it actually is. That's why I believe everyone needs a Coach! A Coach will help us to *ACCEPT* what is real; then help us to *DECIDE* what we want instead. Here a great Coach comes into their own through their knowledge in helping us to *DETACH* from all that's stopping us. Just a little tip though — be sure to work with a Coach that's NLP trained and *accredited* up to Masters — that way you'll be working with someone who really knows how to remove your neurological limitations. As a starting point you'll find accredited Masters here,

http://www.lifebeyondlimits.com.au/our-nlp-coaches.html

So the first step of transformation is to ACCEPT what is *real* and what is *not real*. This is based on what we touched on earlier — our beliefs are so often created from our current Version of thinking and can colour anything we experience. In truth, many of our beliefs are LIES! We've just made them all up. So in order to transform, we need to get real about what is actually going on — it's almost like being the observer of the experience rather than the participant, and abandoning all our beliefs to see with greater clarity. We need to see things as they are, not better than they are, not worse.

It is critical that we remove anything that is not real that we've made up about the situation. For that reason I do not subscribe to *Positive Thinking* as it usually asks us to see everything, even highly emotionally charged negative experiences as a positive and that's delusional or akin to an ostrich shoving its head into the sand. For example; imagine a couple who are going through a marital separation. He sees her as a *bitch* and she thinks he's a *bastard*. We must come to realise that *bitch* and *bastard* are simply *judgemental* words, they're actually lies coloured by limiting beliefs and highly charged emotions. While each individual's behaviour may not be saintly, seeing the other party as a *bitch* or *bastard* will not encourage an amicable resolution. The truth of the matter is that both parties are hurting and like wounded animals, they are striking out to avoid more pain.

So when we *ACCEPT* the situation as it really is, then we create the opportunity to *DECIDE* what we want *instead*. To leverage from the example of the couple aforementioned, then if we truly want to create harmony in our lives or a relationship resolution, we must *DETACH* from all that is making the situation worse than it actually is. This means we must decide to let go of the negative memories, the stories that perpetuate them, the limiting beliefs and the internal conflicts. I know I'm making it sound easy, but it truly is when both parties make a real decision to let go of the pain.

❋
We must accept finite disappointment, but never lose infinite hope.
– Martin Luther

Most arguments are due to two people's beliefs clashing — for whatever reason. The truth is they are unhappy in their relationship and when they blame each other for their unhappiness instead of taking responsibility for their own happiness, that's when men become *bastards* and women become *bitches*.

The second step or the first *D* stands for *DECIDE* what you want. Only then can we create what is really required to have our needs met. I'm still amazed at how few people really know what they want, yet are so vocal about what they don't want — they would gain massively from just this point.

You usually get what you focus on — so decide what you want to focus on. When we have *Accepted* what is real right here, right now and we have *Decided* what we want to happen instead, we are now ready for the final stage, *Detach* — This is 101 Gap Analysis!

OUR STORIES BECOME OUR BELIEFS

The final step is the second *D* for *DETACH*. *Detach* from the stories we're telling ourselves that's perpetuating the problem. The 'He said, She said' blame game stuff that stops us from ever moving on. *Detach* from the emotional baggage that is holding us back or creating what I call a *Stuck State*. *Detach* from the geography, the people and events, anything that is stopping us from getting what we want. While it sounds counter intuitive, to truly transform we must add by subtracting. *Accept + Decide - Detach = Transformation.*

The way we have trained our minds, is we start with *reasons* and then the *answers* come second. In other words, we're telling ourselves stories most of the time about all sorts of situations in our lives and when we believe these stories those stories become us. If we wish to transcend from these stories, we must *Detach* from these stories, simply by stopping ourselves from repeating them in our heads or out loud, particularly if we want to shift our behaviour and transform our lives.

DIVORCE THE STORY AND MARRY THE TRUTH

We all have conditions in the past that we can bring out and magnify. Think about a crappy situation in your life right now and ask yourself: *What crappy story am I telling myself that's perpetuating the problem or situation?* Keep telling yourself *that* story and you'll create associated beliefs that keep you there, stuck in the rut. That's how quickly we can form beliefs — they can happen in an instant and the story around the belief holds it there. When we wake up to our own stories, we'll likely decide to *divorce our stories and marry the truth.* The truth in this case, will truly set you free my friend.

When I was a kid. I used to tell myself the sad old story that I was *weird*, *different* and *poor.* I invested well in removing the *poor* program and it certainly paid off, in multiples! In fact still today I can't believe I held on to that useless program for so long — though I guess I didn't know what I know now. I wish I had. Much of the work I did to remove the *poor program* was by using the *ADD* philosophy in practice. My weird and different programs became the very source of my success — I turned them around — I *reframed* them, to use a coaching term. I'll provide some techniques and resources further into the book.

Regarding *Intellect21*, had I gained my *Billion Dollar Degree* earlier, I could have seen the problem for what it really was and accepted the fact that we were all scared. Then we all could have decided what we needed to be instead and then detached from the fear by talking it out. Instead our egotistical pride got in the way and we all walked away from our vision and the business idea folded. Today our idea is alive, through the many Universities around the world whom are utilising our concept. In the beginning, many of these same Universities said our model wouldn't work, *it couldn't be done* they said. When someone says, *It can't be done* it is simply their belief; or is it a lie? So what are these things called *beliefs*, really?

8
WHAT ARE BELIEFS *REALLY*?

Everything that exists in the world today does so because someone believed in it. While Henry Ford today is well known for his innovative and breakthrough assembly line, where he production lined his Ford motorcar, he wasn't an instant success. In fact, his early businesses failed and he was flat broke five times before he founded the successful *Ford Motor Company*. Most people, particularly in the US are familiar with R. H. Macy's large department store chain, but Macy needed more than a vision, he needed belief in himself. Macy started not one, but *seven* failed businesses before finally hitting the big time with his store in New York City.

Soichiro Honda was quoted as saying; "Success represents the 1% of your work which results from the 99% that is called 'failure'." This saying came from his belief system that began with a series of failures and a fortunate turn of luck (which of course Honda manifested). Honda applied for a job as an engineer and was turned down by *Toyota Motor Corporation*, leaving him jobless for quite some time. He then started making scooters out of his home, spurred on by his neighbours. Finally he backed himself and began his own business, the billion-dollar business that is *Honda®*.[1] Today *Honda®* is a finely tuned business from a finely tuned belief system — *Version 5.0* thinking well before it's time.

Another belief system before it's time can be found in Walt

Disney. Today *Disney®* is a multi-billion-dollar empire, funded by clever merchandising and licensing, movies and theme parks around the world, but Walt Disney himself had a bit of a tough start. A newspaper editor fired him because *he lacked imagination and had no good ideas* (funny that). After that, Disney started a number of businesses that didn't last too long and ended in bankruptcy and failure. His belief in his imagination kept him forging away his ideas and he eventually tapped into an idea and a recipe for success that worked. Though what level of belief in yourself and your ideas would you need to have, to be rejected 1,009 times with the same idea?

Harland David Sanders, perhaps better known as *Colonel Sanders* of *Kentucky Fried Chicken®* fame, had a hard time selling his chicken recipe at first. Though his patience paid off. In 1980 Colonel Sanders passed away and in 2007, 27 years later, KFC posted a revenue of £324.92 million and it had a work force of 24,000 employees. As of December 4, 2012 The Walt Disney Company is worth US$4.807 billion net income. Their total assets are worth US$72.124 billion. Today Honda Motor Company Ltd market capitalisation is $75,011,513,655! By comparison, my beliefs back in 2000 cost me a paltry US$1 billion. So what are our beliefs worth?

Our beliefs constitute a large part of who we are and what we do. They are based on the meaning we place on our perceptions of other people's stories and experiences, our own experiences and knowledge of the world, and how it works. For example, I believe that what you are reading now is written in English. I have beliefs about what objects can do, such as pens can be used to write on substrates such as paper and cameras can capture images. I have beliefs about the world in which I live: why people do what they do; why we get angry; why we get happy among other things. I have beliefs about many other people, including my family, friends, and associates; such as my daughter Sienna loves vanilla ice cream with chocolate topping — lots of it. Zoe my oldest daughter prefers vanilla ice cream and loves having lots of friends but hates it when her friends fight for her attention. I also know that Zoe believes she will be a teacher like her dad and Sienna believes she will work with animals. Because they believe this, it is highly likely to occur. Not guaranteed, but highly likely.

Our beliefs are bundled up in a series of neurons represented in our brain and ready for use whenever we need them. If we were to try to list our beliefs, we would do so using English sentences, such as; *If you fake laugh long enough you'll start to really laugh, really, really hard* and *every year, millions of trees grow thanks to the way nature works to sustain itself and because squirrels forget where they buried their nuts.* We can also state what we don't believe in, such as; *I don't believe when we die it's over — I believe our spirit lives on.* Sometimes beliefs can sound like facts or knowledge — but are they really that?

What are beliefs really? If we really want to know, we need look no further than our lives. Our lives are a mirror of our beliefs. If we believe, for example, that *people are generally lazy*, we'll most likely value *working* highly and mentally beat ourselves up should we dare rest or play. It's also likely that we'll invest our time working for most of our day and it's probable that we'll treat tardiness or laziness with disdain. The chance of one or both of our parents holding the same belief is very high. We accepted that belief without question in our formative years. So while that belief may have fuelled us in the beginning, it has created a pattern, it's what we do and has become our destiny. It is likely that still today, we work, work, work our butts off and chances are we find it easier to work and harder to rest. That's what our beliefs do. As Gandhi's quote at the beginning of this book states:

*"Your **Beliefs** become your Thoughts*
Your Thoughts become your Words
Your Words become Actions
Your Actions become your Habits
Your Habits become your Values
*Your Values become your **Destiny**"*

— Mahatma Gandhi.

If we're working hard, working long hours to make ends meet, then it's likely that that's the very belief that has us working hard — *we must work long hours to make ends meet* — it's actually not true, though for most who believe it is, it is. As a coach, I've noted that people who believe they *must work hard to make ends meet* earn only, what they need, no more.

If we are the CEO or the business owner and we believe CEOs and business owners must work harder than anyone else to succeed — we will. I know this — because I once held those very beliefs close to my heart. Today I work far less than I ever did and earn far more than I ever have. Why? Because I upgraded my beliefs. I learned to challenge the beliefs that stopped me from getting what I *really* wanted. In fact, it has taken me two days to get back to writing this chapter because the surf has been awesome! I'm so glad I changed my beliefs J

Beliefs produce a natural cycle within us that becomes our unconscious patterns. We hardly have to think about them, though these beliefs massively influence our lives — change the beliefs and you'll most likely change your life.

OUR BELIEFS ARE MAGNETS
AND OPPORTUNITIES TO EVOLVE

Metaphorically, beliefs are magnetic in nature. They tend to attract the situations and circumstances that match the belief. For example; someone who believes they're not smart will find that they're cruising through their day, relatively calm with a normal heart rate until they're intellectually challenged and WHAMMO! Their heart rate increases and they trigger a heightened emotional response to the challenge. It is most probable that the part of the day that will be most remembered is that moment when they were challenged. That moment becomes their whole day, their whole challenge, their entire life, their destiny — unless they do something to change their belief. Until they do, they will experience event after event, after event, after event will continue to occur to challenge their limiting belief — until they do something, anything to change that belief. The sooner the masses realise this the sooner humanity evolves.

Here is how *our beliefs become our destiny*. Let's say, for example, we believe we're not smart. We will have a series of (stupid) sentences that we say to ourselves and others, which reinforces this BELIEF. These sentences are our THOUGHTS expressed through WORDS and create the scaffolding for our beliefs. Others will reflect back our words and in doing so, will place the bricks and mortar of our beliefs within the scaffolding framework. The next words we choose either consciously or unconsciously, will cause us do something to change the belief, make a new decision, though for most the words perpetuate the belief and the pattern by stopping us from ever doing anything about it.

What we do or don't do can be viewed as our ACTIONS or non-actions. Our actions or non-actions, become what we focus upon, and what we focus upon most becomes what we VALUE. So we might value time alone, away from people who will prove *we're not smart* or conversely, we spend time in situations that proves our beliefs. Our actions and non-actions become our patterns, namely a HABIT. So we prove to ourselves again and again that we're not smart — it ultimately becomes our DESTINY. Eventually we will program our unconscious to ensure, that in the future we will do anything but *smart*. We will have words for it, say 'dumb' or 'stupid' or some other judgement term will become our IDENTITY and perpetuate the cycle! We will aim to prove it to ourselves by cycling through this PATTERN often. Unless we get some coaching, read a breakthrough book or train it out of us. Break the beliefs that hold the pattern and we're free!

The 7 Phases of a Belief

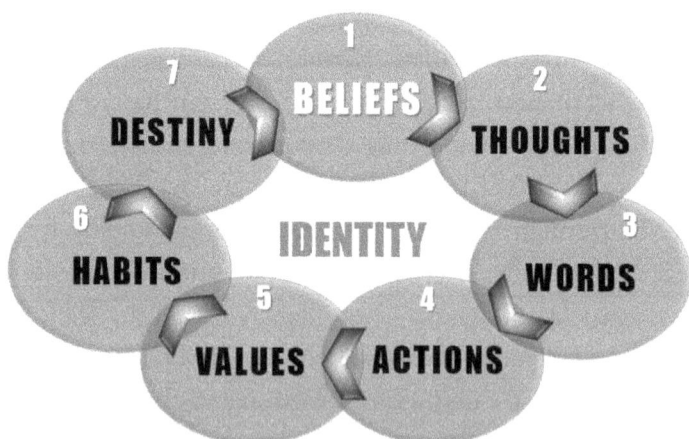

OUR CONVERSATIONS REVEAL OUR BELIEFS

If we are not sure of the beliefs that are creating our lives, we need to start listening to the conversations we have with others and in our head. But instead of engaging in the conversations and stories — become the observer of our thoughts and we will soon hear our beliefs.

When we hear someone say, *study hard and you'll get a good job!* That may well be their belief. Simply ask *why* and you are highly likely to hear their beliefs. Why? — *Because that's what my dad did and he got a good job and I did too.* So the belief is *if you study hard you'll get a good job.* Pretty simple isn't it?

The truth however is that *studying hard to get a good job* is not always true. I recall some people who hardly studied at all and gained high grades at school. Others who studied religiously, tirelessly and gained low or average marks. Others who gained top marks and some who didn't study at all and failed school altogether, today some of them are doing wonderfully in their businesses and careers. Were their results due to their studies or their beliefs, or both?

Ask someone why he or she always does their shopping on Wednesday after work and you'll hear their belief. Ask someone why they earn what they earn and you'll hear their beliefs about the working world or how money works or how it doesn't work. Ask someone what is the key to a harmonious or happy marriage and yes, you guessed it — you'll hear their beliefs on the subject of relationships or marriage.

So it could be said that our beliefs determine our levels of success and what we attain in life. After all, success *begins* the moment that we *believe* it is possible and *faithfully commit* to the actions that move us forward. If we do not believe we will be successful then we will not do what *must* be done — we won't even start! I've witnessed people who go through the motions that lead to success and at the same time believe that they will fail — and surely enough they find a way to prove their belief is true. This belief will have them place one foot on the accelerator of their ideas while placing one foot on the brake. They find the first excuse, the first reason to doubt and they quit or find a justifiable way, even an intellectual way to self-sabotage. While those who really choose to believe in success just keep finding ways over, under and around those same hurdles. Success might not come easily, though it does eventuate with a healthy and empowered belief in self and success.

WE'RE BELIEF-MAKING MACHINES

We are not born with beliefs though soon enough we become *belief-making machines*, creating millions upon millions of synaptic clusters that hold our beliefs within our neurology. We grow more and more beliefs and discard some older, conflicting beliefs as we learn from the environment around us, the creatures and the people we interact with, and the many events that come from all our interactions.

We might experience an event, such as being bitten or frightened by a spider and from that one event we come to believe that *spiders are dangerous* and avoid them at all costs. Perhaps even to the degree that we instil a debilitating phobia that we carry with us for the rest of our lives.

The moment we are bitten by the spider or even the mere threat causes us to create a *tightly wound neural network* that ensures we'll never risk our *life* around spiders again. While the phobia, when it's playing out, might look like an overreaction, it makes perfect sense in the neural world. This is our *Version 1.0* program that moves us into *Survivalist* mode. This electronically activates the associated beliefs by firing off the relevant neurons that activate the program. This program ensures we're safe and do not risk our lives. While a small spider may not kill us — our brain thinks it will and has our body move almost involuntarily to avoid it. *Version 1.0* is our oldest brain and its very motivation *is safety*.

When I learned that most phobias are merely *tightly wound neural networks* my clinic had queues of people who came to me to remove their phobias. Word spread quickly. Though weirdly, after my success with my first phobia clients, I believed it would.

TRANSFORMATION BEGINS BY OPENING OUR MINDS TO NEW WAYS OF THINKING

Every interaction, every event has the potential to create new beliefs. For example; imagine what beliefs would be formed from a ten-year term in a maximum-security prison? What would we form from a one-year working holiday in a third world country orphanage or a month in court trying to resolve a nasty divorce? People who engage in a particular practice are more likely to develop beliefs from that practice — just like Eskimos have about 70 words for snow and people who have never experienced snow have about one — *snow*.

People who engage in the same environment every day will likely build an intimacy and a series of beliefs surrounding that environment. It's like

❋
Minds are like parachutes; they are best when they are open.
— Tommy Deware

pointing your brain at a subject and building all kinds of beliefs around that subject. People who spend their Sundays in church for example will build beliefs around that specific religion, while those who spend their Sundays at the football will crystallize their beliefs around another religion, namely their sport. It's not right, it's not wrong — it's just the way they think — it's their beliefs.

If we want to truly transform, then we must open our minds to new ways of thinking. How do we do that specifically? We simply observe and question our thinking. The very act of doing so will start to evolve our beliefs to *Version 5.0* — *Conscious Awareness*. *Conscious Awareness* is simple, but not easy to do. To start, remain awake to all you and others say, all you think and how you engage with the world — without actually emotionally engaging. In our *Career and Life Mastery (CALM Level I)* training it takes our participants eight days to attain this level of upgrade. Though, its life shifting — that's for sure.

If we're in an unconscious pattern — in other words we're not aware of the pattern itself that is causing us harm or difficulty, then we need to wake up by asking ourselves some hard questions. It's like asking: *What if I'm completely wrong about this?* For some people who have a high need to be right all of the time, that sentence can feel like a death sentence. Though it's the start of an empowering journey and I promise you that what at first might feel uncomfortable, will soon liberate you.

In my first book, *The Secrets of Creating a Life Beyond Limits* I shared a story about a boss who was delivering an enormous amount of challenge my way. I was angry. I made judgements about him and about me. However, the problem moved quickly to resolution when I asked myself: *What if I'm completely wrong about this?* No, it's not easy to accept that we're wrong about something or anything for that matter. No one likes being wrong. But if we get used to being objective, even about our own thinking, we're likely to enjoy realising we're wrong and to start making some wonderful corrections.

Once upon a time I was very wrong about how the world worked, how people worked and how money worked. Opening up my mind and accepting that I could be wrong in the first instance lead me to enjoy the lifestyle I now love. I do what I want, when I want to and I've got a wonderful family and everything that we need. For me, it was more than worth it — it's everything.

WHICHEVER RIVER WE IMMERSE OURSELVES IN, SATURATES OUR BELIEFS

The Formation of Beliefs

Copyright 2013 – Rik Schnabel

We formulate our beliefs wherever and whenever we *invest* most of our time, focus and energy. Our depth of knowledge will expand in that specific area of our focus and will form clusters of new beliefs. *Whichever river we immerse ourselves in will saturate our beliefs.* We'll become who we're being. If we're swimming, we're swimmers; if we're fishing, we're anglers; and if we're drowning, we're flotsam.

To know who we truly have become, all we have to do is follow our journey: the teachers who taught us and how we felt or thought about them; the family that raised us; the friends with whom we associate; the economics of the time; the advertising and media we were subjected to and which ads we believed or hummed or recited. We have become a part of the leaders that inspired us; the events that impacted us; the religion we were exposed to has constructed the core fabric of who we are; and our beliefs keep it all together and perpetuate our very identity! Some or all of these sources might require abandoning. Some information might need to be deleted. Books often serve the purpose of adding new ideas and so new beliefs into our psyche. I trust I'm helping you to shift some limiting beliefs as you read.

As *belief making machines*, we are constantly seeking meaning from the information that gushes into our consciousness every day. Once we conclude what something means, we almost unconsciously construct a belief or series of beliefs associated to the experience. We now support those beliefs as we rationalise them away with explanations, almost always after the event. We thus become invested in the beliefs, forming reasons upon reasons to substantiate and reinforce the belief. Our mind seeks supporting evidence while deleting and blinding itself to anything contrary. It's almost as though the moment we construct a belief, we will do everything we can to retain it.

A belief is like a table. The tabletop is the belief itself, which is formed following witnessing an event or having an experience. We will unconsciously ask: *What does this mean and why did it happen?* We will mind read the meaning and mentally search to uncover the very intention of what we have just witnessed. Then we will form the legs of the table as we form the belief. The legs are the reasons that support the belief — the more reasons, the stronger the belief. Reasons to support a belief will fall into four categories (from strongest to weakest):

1. **Unconscious** — we just believe it. We have never questioned its validity and have no reason to.
2. **Evidence** — we have personally experienced it and verified it to be true.
3. **Doctrine** — authorities have verified it to be true.
4. **Hearsay** — others (a number of them) say that it is true.

The 4 Legs of a
BELIEF

INTENTION MEANING

UNCONSCIOUS   DOCTRINE   EVIDENCE   HEARSAY

Copyright 2014 – Rik Schnabel

Our brain is a meaning-making machine. Beliefs are manufactured with the help of two processes: *meaning* and *intention*. Quicker than a wink, we find meaningful patterns in both meaningful and meaningless data. We infuse those patterns with meaning and imagine its intention. We believe before we reason. Once beliefs are formed, we seek out confirmatory arguments and evidence to justify them. We ignore contrary evidence or make up rationalisations to explain it away. We do not like to admit we are wrong. We seldom change our minds.

We see a man walk out of a shop, he looks left and right and runs. He has a bag in his hand. We ask: *What does this mean (meaning) and why did it happen (intention)?* In our minds, he's already a thief, now we'll build support for this belief. We will listen out for further evidence such as police siren or look to see if someone will run from the shop to chase the man. This process occurs in our minds hundreds of times every day and that's how we form our beliefs.

If we didn't personally witness the event but heard about it from a number of people its *hearsay*. We know to steal is wrong, that is *doctrine*. We just would not even think to steal (but don't know where we got that belief from) — that's *unconscious*.

We seem to make up beliefs as we go along, but how powerful are they? Let me give you one of the stories that I shared in my previous book, *The Secrets of Creating a Life Beyond Limits* to reveal how powerful our beliefs can be.

"In Cleveland, USA a fatal experiment was conducted involving a prisoner. The experiment was designed to compare the strength of one's belief, against the strength of will and intellect, tested the prisoner beyond his previous belief. The event was described in Martin Kojc's book, *The Manual of Life*.

"After eating his last meal and summoned from death row,

the prisoner's time was up. Leaving his cell for the last time and upon entering the execution chamber he was directed to sit upon a chair. He was strapped to the chair, blindfolded and told that his execution was to be relatively painless. A small incision was about to be made to a vein in his neck and he would slowly but surely bleed to death. The prisoner prepared his mind for his inevitable passing. His white-knuckled hands gripped the chair's armrests as he awaited his end. He gasped as he felt a quick movement and felt a sharp pain at his neck. Instantly he heard the sound of his blood streaming from the cut in his neck. It was not unlike the sound of a cow's teat squirting its milk into a pail. The sound horrified him into a cold shiver and soon, he felt his life flow from his veins and died.

"The prisoner died from a brutal experiment, amounting from no more than a bloodless scratch to his neck. Below him, was a metal bucket into which researchers trickled water through a tube to mimic the sound of blood. Prior to his execution, the prisoner was in good health. It seems he died by *believing* that the pain he felt to his neck was an incision to an artery, and his beliefs convinced him, that the sound he heard was his own blood streaming from his neck. He believed what he heard and I would also suggest he also believed what he saw in his mind; a fading picture of his life. Could it be that he died by *believing* that his life-blood was leaving his body?"[2]

"Can beliefs be *that* powerful? Imagine committing this degree of belief to your life! Surgeons among many highly educated professionals appreciate the power of beliefs. Most surgeons are reluctant to operate on anyone who believes that they will die during the surgery.

"Make no mistake; our beliefs hold within them an awesome power. Our beliefs can kill us as easily as they can breathe life into our dreams. As a child, for some the bogeyman existed in the darkness and seemed to magically disappear the moment we found courage over darkness or for those who resorted to turn on the light. Beliefs are a feeling of certainty about something being real; they of course are not necessarily real."[3]

ARGUE FOR YOUR BELIEFS AND THEY ARE YOURS FOREVER

In my training and speaking, I have the pleasure of working with both small and large groups of people to help them to *untrain* their brain so they can get what they want from life, rather than what they're currently experiencing. Over the years I've worked with many thousands of people and it seems that no matter where people are in the world or how intelligent they may appear, I am continually astounded at our open microphone sessions as to how people will defend their beliefs, even though those same beliefs deceive them or disempower them. It's as though our intelligence is in jeopardy should we turn our back on those old beliefs. What's worse, those limiting beliefs play a convenient role in blinding us from our potential. In coaching we call this *secondary gain*. It's where someone gains a benefit for *not* adopting or embracing an empowering belief. If you've ever wondered why someone who wants to lose weight won't take those first vital steps, it's typically because the very decision to do so has them having to give up feeling good when they eat an old time favourite food. Or the mere thought of exercise exhausts them. They are just two examples from the many examples of *secondary gain*.

The fact that we even call some of our beliefs *limiting beliefs* is the reason we have limiting beliefs in the first instance. That's the very first belief that must go. Isn't it true that in life we get whatever we focus upon? So if we're focusing on our limiting beliefs all of the time, they're going to show up a heck of a lot more than if we focused on our assets. Trust me, we can make anything happen in our lives by choosing our focus and making a decision to infinitely focus on it.

IGNORANCE IS NOT BLISS

Just as the medieval clerics who refused to look through Galileo's telescope were afraid to abandon themselves to the power of a new myth, we so often attempt to reason out of existence the sights and experiences that are beyond our understanding. I used to find myself becoming frustrated by some people's blinkered rejection of the realm of potentiality. *There is no magic*, they would say. Others would say — *I'm stuck with who I am and I can't change that*. If that's what they believe, then they're right. How could anyone resist the benefits of a deeper understanding of life? Until I realised that the less a person is *consciously aware*, the easier it is for them to change nothing and do nothing. For some, it is easier to live in *ignorant bliss* until their life falls down around their ankles and they realise that ignorance is certainly not bliss.

Like the prisoner from Cleveland USA, if you can convince your conscious mind into believing that something is possible, that *something* moves through conscious thought and ultimately into our hard drive, our unconscious. Then our very cells will alter to help us to make it happen. We've all heard someone talk about a tickle in their throat on Monday and before long they tell you that they're getting a cold and soon enough the cold takes hold and they are away from work on Tuesday. What about someone who trips and says: *I'm just so clumsy*. They then reveal their clumsiness again and again and again. What drives a tightrope walker to demonstrate amazing balance and a billionaire the courage to build enormous wealth? A belief that *more is possible* is the driver behind success just as a belief that *nothing more than what we know exists* ensures a stagnant life.

Like a computer that deals in 0s and 1s the conscious mind seeks a *yes* or a *no* from the unconscious (our mind's library) before attempting anything new. A *yes* moves the body forward, while a *no* stops the body in its tracks. The unconscious mind is responsible for 95 percent of our functioning while the conscious mind is responsible for the rest. Unlike Richard Branson, Oprah Winfrey, Einstein, Tony Robbins, Edward de Bono, Gandhi, most people really don't like to think outside of their current thinking. Most people resist change or challenge unless they absolutely have to and then they need to consciously focus their efforts.

John Davidson writes in *The Secret of the Creative Vacuum — Man and the Energy Dance* — "…a concentrated mind is able to control physical matter and manipulate the laws of nature. This is how the miracles associated with yogis and holy men are performed. It is also the means by which paranormal phenomena take place. All spiritual practices entail concentration of the mind, whether it is prayer, meditation, telling of beads or some other technique."[4]

Our beliefs are a culmination of what we accept and what we do not. They are summary of our predominant thoughts and experiences. If we

❋

A man becomes what he thinks about most.

– Ralph Waldo Emerson

believe we are able to do a particular thing, we will consciously, and often unconsciously, act to achieve it. If we believe we can't learn French, *c'est la vie*, we won't even try. Believe success is inevitable and we will make it happen. Here we begin to realise that beliefs are not necessarily real, just either *convenient* or *inconvenient*. An inconvenient belief is that we can't remember names and it will limit our social interaction. A convenient belief is that we will soon learn how to improve our memory of names and so find the resource.

A belief is not a notion or a thought, or an idea; it's 100 percent agreement that something is true for us. If we *believe* that something will occur, we will ensure it does, because we also like being right.

Einstein said: "People are boxed in by the boundary conditions of their thinking." Beliefs form the very boundary conditions of our thinking. In other words, we will only speak and act depending upon what we are willing to believe is possible. Anything that we believe is not possible is outside the boundary conditions of our thinking.

Beliefs can either keep us boxed in, or allow us to live bigger lives depending upon the expansion of our thinking. Small possibility thinking has little chance of providing anything other than small results. Just as big thinking can lead to gaining big results. When transformed and empowered, beliefs allow us to fulfil their highest potential. Though if you want more than what you're currently getting from your life, I can guarantee you won't unless you change your beliefs. I have worked with many people who wanted to change their financial lives, so to help you understand some of the beliefs that vary from the rich and the poor, I have put together the following illustration. It shows the difference between some of the beliefs that these two groups hold — as a rule.

Wealth Beliefs

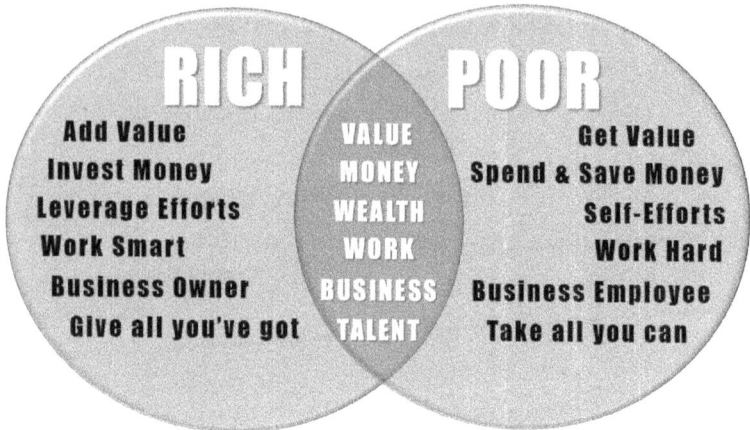

RICH | POOR

RICH	(shared)	POOR
Add Value	VALUE	Get Value
Invest Money	MONEY	Spend & Save Money
Leverage Efforts	WEALTH	Self-Efforts
Work Smart	WORK	Work Hard
Business Owner	BUSINESS	Business Employee
Give all you've got	TALENT	Take all you can

Copyright 2013 — Rik Schnabel

The overlap or centre of the circles is what both rich and poor believe. The words either side, show the different ways in which rich people think when compared to poor people. For example: in the context of 'value' — rich people believe in *adding value* while poor people aim to *get as much value as they can*. Equally in the context of 'talent' — rich people *give all they have to give* while poor people *take all they can*. Each has an almost opposite belief system which determines their financial destiny.

As an NLP and Life Coach Trainer, let me put on my teacher's hat for a moment. Let me offer you the academic answer to what beliefs really are.

Beliefs are generalisations about how the world is and once formed allow us to make decisions about how we engage with the world and its people. Beliefs are the presuppositions or linguistic equivalent of assumptions that we have about the way the world is. Our beliefs either create or deny us personal power. In effect, they are our on/off switch for our ability to do anything in the world. It is important to understand our beliefs, because our beliefs explain why we choose to do what we do.

Beliefs are internal filters within our mind that I often describe as *the rudders of our lifeboats*. They take some of us to the island of *happiness* and some to the island of *sadness*; they only take us to the places we believe in. They will not take us to the island of *wealth* if we do not believe that is our destiny or we don't know how to get there. They will not take us to the island of *love* if we believe that we are not attractive enough or we are destined for *lonely* island.

Beliefs influence our very actions and non-actions. They are convictions, what is held to be true in life. For instance, if someone believes that they CAN learn anything that they put their mind to, regardless of age, then their experience of life is going to be very different from someone who believes they are NOT smart and can't possibly learn anything new. In our *Career and Life Mastery* training, we teach our participants a technique to improve their memory. It's encouraging to see so many people instantly making new decisions about their intelligence and their corresponding beliefs shifting around the concept of intelligence. You'll find *CALM Level 1* here:

http://www.lifebeyondlimits.com.au/calm-i.html

So, now we completely know what beliefs are. We also know that our beliefs do in fact hold a massive amount of power over us and they can equally disempower us. Do we need to change all of them, some of them or none of them?

9

DO YOU NEED TO CHANGE YOUR BELIEFS?

There's a man standing on the ledge of a windowsill. He's on the ninth floor of a ten-story building. He's going to jump or he's certainly threatening to. Do we need to speak to him? Could he do with a belief shift to shift him back off the ledge and back to safety? Most likely. Do we need to change our beliefs? No, not really. As long as we're happy or satisfied with everything that's happening in our world right now. At times however, there are impending reasons for changing our beliefs, let me share a personal story with you.

In my late thirties, I left a secure job at *News Limited* and started working in a whole new industry, in a new position in sales, in a much smaller company selling media. My wife Rebecca had just left her career in Event Management to give birth to and raise our new baby Zoe. We were now a one-income family and my income was paltry to say the least. We could not financially survive on my income and our bank account was down to the last $100. We were financially treading water and worse, we were deeply in debt. Like most average Australian families, we had a sizeable mortgage at the time and we feared that we would have to sell our home. Matters became even worse.

BELIEFS ARE THE LIES WE TELL OURSELVES UNTIL THEY'RE TRUE.

While the company supported me by paying me a regular salary, if my commissions did not cover my fortnightly income in sales, then I owed the company the difference. Alarm bells were ringing in my head and beating through my chest when I was informed that I currently owed the company $35,000! Financially we took the elevator down to the basement — it was empty. I realised that I was unable to support my new family. *Knowledge is not always power.* The familiarity of our situation felt desperate. No matter how well we budgeted and cut back our expenditure, the bills just kept coming and the income was unable to match the outcome. Our debts grew bigger by the week and my earnings showed no signs of improving; the sales just weren't coming my way but the bills certainly were.

Then a most remarkable turnaround occurred. I could say that I couldn't believe our luck, but I know better. Two beliefs were at the very core of my poor results in sales. One of my beliefs was: *Sales people are sleazy and don't care about people, they only care about themselves,* which conflicted with another of my beliefs that remains today and that is: *For the world to be more harmonious, we need to care more about each other.*

Now, let's think about these two beliefs for a moment. If I did become a success in sales, I would have to consider myself as a *successful sales person* wouldn't I? And you know what that means don't you? Of course, I would have to decide which of the beliefs to let go, as they conflicted. According to my beliefs, if I became successful in sales I would no longer care about people and I would have to be sleazy. If you're reading this and you're in sales, please forgive my old self, I no longer believe sales people are sleazy and don't care about people, in fact I know that successful sales people care a great deal about people and that's what makes them successful. Because I had learned how to change my beliefs, I did so immediately. As I am recounting this story I am again realising the power of changing our beliefs. What do you think happened?

In the following six months, my income rose by over 400 percent! Soon I held the top sales position within the company, reaching a landmark position by bringing $350,000 into the company in one month. I finally smashed through another belief; the belief that I couldn't earn six figures. I went on to earn more than John Howard, the then Prime Minister of Australia! And yes, I had to do some quick belief change work around that too!

Beliefs are true if we believe they are. Therefore beliefs are either convenient convictions or inconvenient ones. When I decided to become successful in sales, there was another part of me that didn't want success because of what I believed about sales people. The belief was *inconvenient* in terms of financial success. That belief is now no longer true — thank God for that! (That's only for the believers ;) Beliefs can be whatever we make them.

Now we know that beliefs can conflict and one set of beliefs can stop a dream from ever becoming a reality. We also know that beliefs can be both true and untrue. Beliefs can therefore be lies or truths. The only distinction is that beliefs become lies when they are no longer true and truths when we take the necessary action to make them true. We don't have to change *all* of our beliefs, just the ones that are getting in our way to creating the life of our dreams. Though in order to become dream makers again, we must take *full responsibility* for our lives thus far and responsibly make the necessary belief shifts.

10
WHO'S DRIVING YOUR BUS?

Over the years, science has invested massive resources into researching our cellular system, our nervous system, and biochemistry and of course our brain to find out how we work and function. This incessant focus almost suggests that if we are able to work out the physical, chemical or biochemical influences over us, then we will know what known forces actually power and influence our lives. It's like analysing a rock from the moon believing we'll discover how the universe was created and why. I believe we're looking too deeply and perhaps we're missing the essence of how we work.

We seem to be reacting like we're not in control of this thing we call our brain. We even talk about our brain in ways that assumes it's almost separate to us, such as *my brain has decided not to work today* or *my brain is confused*. I'm sure you get my drift. It's a mystery as to how the brain really works, and the reason I believe we believe that, is because we complicate the crap out of everything we do — and it serves our incessant intellectualism. Let me ask you a question to make a point here.

What tells *you* to eat a particular food? What directs *you* to have a specific thought or follow through on a predetermined action? What tells *you* to cut your toe nails? What has *you* thinking about an old friend you haven't connected to in years? It's *you*! *You* are in control — *you* are driving the bus! It's just at times your unconscious mind is taking the wheel more than your conscious mind because you're allowing it to. Though some people seem to believe that we are controlled by anything but us. Yet I have found that anyone who is highly successful in his or her career or their life for that matter will tell you otherwise. They have mastered their unconscious. They are making the play and calling the shots! Milton Erikson, in my view one of the world's most innovative hypnotherapists once said: "Patients are patients because they are out of rapport with their unconscious mind." So who is driving your bus? We know it is either your conscious or unconscious, but it is still you!

Let's think about this from the level of beliefs. If we believe we're *not* driving the bus, then will we will act as if we're passengers. We will go wherever our unconscious leads us. We will be coerced by our friends, our relatives, our work colleagues our business partners, anyone or everyone other than ourselves. One day we will wake up and realise that our life is not our own! Will we *not* take the wheel; will we *not* take responsibility? If we don't, we will of course have others to blame for everything that's not working in our lives, our careers, our relationships and we won't be at fault at all. Though we'll never create the lives of our dreams, only the dreams of others — our drivers if you like.

If your life is not working out like you had hoped, you are wrong if you think that is not *your* fault. If you decided to give the steering wheel over to someone else — it's your responsibility; it's your choice to give your power away. While for some, this might seem like too big a pill to swallow. To take full responsibility for our lives when we've become so used to blaming others for everything we're not. If you want to create a *life beyond limits* then we must take full responsibility for our lives.

PAY THE PRICE OF SUCCESS OR THE PRICE OF PAIN

Stop blaming others. If you don't like what others are doing in your life, let them know it — in a respectful way of course. But if they're not listening and not respecting you or your wishes, then shift that belief that you can be assertive and shunt them off your bus!

I know some people at this point may say I'm being a bit harsh here. What about those people who have abusive partners, mothers, fathers, others? What about the ones who are trapped in terrible relationships and working with abusive bosses?" I say, get the hell out of there. Drive your bus as far away from abusive people as you can. Either way, you will be paying a price. You are either paying the price of success or the price of pain. My first question is: Which are you paying? And my second question is: Is it worth the price?

If I'm not the one telling you that the path to transformation starts with *you*, then I'm just trying to be another guru, saying, the path of transformation starts with me, and that's nonsense. While it might at times feel easier to shrug responsibility, imagine what life is like letting the bus drive itself while you sit in the back seat! That's right. It's an accident waiting to happen and then we'll have someone else or an event to blame for it all.

I believe there is a lot of *secondary gain* around people not taking responsibility for their lives. It allows them to blame others and never have to self-improve themselves or their situation. While our participants and partners believe our trainings programs such as CALM are gold, I often think to myself — why isn't the whole world in them? The answer is that our courses only attract those people who are serious about taking their lives back. We ask our students to take the driver's seat and grab that wheel and create the life of their dreams — it's not for the faint-hearted. It takes a lot of courage to take ownership of your career or your life. So I want to take this opportunity to thank you for investing in yourself enough to come this far. You've driven yourself all this way! Good on you for backing yourself and sticking it out. Did you know that up to 90 percent of book buyers have good intentions but seldom read beyond the first chapter? Because you have made it to here you are already in the top ten percent! Congratulations — you have what it takes!

TAKE OWNERSHIP AND YOU'LL OWN MORE

Should you now decide to take back the wheel of the bus, in contrast, will you think more thoughtfully, purposefully? Will your actions be more focused and will your acceptance of responsibility be greater if you *believe* you *are* driving the bus? I believe the answer to this question is at the core of most people's problems.

Everyone seems to blame the driver of their bus, when they are in all actuality, driving it themselves! Anyone who doesn't realise this is still playing *the blame game*. To understand the blame game is to realise that the moment we blame someone else for any part of our lives, that's the part we're taking no responsibility for. I'll say that again because it's really important you get this. The moment we blame *anyone else* for any part of our lives, that's the part we're taking no responsibility for.

If we blame our parents for introducing sweet, sugary or fatty foods into our diet, we must become aware that we are not taking responsibility for our health. Like the old adage, if we're pointing one finger outstretched from us at someone else, there are four fingers pointing straight back at us. If we blame our partner for our miserable life, then we are taking no responsibility for our life. We've just replaced our mother or father perhaps?

I know I've been a bit harsh — I've given you a bit of tough love as they say. Though I would really love you to get this, it will free you my friend. I care about your life, but I cannot care too much, I cannot care where you do not or you will just give me the steering wheel of your bus.

It's a truly powerful moment when we take ownership and own up to what we're not doing to create our desired lives, then in a funky and weird way, we'll be a lot happier.

People who take ownership for their lives tend to have bigger, more fulfilled lives. Cyclist, Lance Armstrong for example created a big life. He was large as life because he took full ownership of his life and his actions. Many people looked up to him, admired him. Until of course he *didn't* own up to doping. His lack of ownership of the issue and his incessant delays and denials lost him the respect he held for so long, he lost his medals, sponsorship income and who knows what else. Responsibility is ownership and if you want to own more *in* your life or more *of* your life — Responsibility is the point is where success begins and the old pains stop.

I believe Richard Branson is a success because he takes full responsibility for his successes and failures. In fact, when his company *Virgin®* went public, he realised that because he had relinquished full responsibility of *Virgin®* to the shareholders, he could no longer fulfil the company's promise. He then made a decision to buy back the shares. The reason, I believe Richard Branson is so respected is not only due to his business and brand savvy — it's also due to his level of his courageousness and responsibility.

What happens when we shirk responsibility, what does it look like? Some people for example, who are sick, give over their full responsibility for their health and well-being to the medical system. They believe more in the drugs they're taking for their illness than in their own ability to get well. They give over their power to the drugs, waiting for the illness to rule or the drugs to rule. There's a massive clue here when we realise that many people who are ill improve their health unknowingly using placebos. What do you believe about your own ability to heal your body? Whatever you believe will influence your health.

Speaking of health and beliefs — let me digress for a moment to speak with those people who need an intellectual dose of health. Many years ago I worked with people with cancer. I could tell in that first session if my client was going to live or die by the level of responsibility they accepted for their health. Strangely, their recovery was also dependent upon their willingness to forgive people for their so-called wrongdoings of the *past* and not so surprisingly, their level of interest and enthusiasm for their *future*. While I was never taught to think this way, I felt at an intrinsic level that three things had to happen in order for my clients to become well. I called them *the Six Healing Keys*.

BELIEFS AND THE SIX HEALING KEYS

I'd heard with regularity and from teachers who were practitioners in the field of psychology and coaching, and even those in business psychology, that 90 percent of success is due to a successful psychology. So when I began getting lots of clients who were unwell or clients who had a life threatening illness such as cancer, I began to take my work to a whole new level. This was serious stuff! You can work with someone who wants to achieve more money in his or her life or to be free of depression and yes that's serious too. But have someone sitting in front of you that may die if you don't do the best you can — now that's a whole new level of giving it everything you've got. Though in saying that, your clients must take 100 percent responsibility for their health and their lives and must not give it over to you.

I knew the answers could always be found in the power of your questions. So I thought what would be one of the most powerful questions I could ask. I asked myself this: *If I was my body, what would be the key drivers, the essential things that my mind must know or do in order for me to heal.* It seemed to me that miracles only occur when our psychology allows for them to exist, when we have an empowering positivity or a verve for life. So what takes that verve away from us? That's when I got my key drivers! That's when I was able to help my clients get well again. As long as they really, really wanted it too, that's a key as well.

So in order for us to improve our chances of recovery, here is what I found was essential:

1. **Believe we** *can* **heal our own body. We must believe that we have the psychological power to influence our very cells to heal our bodies. So the process must begin with a full bodied belief, not just an idea or a notion.**

2. **Heal the past**. The process of healing my clients

typically included a series of sessions where we would remove negative or disempowering memories from our past. More so, we would help our clients to learn from those events. So it wasn't just a case of bringing them back to a normal or healthy state of mind about their past, the sessions would raise them above normal, almost to a super empowered state of mind.

3. **Forgive everyone including the self.** Healing the past also meant forgiving people in the past (including themselves). Forgiving individuals and groups for whatever they did that was *wrong,* according to my client. This usually took some persuading as often people feel as though they have to hate their perpetrators so as to punish them for what they did (yes, it's *Version 2.0 Hierarchic* thinking — I'm better than them!). To *not* forgive means that part of you has to stay down there with them to keep them there.

4. **Have something to live for.** I lost my best friend to cancer. I could help all these people but I couldn't help my best friend. My coach had a lot of work to do around this time of my life — it hurt a great deal. The reason I believe he chose to die (yes I did say, he *chose* to die), was because in truth, he had nothing to live for. No dreams, no visions of a truly happy life. He no longer loved his wife and he no longer loved his work. He wasn't happy at home or work. Does that make sense to you?

   We must have something to live for that has real meaning for us. And as we are the architects of our life, the creators of our joy — it's time to get busy and create.

When we have something to live for we'll do all the rest naturally. We'll improve our nutrition, we'll exercise when and however we can, we'll start consuming good psychological material — and to be clear here, that doesn't mean watching murder mysteries and horror movies that are filled with violence.

Another powerful panacea to pain is to help someone else with their pain. Have a reason to live that's bigger than you. Have you ever noticed how many people don't get sick all year round, until they go on holidays? I believe it's because they give themselves permission to get sick. They're too busy to get sick at work.

5. **Remove and resolve all *secondary gain*.** As crazy as this may sound. I've found that some people, at some level, believe that dying or getting sick is better than going to work or living. Think of someone who is having a terrible time in their job, perhaps they're flailing, hardly fulfilling their job description. They're being bullied and harassed every day by their boss and they don't know what to do. They don't have another job option; they don't even see a bright future for themselves. While dying might be an extreme choice — the question is; what do they have to live for? So this is what we call *secondary gain*. It's just a beneficial reason for the problem (in this case illness) to perpetuate. While they're sick or dying, they don't have to go to work!

6. **Take full responsibility for your health**. It is too easy when we are unwell to give our power over to the medical system and anyone else for that matter. It is

critical that we take the driver seat. Do our own research and make our own decisions based on our findings. We must be in charge or our well-being. You might have noticed that I use the term 'we' a lot. I never believed that I was the only one doing the work for my clients. It's a partnership always — yes, that's my belief.

Louise Hay is well known for overcoming cancer and certainly knows that she is *driving the bus*. On writing this Louise is a healthy 87 years old, so my guess is she knows a thing or two about overcoming obstacles. Here is what Louise had to say on the subject of her cancer — "It was marvellous, really, because everything I needed came my way as soon as I became determined to heal myself. I found a nutritionist. He took me on as a patient, and I learned a tremendous amount about nutrition, which I knew nothing of at the time. My diet was not very good back then. I then found a good therapist and delved into much of the childhood stuff that needed to be healed. I did a lot of screaming and beating pillows to get my anger out. I also learned that forgiveness had a lot to do with healing, and I had to practice forgiveness. I had a lot of cleaning up to do."[1]

I would also like to share something else about Louise Hay that I think is gold. She goes on to say: "What I realised, and focused on a lot, was the fact that my parents were born beautiful little babies. I needed to look at how they got from this place of innocence to where they were mishandling me. I pieced together as much as I could of their stories — the stories that had been told, anyway — and I realised that my parents had been brought up under terrible circumstances. If you go into the backgrounds of some of the most horrendous people in the world, you always find a terrible, terrible childhood."[1] Louise

Hay believes that incurable means that it can't be cured by any outer means at the moment.

Six months after being told she had cancer, the cancer was gone. Taking an active role in your health and well-being is one of the most powerful things you can do. Though applying this same *Version 5.0* thinking to other areas of your life can equally be powerful.

I'm sure we both know people who believe more in their employer's ability to create their income than they do in themselves, so they will forever be reliant upon others for their financial well-being. What beliefs could we choose to completely transform our career, our business future or our financial future? For those who want a dose of great wealth, the question for now might be: *What do we currently believe about our ability to earn money?*

There are some people who believe that when they get to a certain age that their body is going to start letting them down, while others seem to defy their age. The latter might be called immature or crazy by the former perhaps — but who is right? Both of course are right and each is paying the price of their belief but only one is getting value for their money. At what age do we decide to believe that our body is going to start letting us down? For those who want a dose of great health, the question for now might be: *Is your body letting you down or are you letting your body down?*

I can recall a time where we created an insane discount to a self-development package we put together. It included one of my books, *The Secrets to Creating a Life Beyond Limits* and one of our most popular audio programs, *Life Beyond Negative Self-Talk*. It went off! It was hugely popular. Just a few days before Christmas when we got another surge of orders, I decided that I was going to personally take those last orders to the post office to make sure the people who ordered them got them before Christmas. I had completely underestimated the weight of all of those packages — man they were heavy.

❋
Argue for your limitations and you get to keep them.
– Richard Bach

In less time than it takes to remove a belief I heard a new belief being formed in my mind. My arms and shoulders were really sore. By the time I got to the post office they were aching and I heard myself say: "Well, you're not as young and strong as you used to be." You see most beliefs start with a small conversation with self into our heads after we've unconsciously found the meaning and intent of a situation or experience. The moment I heard myself say that limiting belief in my head, I said aloud: "What a load of rubbish!" People near the door of the post office turned around to see who I was speaking too. I know it wasn't the smartest thing to say, but nor was creating that stupid belief! I then intellectually rationalised why my arms were sore and that was simple. They were extremely heavy and I carried them for three longs blocks.

The way to take charge of our beliefs is to aim to be more conscious for more of our day because beliefs can be formed so easily with just one slip of the tongue. The beauty of awareness is that it interrupts a pattern and keeps out silly, disempowering beliefs.

To firstly be able to change our beliefs we need to be at the steering wheel of the bus — it's what we call in our *CALM* training, 'Being at cause'. That simply means that we are taking responsibility for the thoughts that create and perpetuate our beliefs, our thinking, our actions, and for that matter our entire lives.

WE BECOME LAME WHEN WE BLAME

Why would we want to take full responsibility for our life? Well let me put it this way; any excuse for not achieving is just an excuse and will not help us to succeed. The moment we make excuses for not achieving something is the very moment we're refusing to find solutions. For example, blaming our parents for not putting us through university is just an excuse for not being brave enough to finance our education ourselves. Blaming our employers for not paying us what we're worth is not valuing ourselves enough or not being courageous enough to state what we're worth. Blaming the economy for our decline in sales is making a decision not to tap into our creativity and brilliance. I think Richard Bach said it well, "Argue for your limitations and you get to keep them."

We become crippled, impaired, weak, inadequate, clumsy and *lame* when we *blame*. Step up to the platform that is your highest life! Own who you are. Be your power by accepting the power of full responsibility for your fullest life. Go on — you can do it. It's the most empowering thing you'll do.

If we're not *at cause* we're at *the effect* of literally everything that can negatively influence our results. The concept of *cause* and *effect* suggests that for any effect to be present, there must be a specific action or non-action that is its cause. In other words and to be specific, if we're ill and want to improve our health then getting sick is the effect of a non-action — that might be *not* looking after ourselves perhaps. Not eating healthily, responsibly or not exercising. An action would be to start looking after ourselves by eating healthily and responsibly or exercising or both.

Those who choose to live at the *effect side of the equation* are typified by telling us that life is happening *to* them. They complain about how unfortunate they are or how people do things to them and it's not their fault. They'll blame their upbringing or the country where they were born, or the fact that their boss doesn't pay them enough or perhaps it's the fault of their parents. They will tend to apportion blame on others and one of their battle cries is: *Why me?*

❋

What the believer believes, the prover will prove.
– Robert Anton Wilson

On the other hand, those who live on the *cause* side of the equation act as if they're responsible for the outcomes in their lives. If something isn't working, it is likely that they'll do something to rectify it. Think, Richard Branson, Tony Robbins, Oprah Winfrey, Nelson Mandela and Mother Theresa, they're big names because they took big action and lots of responsibility for their results. Each is a great example of people at the *cause end of the equation*. Each and every one of these people chose to take a path and became responsible for their actions and therefore their results. They lived at *cause* and as a result they achieved or are still achieving great things.

Those who live at *cause* get *results* and those who live in *effect* create *reasons* for not getting results — does that make sense to you? When people don't succeed and justify to themselves why they didn't make it, they must be aware that this is a form of self-deceit. To justify anything is to give reasons for its existence and therefore perpetuates its existence, otherwise we'd be wrong, wouldn't we? Justifications are simply beliefs that sound like excuses.

Now we know that in order to change our beliefs we must take responsibility for not only our lives, but also the very fact that we've made up stories for why our life is like it is. To change our beliefs we need to take full responsibility for our lives, our careers, our relationships and our destiny and create new empowering stories.

11

WHY YOUR BRAIN OBEYS YOUR BELIEFS

The nineteenth and twentieth centuries gave birth to a number of thinkers believing that we were largely dishonest about how our beliefs actually arise: Friedrich Nietzsche, for example, pointed out that many of the beliefs we hold are due to our need to *fit into the social groups* around us; Karl Marx through his political-economic analysis was focused on how social groups protect their own interests and reproduce their group structures, by a process of *self-justifying their own behaviours*; Sigmund Freud took the view that humans are driven by *instinctual* needs, which they have learned through their own particular individual histories to channel in certain ways and that our self-images are objectively inaccurate and mislead us. In the field of psychology, our thought leaders agreed that our beliefs are as individual as our thumbprint and are self-serving.

While we know that our beliefs are self-serving and they can be truths or lies, what creates them in the first instance? We might be lead to believe that the answer should be as intrinsically complex as our extrinsic world, or at least as complex as our brain, but it's not.

The single determining factor behind our beliefs is due to the *decisions* we make about events in our life and the *reasons* behind them. Our beliefs are created and reinforced by the intellectual process of reasoning. Reasons are simply something that makes something happen or explains why it happened. Now, that's me being practical, but reasons are more than that.

Reasons are the *magic* behind stories and are quite hypnotic in nature. If you watch someone's eyes very carefully as they listen to a long story, you will soon notice their pupils start constricting, their blinking rate slows and their eyes will generally make fewer movements. Their pupils will move much slower and they will start to look relaxed. In this state, time will become distorted where hours will seem like minutes.

Under trance, beliefs can be easily induced and stories are trance inducing. Hypnosis suspends belief, just as for stories to be engaging, we must suspend belief. This is how our brain comes to believe in these stories, regardless of if they are real or imagined.

The conversations we have every day drip-feed into our psyche one belief after another. In 1884, Edwin A. Abbot published a novel that depicts the problem of seeing dimensions beyond your own. In "Flatland: A Romance of Many Dimensions," Abbot describes the life of a square in a two-dimensional world. Living in 2-D means that circles, triangles and rectangles surrounded the square, but all the square sees are other lines. One day, the square is visited by a sphere. On first glance, the sphere just looks like a circle to the square, and the square can't comprehend what the sphere means when he explains 3-D objects. Eventually, the sphere takes the square to the 3-D world, and the square understands. He sees not just lines, but entire shapes that have depth. Emboldened, the square asks the sphere what exists beyond the 3-D world; the sphere is appalled. The sphere can't comprehend a world beyond this.[1]

Our brains aren't trained to see anything other than our

world, and it will likely take something from another dimension to make us understand. Though the moment we venture through a story our eyes can be opened to expand our beliefs.

The process of the story could be explained by: this happens because of that, and when we understand what causes what, we'll find the belief underneath it.

For example the statement: *I robbed the bank because I am poor*, reveals the cause that is *…because I am poor*. The word *because* helps to give us a clue to reveal a person's belief. So the belief could be that *people rob banks because they are poor*.

Once we elaborate upon the story, or colour it with our biases and our stories, the belief may extend to: *poor people rob banks because, they have no other way to survive the escalating grocery prices*. Of course this is a massive generalisation together with some bold assumptions, though beliefs are often just that — *bold assumptions*. They are not always true and often far from it. You can see how our own prejudices adjust beliefs to match our model of the world. Why does our mind continually search for meaning?

WE ARE MEANING MAKING MACHINES

Our mind makes judgements at every opportunity, seeking to understand so that it can pack ideas it calls *knowledge* away into boxes. It likes to *generalise* ideas into clusters, such as they are *rich, middle class* or *poor*. They're either *tall, average* height or *short; smart, stupid* or *average; good* or *bad; generous* or a *scrooge*. Our

❋
Common sense is the collection of prejudices acquired by age eighteen.
– Albert Einstein

minds are *meaning making machines* and what gives us meaning are the very beliefs that give our ideas life.

BELIEFS COME FIRST, EXPLANATIONS FOR BELIEFS FOLLOW

From the earliest of times, our brains search for patterns — patterns insure our survival. From sensory data flowing in through the senses, our brain naturally begins to search for and find patterns, and then infuses those patterns with meaning.

On a still, windless morning in the jungle, it's quiet, almost too quiet. Then suddenly — swish! A blade of grass moves and our brain is on alert to the change in pattern — it could be a lion? A predator! Instantly our body adjusts itself to our amygdala's alert. Our muscles instantly tighten and we're ready for a *fight* or a *flight*. In today's world our jungles have changed, they look very different, though the threat to well-being is still ever present. Threats can be obvious such as trying to cross a road with fast moving city traffic where everyone is in a hurry. Threats can be subtler and less obvious.

It's Sunday morning and we're catching up with some friends, for coffee. We're awake, we're *consciously aware* and we notice that our friends are unusually not themselves; they're quieter, less animated. The patterns have changed. We ask: "Is everything alright?" They all respond with a "Yes!" "Of course," "No worries," their version of, "Everything's okay," but we're *not* so sure. Something *is* wrong. Our meaning-making machine has made up its mind — something is wrong and it starts to search for reasons for this change in pattern. It compares this catch up with the last one. We try to remember what was said — was anyone offended about what we said or didn't say?

Because we are now *consciously aware,* on alert, we soon realise that this is a normal pattern, though it happens only on Sunday mornings. What happens on Saturday nights for this bunch? Then we realise — Aha! They're all single. They like to party and chances are last night they partied hard. They're all hung over and I'm not — I'm not in rapport with them either. So we talk about the last time we were hung over and the group becomes more animated.

Our minds in that moment may even create a new belief: "They drink heavily, I hardly drink at all. We're not the same!" We may even make a new decision that we are no longer safe in the tribe (we don't drink and go to parties with them) and we may adjust our behaviour to gain acceptance (start drinking and going to parties with our friends) — or reject our friends' behaviour by disregarding it altogether, or perhaps cut them loose and search for another tribe. While this example is not right or wrong, it's not good or bad. It's just by having *conscious awareness* that we begin to notice things we never saw before. Only then can we make new choices when we feel they're necessary. The key to shifting our lives is to become *awake* to *patterns* that perpetuate our lives. Becoming awake means to have *Conscious Awareness,* otherwise, we just get more of the same.

The key to a life shift or any shift for that matter is to become consciously aware at first and consciously make new decisions that reshape our lives. What new decision can you make right now to dramatically improve your career or your life?

The Key to a Life Shift

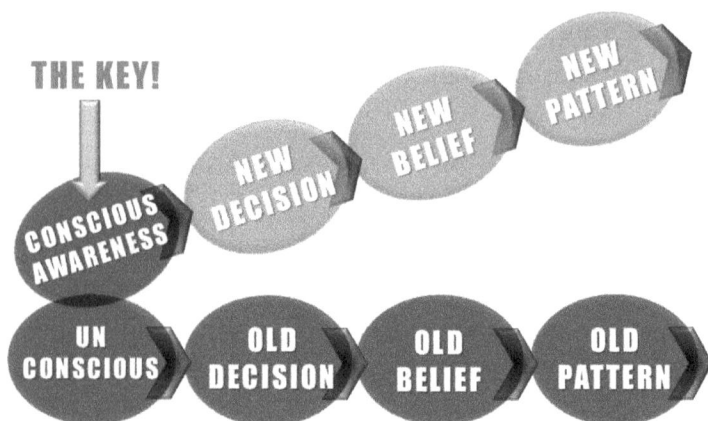

Copyright 2013 – Rik Schnabel

We form beliefs because they serve us. The reasons we do so are a variety of subjective, personal, emotional, and psychological reasons. Although we seldom hear someone verbalise that they are choosing to create a belief, you might, when we get to change our beliefs later in the book.

Typically beliefs come from significant emotional events or any events for that matter; environments created by family, friends, colleagues, culture, and society at large. Once our beliefs are formed, we seldom abandon them, rather we will defend, justify, and rationalise them with a host of intellectual reasons, convincing arguments, and seemingly logical explanations, all of which in coaching, we call stories otherwise known as explanations. Beliefs come first, explanations for beliefs follow. We seldom challenge our beliefs and therefore rarely change them, until our beliefs cause us anguish or a great deal of pain.

I recall coaching one of my clients whom had what I

could only describe as a horrific and grossly, abnormally unique childhood. I believe this is because she's here to do some big things in the personal development landscape, but that's another story. Let's call her Susan (not her real name).

❋
It's never too late to have a happy childhood.
— **Tom Robbins**

As a young girl, my guess is that Susan was curious and as result, very clever and most likely asked her parents lots of questions. Now this can drive any *normal* mother mad, but Susan's mother, I'm guessing, was already mad, angry mad, insane mad, I'm not certain.

Her mother had some strange beliefs and for reasons not known to me, her mother prostituted Susan, to her *associates* (I can't bring myself to call them friends). This was so cruel, I'm finding this hard to write — though it's an extreme example of some *limiting,* or I would call them *sick* beliefs.

Susan was raped, beaten, force fed liquids until she vomited. She was subjected to some extremely cruel and insane stuff. Now as an adult, Susan was aiming to make sense of what happened in our coaching sessions. I asked her to stop trying to make sense of insanity. I said, "Trying to make sense of this insane behaviour will likely make you insane, just to be able to understand it." There was no point in that. This made perfect sense to Susan and stopped her from going over and over and over the events in her mind — which she had been doing all her life. The questions that she was asking herself were perpetuating the very beliefs that were keeping her stuck in life. We were then able to move her on and heal her past.

If I let Susan continue to process and reason what happened, it would not have helped her. It would only have strengthened her memory of the events and likely increased her anger, deepened her sadness and perhaps even had her seek revenge. While some who read this might want to form a lynching party, I don't blame you. But this would not have served Susan — and as a coach, my duty of care is with the client first and foremost. Susan very much needed to move on from her cruel and painful childhood memories. From that moment she allowed herself to let the events go and find some peace in her life. Sometimes we have to stop the *meaning-making machine* from deepening our problems. You will be happy to know that Susan is now doing exceptionally well and is helping other women to overcome the mental anguish of domestic violence.

The fascinating part of all of this is that our beliefs are formed by events, which are experienced by our senses, but our beliefs also influence our senses. So what we see, hear, smell, touch and taste and the sixth sense, what we intuit, forms our model of how the world works. Equally, the very beliefs we currently hold influence our six senses. Like photographic tinkering and untruths, our beliefs create images in our minds, sounds in our heads and feelings in our bodies that are *distorted*, *generalised* or completely *deleted*. Time and again police are befuddled by conflicting accounts of eyewitnesses. In the US where many cultures live together, so often criminal accounts by eyewitnesses will usually follow their prejudice. One individual perpetrator can be described by a group of witnesses as Hispanic, Negro, Caucasian and Indian. How is it possible that a group of people can see exactly the same person committing a crime, but their accounts of who and what happened, conflict?

Could it be that beliefs and prejudice can colour and distort our experience? Can our beliefs have us respond and react in ways that don't always serve us, or anyone else for that matter? Wars demonstrate this prejudice unabashed.

While the events of a war unfold, either side recall something altogether different, even though they have witnessed the exact same event. A factory is bombed and turns to dust. One country views the event as murderous. They see the pain and the fatalities and mourn or avenge their loss, or both. While another country can only see victory and celebrates their apparent win. It's rationalised, intellectualised, yet it's barbaric and primitive actions are the directives of leaders that we are supposed to admire, and worse, follow. In my opinion, wars are the most horrific demonstration of the raging ego justifying itself. Its primitive *Version 2.0* thinking and it's all about who controls who.

Equally, our ego is a distortion filter. It will have us believe that we are right even when we are wrong. What makes one person right and one wrong is due to the filters in our brain that determine our experience. So what are all these filters in our brain and how does our brain work, *really*?

OUR BRAIN DELETES, DISTORTS AND GENERALISES

Everything we experience once reflected and communicated is typically an impoverished view of the world. We see something, we hear something, we feel something and that something is given a name based on our beliefs. As an external event is sensed via our cognitive channels (our mind), it is filtered so that we process only the

❋
As I grow older, I pay less attention to what men say. I just watch what they do.
— Andrew Carnegie

data we understand surrounding that event. In our processing of the data, we delete, distort and generalise what comes in. This also explains why when an event happens to two people in exactly the same way, they sometimes respond differently. Let me give you a real life example of our mind's filters in action.

A group of people go into a meeting to discuss a company's new brand strategy. The Marketing Director says, "We need to redefine our brand in relation to our market and review all communication devices in a more evolved way to meet the shift in a new emerging market of sophisticated buyers." The CEO is asked by the General Manager. "What did the Marketing Director mean?" The CEO replies, "He wants us to increase his budget." The Sales Director doesn't like the Marketing Director and says, "I think he'd like to increase the size of something else!"

Our filters operate every day, in every moment in every office around the globe. They determine what happens and what doesn't. Every day companies around the world are hiring people and unaware of the price they're paying for their beliefs or the invisible filters each employee brings with them. I hope there are some managers reading this as we improve our ability to hire more of the right people when we know what questions to ask to unveil potential candidate's beliefs. In our *CALM Level II* program, we teach people how to know more about someone than they know about themselves with just a few questions — their beliefs spill out of their mouths. It's all in their filters. So let us examine each of these filters in detail to get an insight into how our brain discerns and deceives us.

Let's understand these filters in summary and then we'll go deeper. Every external event that comes to our attention passes through our cognitive channels. The event is filtered and we then process the information and give it meaning — all in the blink of an eye. How do we process information? We *delete, distort* and *generalise* the information. We DELETE what we cannot understand or what contradicts our beliefs. We DISTORT the information so that we can reshape it, rephrase it, so that we can make sense of it and we'll often distort to make it fit whatever we're thinking of at the time. Finally, we GENERALISE the information into clusters of beliefs so we can make decisions about the information we're receiving — though we'll only make it fit into *our* model of the world.

Deletions — There are thousands of events happening all around us at any time so we selectively pay attention to certain aspects of our experience and not others. It has been said that we'd go mad if we didn't delete the things we don't need to focus on.

Deleting incoming information is simply the process of leaving out large amounts of data to avoid sensory overload. Humans selectively pay attention to certain aspects of an experience. Because people get only what they focus upon, they can't experience what they delete or don't focus on. The experience of life is largely dependent upon what remains after individuals delete information presented at any given moment.

An example of a deletion is a person looking at something that's right in front of their face, as they're saying, "I can't find the butter!" Some call that *fridge blindness*. The reason they can't see it even if it's right in front of them is due to their expecting it to be somewhere else or the object doesn't match what they're seeing in their mind's eye.

Another example of a deletion is a woman not recognising a colleague from work at first because he is out of context at the mall on a Saturday. Because the part of our brain called, *The Reticular Activating System* (RAS) is not sorting for that face, in that place, at that time, so it deletes the information. Even though the eyes pick up the information, it never becomes conscious or aware of that information. Deletions help us to simplify our complex world, it's more than just tuning out.

Distortions — As with Deletions, the ability to distort is a very important function of the human nervous system. It consists of creating and imagining, as well as interpreting or ascribing meaning to a set of data. Although people may experience or view the same event, they will likely distort or interpret it differently. A group of friends could see a Broadway show in New York and each end up with a separate internal representation of that show in the form of pictures, sounds and feelings. We'll then express our representation of that event in *our* words or by using *our* physical actions. Upon being asked, "What did you think of the show?" One man shrugs his shoulders, another says, "I liked the joke about the donkey," and his wife says, "What joke about what donkey?" While his other friends are now wondering if they saw the same show.

Another example of a distortion is a woman thinking she sees someone she knows who actually turns out to be a stranger or conversely, seeing her *ex* around every corner, because that person is foremost on her mind.

Distortions are a form of misrepresenting experiences of our reality. It's choosing to see something a particular way because it serves us or fits our beliefs — it's believable. A couple for example, who are looking for reasons to divorce will become overly judgmental, fiercely critical of events that once they wouldn't have paid any attention to. Each may recall an argument and he may describe it as a *disagreement* and she may call it *verbal abuse.*

Hence with distortions, we may even choose to represent something to ourselves in a way to get us to take certain actions, i.e. imagining that we'll get sacked if we don't get out of bed on time will make us leap out of bed if keeping the job is important!

Generalisations — The third and final way we filter information is by generalisations and this is the very core of our belief's generator. By generalising, we organise information to see a theme or overall picture. Generalisation is a valuable process, because it allows people to remember and categorise what they have learned. We see a new show and we say, "That's like *Seinfeld.*" We generalise the show by comparing it to something else that is familiar to us, so that we can describe it to someone else. However, it can also lead to sweeping assumptions.

Generalisations, like the other brain filtration processes, can either benefit or limit individuals because generalisations form our belief systems. Generalisations are based on an individual's experiences as well as on socially and culturally related concepts such as: gender, age, ethnicity, religion and occupation. Generalisations can sometimes sound judgmental, such as; he's too old; she's too young for him; he's set in his ways; she's got her head in the clouds; he's too dreamy.

Unfortunately, many people generalise in ways that eliminate choices for them. For example if we have one or two failed attempts at something and we generalise the experience into a belief, such as: *I could never be successful because…*, or as in: *You can't make money without cheating people.* This is when people use generalising functions in a disempowering way. This is also where we place people in general classes and due to our meaning of those classes we limit our experience by choosing not to associate with this or that class.

When we draw conclusions based on only a few experiences, this is typically a generalisation and our mind does it so quickly that we are rarely conscious of ever doing it. It is a way that we have trained ourselves to learn. If we consider that learning is simply the action of associating something we don't know into something we do know, then by generalising some of the unique experiences we've had and associating them into other known experiences, it gives us an opportunity to compare and learn from our comparisons. We'll hear generalisation's cues with words and phrases like, *everyone, always, all, no-one, never, I must, I should, I shouldn't, you can't, you have to....* These are linguistic clues that the speaker is generalising based on their beliefs.

It is true we've made some generalisations, deletions and distortions in our life and these have created patterns in our thinking that has led us to create the life we are currently living. From the thousands of hours of coaching and training people to help them to move beyond their limitations, I have discovered that many of the deletions, distortions and generalisations come from, seven common beliefs; these restrain people from achieving their goals in life.

In the following chapters I will help you to understand why these beliefs almost guarantee a limited life. I'll also give you a sense of their typical origins and should you decide to hold these same beliefs, I will give you the opportunity to discard them and create new ones. In the final chapters of this book, I will show you three proven ways to change your beliefs. The best way to gain value from this book now is to open your mind and get curious and you'll get much more from reading on. Are you ready?

12

BELIEF #1:
IT'S NOT SAFE TO BE ME

In a world where so many are fearful of being themselves, their true selves, we as a whole miss out on experiencing the real you, of seeing your real talent shine through. Everyone is trying so hard to impress people they hardly know, trying to be someone else. I want the real you to stand up, to take a stand and remove this debilitating belief. *It's not safe to be me* is a belief that stops people from achieving their dreams or ever being their own person. It stifles their true personality. Sadly, this belief is often held by people who had a big personality as a child and allowed themselves to become suppressed or silenced by their parents or carers.

In our formative years, as we start to make sense of language, we hear a word that we aim to avoid for most of our lives. That word is *No!* While *Yes* is approving, we learn pretty quickly that *No* is disapproving. For most, disapproval is emotionally painful for us and is avoided at all costs.

While my wife Rebecca and I are not advocates of hitting our children, many families still do (that's their belief and their programming). The last time I checked, while getting a hit musically might take you to the top of the pops, it can take a child to the lowest of lows. A series of smacks can create what psychologists call a *negative inhibitive habit pattern* which occurs when a child is told *no* enough times to alter their self-talk from *I can* to *I can't*.

A child believes it's not safe to be me when they feel threatened and this belief system can persist within the psychology of a child for the rest of their lives — unless they do something about it. I believe that spanking or hitting children is one of the worst undercurrents that undermine a peaceful planet. It just produces insecure adults who model their parents' behaviour and perpetuate it.

Motivational Speaker and Author Brian Tracy had this to say about the *inhibitive negative habit pattern*: "Fortunately, all fears are learned; no one is born with fears. Fears can therefore be unlearned by practicing self-discipline repeatedly with regard to fear until it goes away."

"The most common fears that we experience, which often sabotage all hope for success, are the **fears of failure**, poverty, and loss of money. These fears cause people to avoid risk of any kind and to reject opportunity when it is presented to them. They are so afraid of failure that they are almost paralysed when it comes to taking any chances at all.

"There are many other fears that interfere with our happiness. People fear the loss of love or the loss of their jobs and their financial security. People fear embarrassment or ridicule. People fear rejection and criticism of any kind. People fear the loss of respect or esteem of others. These and many other fears hold us back throughout life.

FEAR PARALYSES ACTION

"The most common reaction in a fear situation is the attitude of, *I can't!* This is the fear of failure and loss that stops us from taking action. It is experienced physically, starting in the solar plexus. When people are really afraid, their mouth and throat go dry and their heart starts pounding. Sometimes they breathe shallowly and their stomach churns. Often they feel like getting up and running to the bathroom.

"These are all physical manifestations of the *inhibitive negative habit pattern*, which we all experience from time to time. Whenever a person is in the grip of fear, he feels like a deer caught in the headlights of a car. This fear paralyses action. It often shuts down the brain and causes the individual to revert to the *fight-or-flight* reaction. Fear is a terrible emotion that undermines our happiness and can hold us back throughout our lives.

VISUALISE YOURSELF AS UNAFRAID

"By visualising yourself performing with confidence and competence in an area where you are fearful, your visual image will eventually be accepted by your subconscious mind as instructions for your performance. Your self-image, the way you see yourself and think about yourself, is eventually altered by feeding your mind these positive mental pictures of yourself performing at your best.

"By using the *act as if* method, you walk, talk, and carry yourself exactly as you would if you were completely unafraid in a particular situation. You stand up straight, smile, move quickly and confidently, and in every respect act as if you already had the courage that you desire.

"The *Law of Reversibility* says that *if you feel a certain way, you will act in a manner consistent with that feeling*. But if you act in a manner consistent with that feeling, even if you don't feel it, the Law of Reversibility will create the feeling that is consistent with your actions.

"This is one of the greatest breakthroughs in success psychology. You develop the courage you desire by disciplining yourself repeatedly to do the thing you fear until that fear eventually disappears—and it will." [1]

An April 2012 study published in *Child Abuse and Neglect* revealed an intergenerational cycle of violence in homes where physical punishment was used. Researchers interviewed parents and children aged three to seven from more than 100 families. Children who were physically punished were more likely to endorse hitting as a means of resolving their conflicts with peers and siblings. Parents who had experienced frequent physical punishment during their childhood were more likely to believe it was acceptable, and they frequently spanked their children. Their children, in turn, often believed spanking was an appropriate disciplinary method.

On the international front, physical discipline is increasingly being viewed as a violation of children's human rights. The United Nations Committee on the Rights of the Child issued a directive in 2006 calling physical punishment *legalized violence against children* that should be eliminated in all settings through *legislative, administrative, social and educational measures*. The treaty that established the committee has been supported by 192 countries, with only the United States and Somalia failing to ratify it.

Around the world, 30 countries have banned physical punishment of children in all settings, including the home. The legal bans typically have been used as public education tools, rather than attempts to criminalise behaviour by parents who spank their children, says Elizabeth Gershoff, PhD, a leading researcher on physical punishment at the University of Texas at Austin.[2]

If we think about it from this perspective; the moment we are hit by someone, regardless of what we have done to *deserve* it, what is the first thing that we want to do? I'm guessing I don't even have to spell it out.

SMACK AND BE SMACKED

For those who would benefit from a real belief shift around smacking children, consider this next insight as a conscious lesson in awareness, which is the first step to a belief shift.

Spanking on the buttocks, an erogenous zone in childhood, can create in the child's mind an association between pain and sexual pleasure, and lead to difficulties in adulthood. *Spanking wanted* ads in alternative newspapers attest to the sad consequences of this confusion of pain and pleasure. If a child receives little parental attention except when being punished, this will further merge the concepts of pain and pleasure in the child's mind. A child in this situation will have little self-esteem, believing he deserves nothing better.[3]

Women's breasts like buttocks are a sexual or erogenous part of the human anatomy, even though they are not actually sex organs. This is why baring one's buttocks in public is considered indecent as well as unlawful and why their exposure in movies or on television constitutes nudity. It is also why someone, who uninvitedly fondles another person's buttocks is treated by law as a sexual offender. The sexual nature of the buttocks is explained not only by their proximity to the genitals, but also by their high concentration of nerve endings that lead directly to sexual nerve centres. Hence, the buttocks are a major locus of sexual signals.[4]

As children we learned quickly to adjust our behaviour to avoid a *no* response or to reduce the risk of getting a smack. It makes logical sense. In practice, we consciously adjusted our behaviour until our *approved* behaviour seemed to run itself, without our having to consciously think about it. Once we progressed to running our neural programs without thinking, a process I call, *unconscious patterning*, our lives seemed to improve as we gained more approval from our parents or carers.

The aim was to produce what our parents deemed as *good* behaviour. When we produced *good* behaviour our environment became peaceful and we felt more secure and safe. Whatever we had to do to produce that behaviour is no longer our parent's problem — it's now ours. We may have had to suppress who we really were, to shut up or stop our expression somehow. Perhaps we became *yes people* and agreed with anyone who was bigger, smarter or faster. I would hazard an educated guess that the large majority of my clients had early behavioural dysfunctions brought on by their parents, as a cause to many of their problems as adults. This environment and conditioning is largely why I believe we try to be like others instead of being ourselves.

As children, we may have heard the verbal signal that told us all is well, words such as *good boy* or *good girl*. The physical signals perhaps were hugs, cuddles and approving interactions or at worse we were left alone with no physical pain. We are now meeting our parent's approval and therefore we get food, nurturing, and gifts perhaps, we get looked after. We're okay and we can sleep safe in our beds again tonight. The real learning I want us to get from this is that those early-formed patterns are still likely to be operating in us today. We're most likely still adjusting our behaviour to meet other people's approval.

It's pretty easy to know if we're seeking approval by honestly considering how we behave in the presence of our parents, our employers, police or authority figures, teachers or people we admire and look up to. Do we speak passionately? Do we fully express who we are or do we fall into someone or something we're not? Are we playful with a big smile on our dial and risk the moment with a bit of fun or do we sit quietly and wait until we get permission to engage perchance?

OUR THOUGHTS AND ACTIONS ARE KINETIC

Gandhi said: "Be the change that you want to see in the world." This statement makes sense when we examine it scientifically. Like *Newton's Cradle*, aggressive action will typically and kinetically generate aggressive action. How does that apply to the violence we see in the world today? Perhaps what we're witnessing is an angry population, who as children were hit, and now as adults are hitting back.

I therefore hypothesise that what happens in our homes happens in the world. Our micro worlds simply become a reflection of our macro worlds. Our thoughts derived from our parent's thinking and patterns, kinetically affects our own family. Our family determines what happens in our communities and our communities define our countries and our countries mimic our families. It therefore sequentially and logically suggests that our countries impact the world at large. Sometimes, when I'm coaching my clients, I'm quietly thinking to myself that I really should be working my client's parents. Because my client's issues mostly, all started there. I also realise that as we train and coach individuals that we are impacting the world, sometimes one person at a time.

EVOLVE YOUR FAMILY AND YOU EVOLVE YOUR WORLD

I recall the father of one family who attended one of our weekend workshops — *Breakthrough*. He volunteered as a demonstration to show the audience how quickly we can change our beliefs. He was drinking 15 to 20 cups of coffee a day — he *loved* his coffee. After the 15-minute process his life changed. He went from drinking all that coffee, to just one or at most two a day and then none.

He was so impressed with how he changed his beliefs so quickly that at the next workshop he brought his wife — then his two sons. As a result they all enrolled into our *Career and Life Mastery Program*[5] and I've watched this family as a unit evolve not only individually, but also as a tight and loving family unit. The father more than doubled his income; his wife became completely empowered, as did their two sons. My prediction; their two sons will be superstars in their chosen field. Once we become aware and conscious of our thinking, and change at an unconscious level, we can't go back to those old limiting patterns — of course unless we consciously decide to do so.

WE EARN WHAT WE LEARN

Personally, I believe that our evolutionary work in thinking will be best focused on the family. Should we do so, we create the potential to remove patterns that have plagued the family for generations. It's almost as if we stop a debilitating pattern at the generational level, it therefore no longer affects the lineage.

Entire dynasties are poor because of poor thinking just as much as alcohol and drug dependence is modelled and hops from one generation to another. We earn what we learn and learn we do — from our preceding generations.

From a child's perspective, we quickly learn that the most important means of survival is through our parents. Innately we crave the love and the care of our parents. In our formative years, parental love and care is typically demonstrated through the positive affirmations that reinforce a child's *cute* behaviour or a child's *good* behaviour. Though in the very early stages of our connection to parents, we have learned the most powerful of all affirmations; the ones that tell us that we're okay, namely caring shown through loving touch. Touch has emerged as an important modality for the facilitation of growth and development; we desire it, we need it and we'll die without it.

TOUCHING THRIVES LIVES

Early orphanages, called *orphanotrophia*, were founded by the *Orthodox Church* in the 1st century and yet only a hundred years ago, the large majority of babies given to orphanages in the United States died before they were seven months old. Unwanted babies were deposited into these institutions where antiseptic procedures and adequate food seemed to guarantee them at least a fighting chance for a healthy life. But the babies died. Not from infectious diseases or malnutrition; they simply wasted away in a condition called *marasmus*. Sterile surroundings didn't cure it; having enough food made no difference. These babies died from a completely different kind of deprivation; lack of touch. When babies were removed from these large, clean but impersonal institutions and moved to environments where they received physical nurturing along with formula, the marasmus reversed. They gained weight and finally began to thrive. Loving touch is vital for survival in the very young and is a symbol of acceptance, and we'll do almost anything to get it.[6]

Our parents are the key in helping us to feel that *it's safe to be me*. If we don't get it from our parents, we'll seek it from everyone else through our lives and still not feel safe. We are trained from a very young age to seek acceptance. First we seek the acceptance of our immediate caregivers, then our extended family members, friends, our employers or our clients and customers. Literally anyone who we believe ensures our survival, we will bow down to, acquiesce and even give up our true selves to gain their approval. We believe at some level, that it is not really safe to be the real me.

I hope I have given you a logical perspective to add some insight to the questions I am about to ask you. To help you gain some understanding of things you may do to be safe, here are my questions. Though understand these are to help you gain some clarity of your behaviour, *not* to criticise you.

In your relationships:

1. What part of yourself do you give up to ensure that you keep your relationship, your friendships or your marriage intact?
2. When do you bite your tongue instead of speaking up?
3. When do you just do what you're told rather than risk an argument?
4. Do you work late or go out with friends, indirectly avoiding coming back into contact with your partner?
5. What sort of relationship would you prefer to be having?
6. Are you willing to be the *real you* and risk your relationship?

In your career:
1. What part of yourself do you give up to ensure you keep getting paid?
2. Do you follow the lead of someone you hardly respect and find yourself nodding and smiling at them, when deep inside you feel like telling them how you really feel?
3. Do you do more than you're being paid to do or do you get out of bed earlier than you would normally do to get to work?
4. What would you rather be doing or being?
5. Are you willing to be the *real you* and risk your income?

If we move to the core of the belief (It's not safe to be me), it's just a fear of transitioning from one circumstance to a preferred one. It requires courage. I wish I had an easier answer for you but I haven't. In all my years of psychological study and practice, I have found that the most powerful formula to move you from *fear* to *courage* follows:

Step One: Make a new decision
Step Two: Determine the price, and
Step Three: Pay the price. Take the necessary action. Only after taking action will you gain the reward and find the courage you desire.

The Path to Courage

A NEW DECISION FEAR **= A NEW YOU**

Copyright 2013 – Rik Schnabel

To take the necessary action, we need to *create a compelling reason* to take that action, make it worthwhile for you and the people in your life. Then sit down, use your imagination and create and write a *new* story. Paint a *new* vision (what does it look like?). Shift your energy to build a *new* state (what do you need to feel like?) and create a *new* story (how does it all unfold, ideally?) It might take you a few minutes or at worst a few hours, or you can put up with the pain, for the rest of your life. As harsh as that may sound (sorry), it's true, it is your choice and one I cannot make for you.

It is safe to be you, the *real* you! Believing it's not safe to be the real you is not a life, it's a *lie*! It really is an illusion. You're just running off some old patterns that were installed when you were a child that didn't know better, and those patterns can be changed. Become aware of what you're sacrificing for love, for acceptance, for income and ask yourself, is the price worth it? If it's not, start being the *real* you or if you've forgotten who that is, create a version of you that's really appealing.

✳

WHAT ARE FOUR POSSIBLE OUTCOMES THAT COME FROM THE BELIEF *IT'S NOT SAFE TO BE ME*?

1. We will live our life according to others
2. We will never experience what we can *really* achieve
3. If we believe in past lives, perhaps we'll be back to do it all over again
4. If we think we're doing it for the sake of everyone else, then no one will respect us for it.

PERHAPS A BETTER BELIEF COULD BE:

IT IS SAFE TO BE THE REAL ME, AND THE WORLD BENEFITS WHEN I AM REAL!

13

BELIEF #2:
I'M NOT LUCKY

From the moment that humankind witnessed the very first miracle, some have come to believe in luck and some have done whatever they could to attain it. Whether through the use of magical potions, spells or crossing one's fingers, people over the centuries have aimed to harness and attract luck.

Others have tried alternate methods of attraction, such as wearing lucky underpants, charms, knocking on wood, thought to date back to pagan rituals aimed at eliciting help from the powerful tree gods. Even today, some people still knock on wood in an attempt not to curse the mention of a hopeful future outcome, though few, if any of us worship tree gods. So why do we pass this and other superstitions down from generation to generation? The answer lies in the belief of the power of misfortune and fortune — most call it *luck*.

While the dictionary suggests the meaning behind luck is: *The force that seems to operate for good or ill in a person's life, as in shaping circumstances, events, or opportunities.* The word *luck* originated in the 1200s and evolved from the Old Norse word, *Hap* which means, *chance, a person's luck, fortune, fate.* By the 15th century the Germans shortened *Gelücke* meaning *happiness* or *good fortune* to *Lücke.* At the same time *luck* entered the English language along with all its superstitions and belief systems intact. A religion also claimed *luck* and *fortune* suggesting they originated from the sun-deity *Lucifer*. Luck is the abbreviation of the name *Lucifer*. The idea of having *luck* and *good fortune* is unscriptural and points to a belief in *Gad*, the Syrian/Canaanite deity of *good luck* or *fortune*. Enter the concept of *good luck* and *bad luck*. Today, we have come to know *luck* as being a force of *ill will* or *good will*. So how do we summon it into our lives? Does it exist or is it just an old belief system that came from our mysterious past?

REASONS COME FIRST AND ANSWERS COME SECOND

While some pray and ritualise luck, others avoid walking under ladders, in front of black cats or refrain from stepping on pavement cracks. Some have no idea where their belief in luck originated, though will never open an umbrella inside the house, particularly on Friday the thirteenth.

Opening an umbrella indoors is supposed to bring bad luck, though the origins of this belief are murky. Legends abound, from a story of an ancient Roman woman who opened her umbrella moments before her house collapsed, to the tale of a British prince who accepted two umbrellas from a visiting king and died within months. When we can't understand something, we literally make stuff up. *Reasons come first, answers come second*, regardless of how illogical they may seem.

In the USA, *Detroit Tigers* manager Jim Leyland couldn't explain his team's 12-game winning streak and refused to change his underwear believing his underwear was lucky. Jim's a smart guy and so is Michael Jordan who wore his lucky old North Carolina winning shorts under his pro uniform.[1]

Wearing lucky underpants might sound silly as superstitions typically do; though do we risk our luck by not believing in its existence and does our belief in luck help it along? While luck can be seen as inconsequential creations of irrational minds, according to researchers, it also seems to work.

Subjects in an experiment who were verbally wished *good luck* before attempting a task completed that task much more quickly than those who were not granted the same wish. Others who had some sort of *lucky charm*: a key chain, special stone, a photo, a sentimental piece of jewellery, etc. performed better on mental tests, working harder and sticking with it longer than participants without lucky charms. When it comes to golf, lucky golf balls are a must (I think they're talking about the white dimpled ones ;). Students at Colorado College who putted with what they were told were *lucky* golf balls performed significantly better than those who didn't.[1] Why?

❋

Can luck be conjured within the beliefs of an individual or embraced by an entire group? Golf balls, charms and individual rituals might not have any special powers or do they? Underwear itself may not have any lucky field of energy surrounding them either. Instead, like a placebo the power seems to derive from the believer's beliefs. Believing that our lucky underwear will bring us good fortune can increase our propensity to extract our fullest potential, our highest level of self-confidence and give the task at hand our best. When we are more confident, we are more enthusiastic. We're more

❋

Luck is preparation meeting opportunity.
— **Oprah Winfrey**

patient. We're more relaxed. We think more clearly. We're more focused. All of which leads to better performance or better luck.

WE SEE WHAT WE BELIEVE

UK Psychologist, Richard Wiseman, writing for *Readers Digest* **detailed a fascinating survey where f**our hundred men and women aged 18 to 84 from all walks of life participated in a ten-year *luck experiment*. Subjects were asked to complete diaries, personality questionnaires and IQ tests, and invited to laboratory experiments. The result was that *lucky* people get that way via some basic principles — seizing chance opportunities; creating self-fulfilling prophecies through positive expectations; and adopting a resilient attitude that turns bad luck around.[2]

Consider chance opportunities: lucky people regularly spot them; unlucky people don't. If you believe you're lucky, you will set the focal part of your brain, your *Reticular Activating System (RAS)* to sort for opportunities of luck — it's that simple. *We see what we believe.*

To determine why a group of people who considered themselves to be *lucky* or *unlucky* classified themselves as such, an experiment was conducted. Each person was given a newspaper. They were then asked to count how many photos were inside. On average, people who considered themselves *unlucky* spent about two minutes on this exercise, while those who considered themselves *lucky* spent seconds. Why? Because on the paper's second page, in big type was the message, it read, "Stop counting: There are 43 photographs in this newspaper." Lucky people tended to spot the message immediately. Unlucky ones didn't. Half way through the newspaper there was another message that read, "Stop counting, tell the experimenter you have seen this and win $250." Again, the unlucky people missed it.

The lesson: Unlucky people miss chance opportunities because they're too busy looking for something else. Lucky people see what is there rather than just what they're looking for.

Subjects were also tested on their luck during a moment of misfortune. Each was asked to imagine being in a bank. Suddenly, the doors burst open and an armed robber enters and then fires a shot that hits them in the arm. Unlucky people tended to say this would be their bad luck to be in the bank during the robbery. Lucky people said it could have been worse, "I could have been shot in the head." The latter thinking makes people feel better about themselves. It keeps expectations high and increases the likelihood of continuing to live a lucky life.

Can we learn to become lucky? A series of experiments were carefully created, examining whether thought and behaviour could enhance good fortune. First came one-on-one meetings, during which participants completed questionnaires that measured their luck and their satisfaction with six key areas of their lives. The ideal conditions to create luck were outlined as *principles of luck*. Techniques were designed and given out to help participants react like lucky people. For instance, here were some of the keys to luck!

1. They were taught how to be more open to opportunities around them.
2. How to break routines and unlucky patterns.
3. They were also taught how to deal with bad luck by imagining that things could in fact be worse.

Each participant was asked to carry out specific exercises for a month and then report back.

The results of the experiments were dramatic! In conclusion, 80 percent of the participants were happier and more satisfied with their lives and luckier. One unlucky subject said that after adjusting her attitude, expecting good fortune, not dwelling on the negative, her bad luck had vanished. One day, she went shopping and found a dress she liked. But she didn't buy it. A week later, when she returned to the store, it was gone. Instead of walking away disappointed, she looked around and found a better dress, for less. Events like this made her a much happier person. Her experience revealed how thoughts and behaviour affect the good and bad fortune we encounter. It proves that the power of luck is available to us all.[2] Particularly when we have the right attitude!

Prior to travelling to a conference in Florida, USA, I was teaching our *Career and Life Mastery Level II* program in Melbourne, Australia. It's a program where we explore beliefs in detail and our participant's learn to change their neurological blueprint to meet the lives that they design for themselves. Here is where it got interesting. One of our students, a doctor, made a decision to change one of his beliefs from *I'm unlucky* to simply, *I'm lucky.* It worked wonders for him in his private life and his career. He and I were both so pleased with his results.

After changing his belief, he said that he found it much easier to attract new clients into his business and he recited many examples following the program that were unquestionably lucky events that seemed almost magical. He was making more money, attracting more clients and overall he was much happier — the result of changing just one belief.

While flying into Orlando International Airport I had an idea. My student's *I'm lucky* belief worked so well for him, I thought I would try out too, I'd never thought of changing this belief — why not, it would be fun! I had to drive from Orlando to Florida and afterwards head south to Boca Raton. I approached the car hire desk and a lovely lady with a big warm smile greeted me. The weather was gorgeously warm, as Florida often is and you could imagine how lucky I felt when the smiley lady upgraded me from a Toyota Corolla to a Volvo C70 convertible.

While I was in Orlando, I had a day off. I thought about what I could do to enjoy the time so I decided to visit *Universal Studios*. Now I'm a big kid at heart and I love the scary rides. You probably know that it is impossible to enjoy all that's on offer due to the typically long queues and the time it takes to get to all the rides, particularly during school holidays. Not for me! After paying for my ticket and enjoying a conversation about Australia with the guy in the ticket booth, he piped up and said, "I almost forgot to tell you about our Fast-Pass!" And he gave it to me at half price! I felt like royalty as I kept walking past massive queues of people only to find myself at the front of *every* queue. I seemed to be the only person with a *Fast-Pass*! Not only did I get to experience the entire park and go on *all* the great rides, some of them I enjoyed twice! What's more, I even lost my favourite hat on *The Incredible Hulk Coaster®* and it turned up at lost and found. I still have my favourite hat today. How lucky was that!!! It didn't stop there!

The funniest thing happened at LAX. When I got to Los Angeles International Airport, to amuse myself while waiting for my next flight, I meandered through the shops and in one shop, a flashing key tag in the distance caught my attention. It had a solar panel causing the words on it to flash. Can you guess what the flashing words were? You guessed it, *I'm Lucky*! What luck!

By now I'm deducing that you know that you create your own luck. Luck isn't due to kismet, karma, a lucky rabbit's foot or because you're blessed (you have always been blessed). Luck is created by the creator — you. There are some things that you can do however to improve your fortune. There are many, though here are four which may help…

1. Expect good luck and opportunities to come your way and keep open to them.
2. Attune your *Reticular Activating System* (your mind's filters) to see, hear and feel luck. You do this by noticing luck when it happens and recording those lucky

moments in a journal or committing them to memory, even the little wins such as finding small change on the ground are lucky events.

3. Change your beliefs from *I'm unlucky* to *I'm lucky (you can learn to do this near the end of the book)*.

4. Make up new stories and generate empowering inner self-talk to create convenient meaning behind every incident (refer to — *Life is Good or Bad*).

THERE ARE ONLY *CONVENIENT* OR *INCONVENIENT* BELIEFS

We can hold a *convenient* belief or an *inconvenient* belief — I would say that believing you're lucky is a pretty convenient one — wouldn't you agree? Later into the book I'll show you how to change your beliefs in a step by step process in — *The Five Step Belief Change*, although the first pre-step of any process is to make a decision to actually do the process, as Clint Eastwood in *Dirty Harry* once said: *Do you feel lucky punk*?

Unlucky is a LIE! So is *lucky* — so choose your preferred lie and make it true. Perhaps as Oprah Winfrey suggested, you can *prepare for opportunity and create your own luck*. Luck is what you make it. Make it awesome!

✳

WHAT ARE FOUR POSSIBLE OUTCOMES THAT COME FROM THE BELIEF *I'M NOT LUCKY?*

1. We'll look for reasons why we're unlucky, and worse, we'll find them.
2. We'll unconsciously and consciously avoid opportunities, just in case we're disappointed. This is where I often see people missing great prospects thinking they're too good to be true (which is often an inconvenient belief by the way. Some opportunities are too good to believe — but they're still good).
3. If we believe we're unlucky, our *Reticular Activating System* (our sorting filter) may only register *unlucky* experiences.
4. If we're religious, we may even blame our deity for our misfortune.

PERHAPS A BETTER BELIEF COULD BE:

I'M LUCKY.

14

BELIEF #3:
IT'S EITHER GOOD OR BAD

This belief activates our internal judger, which often sounds like one or both of our parents. When we judge we close our minds to anything other than our own (often limited) perceptions. While we know that we must judge in order to make decisions, the suggestion is to keep our minds open. The ancient *Huainanzi* text further into this chapter will help you to see this more clearly.

Believing that anything is either *good* or *bad* will so often have us missing out on many opportunities to *evolve* our lives. It can cause us to feel unlucky, hard done-by and can even have us sending out invitations for our very own pity party. Shift this belief and you will expand your experiences and so grow your wisdom a hundred-fold!

Intuitively, many of us get a sense that to suspend the judger will open our minds to evolve us and open ourselves up to more wonderful experiences — so why at times, do we defy our own intuition?

The human brain has evolved a particularly strong capacity to detect what neuroscientists call *Errors*. *Errors* are perceived differences between what we *expect* and what we *actually experience*. It's like looking at tomorrow's weather, knowing it will be sunny and experiencing rain on awakening. Think about biting into an orange, expecting a sweet taste, and instead experiencing the sour taste of a lemon.

Here our brain emits strong signals that use a lot of energy, showing up in imaging technology as dramatic bursts of light. It happens whenever there is a *mismatch* between our experiences and expectations. Edmund Rolls first illustrated this at Oxford University in the early 1980s, with a study involving monkeys. Dr Rolls found that *errors* in the environment produced intense bursts of neural firing, markedly stronger than the firing caused by familiar stimuli. In this high expectation world we live in, you could imagine that this part of our brain is (often) in high alert status.

These *error* signals are generated by a part of the brain called the *orbital frontal cortex*. Located above the eyeballs, it is closely connected to the brain's fear circuitry, which resides in a structure called the *amygdala*.[1]

Like Dustin Hoffman's autistic savant character Raymond Babbitt in the movie *Rain Man* our *orbital frontal cortex* will almost have us recoil at anything that doesn't appear to be *right*. In other words, anything that does not fit with previous patterns will send warning signals to our brain. This makes sense why we will be challenged to create the dreams that we're not living now. The dream actualising thinking produces different neural patterns than those that we're running today. We'll view anything we're doing out of the norm as *not right* or *bad* and so never create the patterns that will deliver our dreams, unless of course we consciously ignore our *orbital frontal cortex* fear response. To do that we must first upgrade to *Version 5.0* thinking. We must become *conscious* and *aware* and do the necessary work.

While our *orbital frontal cortex* will ensure we avoid anything that's *different*, our generalisation filter is a *meaning-*

making machine. It will make black and white distinctions about anything we experience and place them in a metaphorical box. Our experiences and perceptions are neurologically placed in either the *good* box or the *bad* box.

Our beliefs that certain people, events and things are either *good* or *bad* prevent us from learning and evolving. At the risk of going to an extreme to make a point — judging Adolf Hitler as simply being a *bad person* might have us miss a vital lesson. For example; how did one man initiate a world war? Perhaps studying the merits of Hitler may give us the answers, the solutions to world peace? What if we modelled his ability to *convince* a nation but instead directed it towards the promotion of a harmonious world?

A *SOLUTION FINDING MINDSET* VS. A *PROBLEM PERPETUATING MINDSET*

If instead of searching for the lessons in *any* given situation, seeing things as *bad* means we will also move to blame. This will have us making unconscious decisions, not to own our problems. Hence we will move out of a *solution finding mindset* and into a *problem perpetuating mindset.*

I'm sure you'll agree that avoiding our problems does not solve them. Seeing things as *bad* means we have instantly moved to judger and will likely avoid our problems, or hope to God they go away. It's what keeps the multitudes stuck in emotionally debilitating states and patterns that perpetuates this myth. I would go as far as saying that this belief is a *problem generator*!

While you might at this juncture start believing that conversely, viewing things as *good* is ideal, think again. If we view events and circumstances as *good*, it typically means

❋

There are two ways to be fooled. One is to believe what isn't true; the other is to refuse to believe what is true.

– Soren Kierkegaard

that they have gained acceptance from the *orbital frontal cortex* and we can fall back into our hypnosis, our unconscious bliss. Some patterns that we currently succumb to may well be perceived as *good* patterns: such as binge drinking with the guys every Friday night; congregating around the cafeteria with your friends criticising others; laying on the sofa in front of the *Time Vampire* (TV) each night with a big bag of chips and a bottle of soft drink is not *good* or *bad* — it just perpetuates the pattern which we might call *unhealthy*.

Let me help you to understand this myth, this belief, by sharing my account of the Chinese story, adapted from the ancient *Huainanzi* text. It is one of the classics that form the fabric of Chinese culture. The Chinese people know the story well, and have coined a phrase to summarize it: *Sai Ong loses horse. Who knows if it isn't a blessing?* Who knows if it is *good* or *bad*?

SAI ONG LOSES HORSE. IS IT *GOOD* OR *BAD*?

In a tiny and poor village there lived an old woodcutter who was envied by all, yet he was poor. He owned a beautiful, tall white horse with a black diamond on its head, above its eyes. A horse like his had never been seen before and even the King admired the old man's treasure.

One morning the King sent his wisest noble men to offer the old man anything and everything he desired for the steed.

But the old man refused. "This horse is not a horse to me," he said. "It is a person. How could anyone sell a person? He is a friend, not a possession to be sold." The old man was poor and the temptation was certainly great. But he never sold the horse. The noble men respected the old man's wishes and left without the horse.

One morning a group of villagers saw the old man's horse break free from its enclosure, gallop away toward the forest and soon the gallant steed was out of sight. They laughed at the old man's misfortune and stupidity. On telling the other villagers, the entire village came to see the old man who was now truly poor. "You old fool!" They scoffed, "We told you that you should have sold your horse to the King. You could have gotten whatever price you wanted. No amount would have been too high. Now the horse is gone and you've been cursed with misfortune." The old man showed no sorrow and replied, "Judge not so hastily. Say only that the horse is no longer in my stable. That is all we know; the rest is judgment. Have I been cursed, how can you know? How can you judge?" The villagers contested, "We are not the fools! We may not be philosophers, but great philosophy is not needed. The fact remains, because your horse is gone, it is a curse." The old man spoke again. "All I truly know is that the stable is empty, and the horse is gone. Whether I am cursed or blessed, I can't say. All we can see is a fragment of time. Who can say what is to come next let alone eventuate?"

The villagers all laughed. They thought that the old man was crazy. They had always thought he was a fool, if he wasn't, he would have sold the horse and lived happily off the money. But instead, he was a poor woodcutter. Each day he would still have to cut firewood and drag it out of the forest and sell it to survive. He was unlucky. He lived hand to mouth in the misery of poverty. Now he had proven that he was, indeed, a fool.

To the villager's surprise, a fortnight had passed and the horse miraculously returned. Not only had he returned, but also he had brought with him a dozen wild horses. Once again, the villagers gathered around the woodcutter and the eldest of them spoke with shame. "We are sorry old man. You were right. We were wrong. What we thought was a curse is in fact a blessing. Please forgive us for our hasty judgment." The old man responded, "Once again, you go too far. Say only that the horse is back. Say only that a dozen horses returned with him, but don't judge. How do you know if this is a blessing or not? You see only a fragment. Unless you know the whole story, how can you judge? You read only one page of a book. Can you judge the whole book? You read only one sentence of one phrase. Can you understand the entire phrase? Life is so vast, yet you judge all of life with one page or one sentence. All you have is one fragment! Don't say that this is a blessing. No one knows. I am content with what I know. I am not perturbed by what I don't."

"Maybe the old man is right," they said to one another. So they said little. But deep down, they believed he was wrong. They believed it was a blessing. Twelve wild horses had returned. With a little work, the wild animals could be tamed, trained and sold for a great deal of money. The poor man would become a rich man with little work.

The old man had a son, an only son, and he was helping his father to tame the wild horses. One afternoon, the old man's son fell from one of the horses and broke both legs. Once again the villagers gathered around the old man and cast their judgments at the old man. "You were right," they said. "You have now proved you were right. The dozen horses are not a blessing. They are a curse. Your only son has broken both his legs and now in your old age you have no one to help you. Now you are poorer than ever." To this the old man quietly replied, "You my friends, are obsessed with judging. Don't go so far, don't judge so quickly. Say only that my son broke his legs. Who knows if it is a blessing or a curse? No one knows. We only have a fragment. Life comes in fragments."

It is harder to crack prejudice than an atom.
– Albert Einstein

A few weeks later the country engaged in a bloody and violent war against a neighbouring country. All the young men of the village were required to join the military. Because of his broken legs, only the son of the old man was excluded, he could not walk. Once again the people gathered around the old man, crying and screaming because their sons had been taken. They believed that there was little chance that their sons would return. The enemy was strong and the war would be a losing struggle. They would never see their sons again. The eldest man of the villagers said, "You were right again, old man." Through tears and gritted teeth he said, "God knows you were right. This proves it. Your son's accident is a blessing. His legs may be broken, but at least he is with you. Our sons are gone forever."

The old man spoke again. "It is often difficult to talk with you. You always draw conclusions. No one knows. Say only this. Your sons had to go to war, and mine did not. No one knows if it is a blessing or a curse. No one is wise enough to know. Only God knows."

This is a lesson that we all need to remind ourselves of every now and again — me included. When we upgrade our thinking to *Version 5.0* — we gain *Conscious Awareness*. Rather than becoming consumed by our emotions and sucked up into the stories we hear from others and the ones we tell ourselves in our heads — we can choose what to accept into our belief system.

EBB IN ORDER TO FLOW

The sages teach us that *everything* happens for a reason. Temporary defeats and disappointments all contain the golden kernel of a lesson, custom-made for us to learn. Just as we must lower ourselves in order to jump higher, ebb in order to flow; learning the lesson in a spirit of humility will give us the extra energy we need to fly over the next hurdle. And when we look at it this way, is it possible that the so-called *negative* stuff is good news in disguise?

Any day that appears bleak or clouded is an opportunity to create clarity. Equally can a deceit be an opportunity to learn to become honest? Just as any moment of anger is an opportunity to learn how to create calm. There is always a lesson begging to be learned, waiting for us to be brave enough to see training in tragedy, hope in hopelessness, and lessons in the lousy. Just as gratitude overcomes greed, peace annuls anger and love dissolves hate. It is only when we experience these opposites, that we truly can gain everlasting wisdom. When we're all full of ego and self-focus we sometimes miss the value of gold in a downturn. In fact, in the *global financial crisis* many did in fact miss the gold as it massively increased in value — literally.

Observe anyone who has grown a large company or someone who is self-made and you will mostly witness someone who has learned this lesson. They know that with life come obstacles, however they give those obstacles their attention and learn from them – you can too.

THE FIVE LIMITERS OF LIFE:
ANGER, SADNESS, BLAME, GUILT AND FEAR

The Tao is all about balance. So the other side of the teaching is just as valid and valuable. If we do not gain the lesson, then it is likely our negative emotions are blinding us. We can see how we need not dwell on *The Five Limiters of Life*, namely *anger, sadness, blame, guilt* or *fear* to the point where they rob us of the ability to act. The flip side of the coin is just as true. That is, when we encounter something that appears to be an advantage, we need not let ourselves get carried away with ecstatic excitement, to the point where we become blind to the seed of adversity hiding inside the advancement. Every dark cloud does in fact have a silver lining. Conversely, the silver lining frames a dark cloud. Or as chapter 58 of Tao Te Ching expresses it: "Misfortune is what fortune depends upon. Fortune is where misfortune hides beneath."[2]

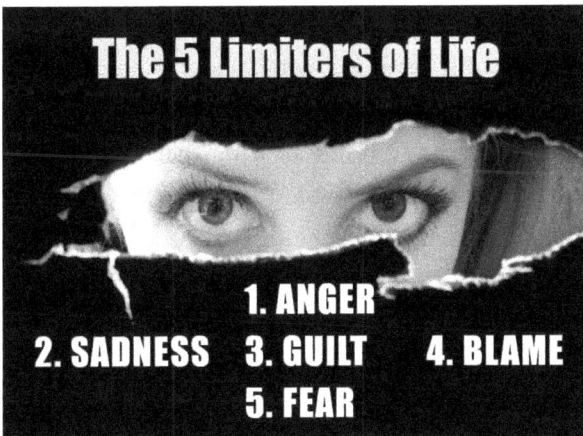

The 5 Limiters of Life

1. ANGER
2. SADNESS 3. GUILT 4. BLAME
5. FEAR

Copyright 2013 – Rik Schnabel

It is not so much, about what happens to us, it is what we make it about, that's important. In other words — it's about mastering our emotions. In our *CALM Level I Program* we teach a process called *Timeline*, which is specifically designed to reduce the impact on our lives from *The Five Limiters of Life*: anger, sadness, blame, guilt or *fear*. Life is about mastering our emotions. We've been running this program for the last ten years now and I still marvel at how our graduates seem calmer and more together after the program. Those negative emotions are keeping us stuck in negative associations of the past and leaching our very life-blood.

The purpose of the *Timeline* process is two-fold. It is brilliantly designed in a way that reframes past *negative* events that cause our limitations and in so doing reduces the impact from those events in our current lives. The second purpose is to help us evolve from those events by extracting specific lessons, insights and learnings that we can now use in our lives. I continue to marvel at how this one process seems to almost magically remove the *limiters* — instantly evolves us and grows our wisdom.

Louise Hay, founder of *Hay House* has in my view completely embraced the ancient *Huainanzi* text. Let me share a quote directly from her book with Cheryl Richardson, *You Can Create An Exceptional Life,* she says, "Everything is perfect. At first, hearing this phrase is like hearing that everything happens for a reason. It's a tough message to swallow when faced with tragedy or deep pain of any kind. But by training ourselves to see perfection in our most difficult moments — a perspective that can often only be seen in hindsight — we learn to trust life. We come to understand that, while we might not like a certain outcome, life may be leading us in a new more appropriate and beneficial direction. Everything happens for a reason or everything is perfect are beliefs born from a decision to see life as a school room. When we choose to become students of life who learn and grow from our experiences, everything does in fact happen for a reason. In this way, we make our most difficult moments mean something by using them to our spiritual advantage."[3]

RISKS ARE THE LIFE-BLOOD OF THE SOUL

In short, our judgments about things: events, experiences and people being *good* or *bad* potentially stops us from taking *risks* in our lives. To no longer risk is like dying. In business especially, we have to learn how to handle risks because almost everything we do that is new is a risk on so many levels. Though risks are the life-blood of the soul, the learnings that come from them, the falls and the achievements add a greater depth to our soul. In an earthly sense, they can also make us faster, better, smarter — and more humble so that we can accept all things, all people, and all experiences. Remember, *acceptance* is the first step to our transformation using the *ADD* formula.

The late Victor Kiam coined the phrase *Go for it*! It was this fearlessness, which lead to his belief that, "Even if you fall on your face, you're still moving forward." Victor Kiam made his fortune by letting go of fear and became famous for buying the company that manufactured his favourite razors, *Remington®* razors. Choose to release your fears, open the door to a life that up to now you have only dreamed of.[4]

Recently I was coaching a client who wanted to have more fun and playfulness in his life. Working together as coach and client we quickly realised that his unwillingness to *risk* was causing him to live a fearful and far too serious life. It was anything but playful and fun. After the coaching session he played with *risk* and guess what happened? That's right — he enjoyed his life much more and now has more fun. Success and joy at times can be that simple.

All events are just events, though our prejudices make them *good* or *bad*. *Good* is only a judgement created by the beliefs that we have formed, so is *bad*. Einstein once said, "Common sense is the collection of prejudices acquired by age eighteen." While one thing may, at the time, appear as *bad,* if we look with the eyes of wisdom, we may soon discover its blessing. All we need do is open our minds to see how it all eventually turns out — and that opportunity happens on the last day of our life. So let's not wait until then to define our life and all our experiences. As Tom Robbins once said, "It's never too late to have a happy childhood."

❋

WHAT ARE FOUR POSSIBLE OUTCOMES THAT COME FROM THE BELIEF *EVERYTHING IS EITHER GOOD OR BAD*?

1. We'll start classifying every experience as either *good* or *bad* and miss the learning.
2. We'll become more judgemental and perhaps even overly critical.
3. Depending upon if we also believe we're lucky or not, our mind's sorting filters may only register *bad* experiences, creating the illusion that there is more *bad* than *good* in our world.

4. If we adopt any of the above as a result of this belief, we may find that people come to avoid us or overlook us when it comes to any opportunities for career advancement.

PERHAPS A BETTER BELIEF COULD BE:

NOTHING IS GOOD OR BAD.
EVERY EXPERIENCE IS
AN OPPORTUNITY TO LEARN.

15

BELIEF #4:
I DON'T HAVE ENOUGH MONEY

This belief in my view is often just an excuse. It is the number one excuse most of us use for not investing in ourselves. And as a result, we will never have enough money. However, if we improve our psychology, grow our selves and we can truly become self-made. However the big question is: *I don't have enough money* — for *what*?

TO GROW YOUR INCOME, GROW YOUR PROMISE

If we don't know *why* we need money or *what* we need it for, we'll seldom get the money that we need. We rarely get the money we want, we mostly get the money we need. If we grow our *needs* we grow our income, we raise our profits and grow our companies. This all happens by expanding our vision. Creating a bigger vision or making a bigger *promise* makes way for more money. For example, if our promise is to put food on our table, then we shall enjoy the income that matches the promise — our unconscious and conscious actions to attract funds will likely be no more than your cost of living (putting food on the table).

According to the World Food Program (WFP) — the world's largest humanitarian agency *fighting* hunger (*fighting* —

an interesting choice of word); calculates that **US$3.2 billion** is needed per year to reach all 66 million hungry school-age children around the world.[1] If our promise is to reduce that number to even 33 million, then our actions must be much greater and so our income attraction will be much more. For those 33 million starving children, what would it be worth to them for us to change our beliefs around our ability to attract money?

Now that we know all of this, where does this silly belief come from, and what does it really mean to hold the belief — *I don't have enough money*?

We know that beliefs are absolutes and that's the main reason that we rarely make a conscious decision to change them — after all they are true, are they not? When it comes to absolutes, money is a subject that seems littered with absolutes and the belief that *I don't have enough money*, ensures that the multitudes don't ever have enough money. Not surprising.

At this very moment, as we look over our bank statements, perhaps we may be able to provide some absolutes around money. We may even be able to conjure evidence and substantiate why the belief, *I don't have enough money* is true for us. Though to remain open to why this belief is a LIE creates the opportunity for more money to come into our lives. I think that's a pretty good reason to do so — wouldn't you agree?

Beliefs are not written in stone. They can be changed. So our current beliefs around money are either *convenient* or *inconvenient* and I would suggest the belief *I don't have enough money* falls into the latter — unless of course there is some *secondary gain* around it. It is not a matter of the belief being true or not, it's more about realising that having this belief is most likely why we're in our current financial predicament. The problem with this particular belief is that we will either consciously or unconsciously aim to prove that it is true.

Back in 1988 I started *Schnabel & Knights Advertising* and founded it in Western Australia. It was after Alan Bond had won the fiercely contended *America's Cup*. It was a huge win for Western Australia and Australia as a whole. The world's eyes were on a state of Australia that prior, hardly gained much attention. After winning the *America's Cup*, Western Australia had more millionaires per capita than anywhere else in Australia — some said the world. So I moved to Perth from Melbourne because it seemed the prosperous place to be at the time and I loved the wonderful sunshine and warmth.

At first, my company grew fast and then just as fast, like turning off a tap, suddenly we went into a major financial backslide. This happened during Paul Keating's reign as Australia's Prime Minister. Remember him? He was quoted as saying that the recession of the 1990s was, "The recession we had to have." Australia went from *boom* to *bust* based on the collective beliefs of a nation — truly! Money didn't disappear, *confidence* did! Later, my advertising agency was engaged by Alan Bond. Alan told me that he and his inner circle had known for some time that the recession was coming. Though the moment the masses lost confidence in the economy it was near impossible to get their money out of the market. Investments dried up, companies went bankrupt, many overnight. So many people lost their life savings and as a result, the *belief* in the economy diminished.

The talk of the recession and the incessant news articles shouting *doom* and *gloom* gave me *reasons* to substantiate my belief that times would be tough. It made sense to me why my clients were going broke — I had personal *evidence*. What didn't make sense was why my company became responsible for *their* debts. It was my baptism into the world of business, money and not money.

Leading up to my car accident, remember the one I told you about at the beginning of the book, I was approaching my 30th birthday. I sat down one evening and worked out how much debt I had accumulated. Based on my best income and the level of my debt, I calculated that I would be working until I was 70 years old just to pay off my debt. What do you think that did to my beliefs around money? This part of my life could have shed some light on the world of money and business and granted me wisdom. But at the time, I was engaged in my negative emotions and my stories. Which by the way I repeated to anyone who would come within ear-shot — until no one wanted to anymore. At the time, all this experience did for me, was place a veil of darkness over my money beliefs. I believed money was hard to make, easy to lose and what's worse, at the time, I was right.

SOMETIMES YOU NEED A SHAKE UP TO WAKE UP

My guess is you've heard of *money magnets* and *money magnates*. During this period I was the opposite. I'd become a powerful *debt magnet*. My beliefs in myself, my abilities and my future became a shade of grey, let's call it *black*. If I had to describe where I was at, as a place, I would call it *The Hole to Hell*. When your life is *The Black Hole to Hell* you're not that attractive to anyone. I tried as much as possible to stay away from people and they stayed away from me, which isn't a great thing to do when you're in business. Perhaps I was ashamed of myself. But I didn't completely give up, not yet because my circumstance hadn't gotten bad enough to shake me and wake me up!

In an attempt to claw my way back out of the hole and out of this massive debt, I got up at 6am every morning to head off to the agency. The team and I worked our butts off to just make ends meet. I usually finished work no earlier than midnight and sometimes I'd actually sleep at the agency. At the time I was living with my English fiancé, Sue and her two young boys Paul and Gary. I only saw them on weekends, but you can guess I wasn't exactly a ball of fun and enthusiasm. Most Friday nights and weekends, I would be self-salving in alcohol.

Sue had a catering business called, 'The Scrumptious Food Company' and sold it around this time. She used the money to take her boys to England for a holiday and never returned. It was no surprise to anyone else, but it came as a shock to me. I wasn't awake — I didn't have any *conscious awareness*. Later Sue asked for almost everything we had in our home. I was so low at the time that I just agreed. They did leave me Goldie our golden border collie, a little bit of furniture, a house we bought together and Sue's car. The house and the car however were worth less than we owed to the banks for them. The recession was not a great time for me. Oh well. Maybe I could work another 20 more years and pay those debts off too — that would have me debt free at 90! Why I didn't do what my clients did and declare myself bankrupt I'll never know. Perhaps it was a sense of pride, I don't know.

My heart was empty, my home was empty and my bank was empty and my overdraft was overdrawn. It seemed like one tragedy lead to another after another, after another. One night my home was broken into and what little I had was stolen; my car was broken into; Sue's dog got hit by a car and I couldn't even afford the vet bills. Though I just added it to my debt, after all, my dog seemed like my only friend at the time. I felt like a living country music song! So there I was empty. Can you guess what sort of beliefs I held at the time? Let me give you one more clue.

I ran out of useful ideas so I tried a useless one. I decided to get drunk, really drunk. I remember it was a Sunday night and I couldn't bear it anymore. I couldn't go back to work on Monday, I couldn't see a way out. I had no idea what to do and it all seemed hopeless in this emptiness. So I took what seemed to be the next and only step. I stood at the edge of the deep end of my pool. I used to, in the good days, swim under water from one end to the other holding my breath to see how many laps I could do. I decided to break my record. But I really didn't give a damn about the outcome. I'd had enough and so I dived in.

WHEN THINGS ARE NOT WORKING, MAKE A NEW DECISION

I recall one conversation during my adolescence with my surfing buddies. We were sitting on our surfboards, out the back behind the waves. I don't know why, but we started talking about getting snagged in the kelp and drowning. My best mate Steve Wilkie said he had heard that drowning was the most euphoric way to die. Apparently you take a breath of water into your lungs just before you die and it is like a dream state. Sorry Steve, one word — crap! It's not like that at all. When I took in my first gulp of water it burned like hell. It felt like I'd been punched in the chest and it shocked me into a lurch to the surface.

Well… that hadn't worked. But what did work was making a decision at that very moment to fix my life. To fix everything! That one decision helped me to slowly evolve my beliefs and then advance my life. Can you now guess what my beliefs were that lead me to trying to take my own life? Here they are:

✿

To get out of a hole we must become whole.

– Rik Schnabel

1. My life is *bad*.
2. I don't have enough money.
3. I don't have enough time.
4. I'm not enough.
5. I'm not lucky.
6. It's not safe to be me.
7. It runs in my family, it's genetic — they are all poor too!

These beliefs were driving my life down the toilet and drove me into a pool of sadness. It could have been the end of my life. It's no surprise to me that, after attempting to take my own life that in my early coaching career I worked with so many people who felt like they were in the *Black Hole of Hell*. To get out of that *hole* we must aim to become *whole* and when we're whole we can give some of what we have.

WAKE UP TO GET UP

In a weird way, there is no better way to get yourself out of a hole than by helping others to do the same. In a sense we almost become holy — no pun intended. To become whole we must be aware of our beliefs that are taking us down. We must first wake up to get up — our life rope is *Version 5.0* thinking, *Conscious Awareness*. Remember the formula to evolve us, the one that will take us out of the depths of despair is to *Accept + Decide - Detach = Transformation*. *Accept* what is, make a new

Decision and *Detach* from everything that stands in our way.

The upshot of making this new decision helped me to become resourceful. Making a new decision is always a turning point; it can completely turn our lives around. I turned around my thinking and within days I found a solution that was right under my nose. I realised that while my company was in debt, it was still generating profits and so I sold enough of my company's shares to remove most of the debt. In that year our new investor helped us to grow by over three thousand percent! A massive turnaround! I also learned a great lesson that I would love to share with you:

SUCCESS MAKES DECISIONS QUICKLY AND CHANGES THEM SLOWLY — FAILURE MAKES DECISIONS SLOWLY AND CHANGES THEM QUICKLY

If there is a problem, address it quickly, make a decision otherwise the problem will likely grow and you won't. Now let us get to this old money belief that there isn't enough. I'm just curious. Why is it that every year there is at least four trillion dollars that pass from one hand to another and yet it keeps ending up in the same hands of those few who put their hands up and say, "I'm claiming some!" — a clue perhaps?

MONEY FLOWS TO THOSE WHO BELIEVE IN IT

One of my big lessons in life is that money flows to people who believe in it, to people who value it more. Conversely, the people who believe *money is bad* or *money is the root of all evil* or *the desire for money comes only from greed* will ensure that they are right. I'm the bearer of good news folks. Money is just money and our *meaning making* friends have made money into much more than it really is.

If you want to change your money situation, change your money beliefs! Don't think that if you believe that to make more money you need to work harder! Because then you'll just keep working harder and perhaps have little to show for it and surprise, surprise — you'll have to keep working harder! Otherwise if you had $12 million in the bank you would likely stop working altogether and that too would conflict with your beliefs. Is this starting to make sense? Or should I say, is it starting to make *cents* or better still *dollars*?

THE TRUTH WILL SET YOU FREE, BUT AT FIRST IT'S GOING TO PISS YOU OFF

The truth will really set you free, but you've got to be brave enough to hear it and more so, to do something about it. Here's the truth. If you're broke, it's because you want to be. If you're rich, it's because you want to be. So consciously or unconsciously, we'll take either poor action or rich action. *Acceptance is the first step in transformation.*

Our unconscious beliefs drive us daily (they're the ones we're not even aware of). They perpetuate our patterns and as a result preserve our lives. It really sucks when we realise what's going on, but now that we know this we can choose to change. I believe Gloria Steinem, feminist and journalist and once a key figure in the women's movement said it well, "The truth will set you free, but at first it's going to piss you off!"

As I detailed in my opening chapters, many of our unconscious beliefs were formed when we were growing up. I have often said that how our parents reacted when bills arrived in the mail

❋
The truth will set you free, but at first it's going to piss you off.
– Gloria Steinem

determined our beliefs around money. On opening letters with requests for monies owed, I recall my parents say things like, "How are we ever going to get ahead if we keep getting these bills?" And, "This bill is highway robbery!" or "Do those crooks think we're made of money?" Though my personal favourite must be: "Well enjoy your last meal; we can't even afford to eat anymore!" These were typically said with lots of emotion attached, a perfect formula for establishing and cementing beliefs into our unconscious. These phrases might sound crazy to you — or perhaps they're bringing back some old memories. Though this is how beliefs are formed and if we hold these beliefs we'll marginalise ourselves. We'll even go blind to opportunity when we've got gold on our doorstep.

AFFLUENCE ACTS AND POVERTY PAYS

I recall one Asian gentleman who was a member of our *WealthClub*. One evening I gave him what I believed to be a multi-million dollar idea. I get ideas all the time and of course I can't do everything, so I'm okay about giving my ideas away, particularly to our *WealthClub* Members. Though it really annoys me when people want *what* the idea will give them, but they don't act on the idea.

When we next met, he changed the idea to meet his low self-esteem. He turned a multi-million dollar idea into a low margin, low profit idea and what's worse, he didn't even move on the idea. I have a saying: *Affluence acts and poverty pays.* In other words, it's the action takers in this world who create the wealth and it's usually the poor people who pay the price of not taking any other action other than consumerism. Here's a belief worth noting — *Rich people invest their money, poor people spend their money while average people save their money.*

I can even recall showing a group of people how they could all work together as a team to create an income for each of them of around $30,000 per month. It would have taken them a year, maybe five at the outset, investing around five hours a week. Even though I handed it to them on a platter, less than five percent of them took on the business idea that ensured it was under resourced and while the five percent made some money, they didn't meet the $30,000 mark. People are broke because they want to be. If we want to make lots of money or we want to be financially independent or financially free, it's time for an upgrade — don't you agree?

When I went from *Version 4.0* thinking to *Version 5.0* my income grew by more than three thousand percent in the first year! Today I have more time and more money than I've ever had. It's thanks to my investment in my self-development and a decision to do what I had to do, to shift to *Version 5.0* thinking.

Some people keep themselves poor because they don't want to be judged by their poor peers. Some don't want it because of all the poor people in the world — they don't want to contrast poverty. We must realise that we cannot help anyone out of a hole while we are beside them. We must rise above the hole. Charity comes from the opportunity to share our wealth. In 2011, remittances from all nations to the developing world amounted to $373 billion, showing an eight percent positive growth from the 2010 total of $325 billion.[2]

You've got the potential in you, to create all the money you need, you're perhaps just not realising your potential at the moment while staring at your bank statements. Thinking you don't have enough money is a momentary LIE! You could change your financial situation in a heartbeat. The right idea! The right connection or a fortuitous moment could change it all.

Perhaps you're still running off some old patterns that were installed in you when you were a child. Remove them. There's trillions of dollars floating through the air every day, going from hand to hand while some choose to live hand to mouth. It's their beliefs; it's their decisions that make it so. Please don't give me, "the starving Africans didn't decide to be poor." I'm not talking about them — I'm talking about you. Perhaps it's now time to put up your hand and stake your claim? I've been rich and I've been poor and I'm not going to delude you and say it's okay to be poor, because it's not — not for me. I can do much more for others now than I ever could. If you want to help Africa, get rich.

❊

WHAT ARE FOUR POSSIBLE OUTCOMES THAT COME FROM THE BELIEF *I DON'T HAVE ENOUGH MONEY*?

1. We'll ensure we never have enough money. Even if we do improve our financial position, statistics tell us that we'll squander our money gains to meet our beliefs.
2. We'll judge others with more money than us, calling them *greedy* or *bad*, thus believing we're the opposite (when we're really not).
3. We'll do everything to ensure we're average, including avoiding risks or entrepreneurial ventures. However

we'll most likely become a sucker to scams or poor investments as this supports our beliefs (as crazy as that may sound).

4. Money may even have become a dirty word in our household. (Pardon my language here, though I'm making a point) We may even prefer to use the phrase, *Those F#@*ing rich people* than use the word *money* or even talk about money in our homes.

PERHAPS A BETTER BELIEF COULD BE:

I CREATE ALL MONEY I DESIRE, EASILY.

16

BELIEF #5:
I DON'T HAVE ENOUGH TIME

Time is another of life's illusions that seems to confuse us at every opportunity. The clock sneakily speeds up and slows down, depending upon how we *observe* time, the way we *experience* time and *watch* time. We of course know that the moment we make a decision to watch time, like the idiom, *a watched pot never boils*, time seems to move at snail's pace — it takes forever. As a child, we may recall how long the time dragged to get to Christmas or our birthday, though the moment they arrived, time shot past us like a bullet. This may be the very reason that time moves slowly for people who *wait* for things to happen and races for people who take action.

It's true. Time moves much faster for active people, people who pack more into their lives — particularly if they're enjoying the experience. While time is measured in units, from seconds to minutes, hours to days, days to weeks, months to years and decades to eons, it suggests that time is linear and each specific unit of time is exactly the same. Time, my friends is not linear, while the illusion of our measuring devices would have us believe so. Time is relative, just as

❋
Live life to the fullest because no one gets out of here alive.
– Carole Mirla Bach

Einstein said it was. Time changes depending upon the meaning we place upon it.

THINKING ALTERS WITH TIME AND TIME ALTERS WITH THINKING

David Rock and Jeffrey Schwartz explained the altering of time in *The Neuroscience of Leadership*. Neurons communicate with each other through a type of electrochemical signalling that is driven by the movement of ions such as sodium, potassium and calcium. These ions travel through channels within the brain that are, at their narrowest point, only a little more than a single ion wide. This means that the brain is a quantum environment, and is therefore subject to all the surprising laws of quantum mechanics. One of these laws is the *Quantum Zeno Effect* (QZE). The QZE was described in 1977 by the physicist George Sudarshan at the *University of Texas* at Austin, and has been experimentally verified many times since.

The QZE is related to the established *observer effect* of quantum physics: The behaviour and position of any atom-sized entity, such as an atom, an electron, or an ion, appears to change when the entity is observed. In the QZE, when any system is observed in a sufficiently rapid, repetitive fashion, the rate at which that system changes is reduced.

One classic experiment involved observing beryllium atoms that could decay from a high-energy state. As the number of measurements per unit time increased, the probability of the energy transition fell off: The beryllium atom stayed longer in its excited state, because the scientists, in effect, repeatedly asked, "Have you decayed yet?" In quantum physics, as in the rest of life, *a watched pot never boils*.[1]

It is much easier for us to think in linear terms, and what we believe are logical ways, than it is to understand the world of quantum physics. One plus one does equal two because someone created it, made it so, sold it and we bought it. We are not completely clear who created the modern number system we use today. Although called *Arabic numerals* because it came to Europe through the Arabs, the Arabs themselves call it "HindSaa" meaning — *given by Hindus or Indians*. The Persians copied the Indian number system and then passed it on to the Arabs. Then Fibonacci, an Italian mathematician travelled to Algeria to study. When he came back home, he brought the Indian numerals with him. He wrote about the system in his book *Liber Abaci*. This system soon gained wide acceptance throughout Europe. Today this is the number system used by practically the whole world and why we now believe that *one plus one equals two*. A large majority of the population believes that one plus one does in fact equal two, though most entrepreneurs do not. Entrepreneurs believe that one plus one equals at least eleven! They believe that one action should cause a multi-result; they call it — *leverage*. One person doubles (at least) the efficiency of another, equalling at least four.

Leverage has the power to completely alter what is possible. Leverage can equally alter time. While one skilled carpenter can build one chair in one day, one entrepreneur can have that same carpenter teach ten others and now we can build eleven chairs in just one day. It is the same time, it requires the same effort, but we get a completely different result. The power of leverage creates multiplier effect.

While it may seem easier to think in linear terms, at times our linear thinking will create problems in our mind by adding our one plus ones; let me elaborate. There was a *time* in my life when the previously mentioned belief: *I don't have enough money*, was real for me as it was true, or at least I thought it was true because the evidence was there.

EXTRAORDINARY PROBLEMS REQUIRE ANYTHING BUT LINEAR THINKING

Elaborating what I shared earlier in the book — after working for 12 months in a new sales career in Melbourne, Australia, I was $35,000 in debt and only had $100 in the bank to show for all my work. Besides believing I was the worst sales person on the planet, linear thinking could safely assume that in the next twelve months I would be $70,000 in debt, unless of course I changed part of the formula. *Extraordinary problems often require anything but linear thinking.*

I decided to embrace some extraordinary thinking. At the time, my friends and relatives thought I was crazy when I decided to invest almost $30,000 in learning *Neuro Linguistic Programming* (NLP) and *Life Coaching*. Few of them had ever invested in self-education and in their minds, this did not solve my problem, it just put me deeper in debt. The math will tell you that I now had a debt of $65,000. I knew that NLP helped people to turn their thinking around and what I needed was a complete turnaround! The result was that learning NLP seemed to accelerate time itself!

❋

Time is an illusion, albeit a convincing one
– Albert Einstein

While making more money in less time was previously outside of my beliefs, during my training, a fellow student in my class helped me to change my beliefs and it resulted in me earning two years income in just three weeks! Now I know that might sound incredibly bizarre or perhaps it doesn't even stack up mathematically, but sometimes you can change just one belief and life does a quantum leap on you. The training completely fixed my problem and the bonus was I learned to become a *Life Coach*, a *Life Coach Trainer* to boot! I decided to continue training until I attained my *NLP and Life Coach Trainer* qualification. I now had new skills, new thinking and new money. This one extraordinary decision changed my entire life and it is the very reason you're reading this book right now. I mastered not only how to change my beliefs, I seemed to master time itself.

How did I do it? I'll show you in detail at the end of the book though please don't skip to there yet, take your time and fully understand what you're about to read. You need a few more pieces to come together first before you start changing your beliefs.

To change my financial future, present and past, I learned to release the pain and emotional anguish I held around money. I made peace with my childhood at not being given any pocket money. I made peace with every moment I compared myself to successful people and looked down at myself and judged myself harshly. Then I discovered which beliefs were creating what outcome. I learned how to change my *poor* beliefs, my *I'm doing it tough* beliefs, my *I'm not worthy of keeping my money* beliefs, my *I haven't got enough time* beliefs and *I'm not a leader* beliefs, among many others.

I'm sure we both know of people who can make the average persons' annual income in literally weeks or days or even minutes. If we removed rich people's businesses, their money and all their assets and placed the poor and rich at the same starting blocks — what do you think would happen? The only things that will separate them are their beliefs. We can all gain knowledge and learn skills, though the rich and the poor have differing beliefs. It's those very beliefs that will, over time, have the rich create their wealth again.

Okay! Some people may judge what I just said rather harshly — perhaps they may completely disagree. But it's true and sometimes the truth is not pretty or generous. Sometimes it's this very disagreement that has them stuck in some sort of financial rut. Some people will start dredging up all the reasons why the rich are rich and the poor are poor — judging the rich harshly for err, um — being rich! Judgments have to come from somewhere and these may have something to do with the judgers' family, their education, their intelligence, their lack of luck or some other load of BS (Belief Systems). History however has shown us that people have succeeded without education, with little intelligence and despite their family or the *time* they have at their disposal. It's that *good* and *bad* belief system again.

Many of our beliefs were formed as children and teenagers, well before we realised the consequences of holding those beliefs. Most of the world's population will retain their foundational beliefs for their entire lives, even though those same beliefs drive them into brick walls every day. Then some extraordinary life changing event modifies their beliefs or they consciously change them and voila! Their lives become almost magical.

It is almost near impossible to believe that we won't win a race and yet win it. I know there are some flukes in life and history, though try to win with a belief that you won't. If we believe we'll never be rich or happy or successful, we'll unconsciously ensure we never try. People have been given a path to success, without believing in success and success rarely ensues.

Our beliefs are the thin line that separates failure from success, obscurity from stardom and rags from riches. It sometimes seems like two people can be on the same planet but on two completely different wavelengths or perhaps two different planes of time. So let's get back to time and view it from a completely different perspective.

While Japanese females are expected to live to 86, if you were female and lived in a small republic in Africa, the Republic of Sierra Leone, you could only expect to live to 47. According to *United Nations World Population Prospects Worldwide*, the average life expectancy at birth was 67.88 years (65.71 years for males and 70.14 years for females) over the period 2005–2010.[2] If we take the average life expectancy of 67.88 years and round that number up to 68, let's look at time in another way.

We can look at time in years, months, weeks, days, minutes, seconds and even micro seconds! Though if we examine 68 years in a different unit of time, time seems to alter. At birth with 68 years' worth of life left, you start with approximately 3,536 weeks or 24,752 days or 594,048 hours, 35,642,880 minutes or 2,138,572,800 seconds. Now let's just work with minutes, as I'm sure we could achieve a lot with almost 36 million minutes. Upon writing this and at 51 years old, I have realised I have less than 36 million minutes left. Based on an average life span and my current age in years and months, I only have 8,539,200 more minutes to live, and while that might seem like a big number to you, a minute passes quickly. In fact when I first wrote this chapter, I had 8,539,200 minutes. Now as upon my final edit before this goes to my publisher, that number has reduced to 8,272,800. In that time, 266,400 minutes have elapsed! Every day that passes, we lose 1,440 minutes — so I'm guessing I better get on with it.

When we view our life in minutes it changes our perspective of time. While my eight million or so minutes might seem like a big number, the rapid rate that a minute flies by makes the end of my life seem more imminent than the 16 years I have left. (Well I think I'll live longer than that because I'm far from average!) Though who knows, I might already be gone by the time you read this? I hope my time invested here was worth it for you.

What would happen to your productivity if you were paid by the minute instead of paid by the hour? Lawyers for example charge in six-minute blocks while accountants charge per hour. Who values their time more? Who earns more? If we view our life in years, we will perhaps not value the hours or minutes that pass us by. Now of course when we observe what we see in a different way, it gives us the chance to hear our beliefs rise up into our conscious thoughts. For example: what do you believe about lawyers? What do you believe about accountants? What do you believe about your time now? Let's focus on you now…

HOW MANY MINUTES DO *YOU* HAVE LEFT TO LIVE?

If you completed this formula, you'll get an idea of how many minutes you have left (I've omitted leap years just to keep the formula simple).

68 years −_____ your age = _____ years x 525,600 minutes = _____ minutes left.

When we look at time that we have left visually, it again can seem quite different. In the following illustration, shade off all the boxes to make up your current age. In other words, if you're 30 years old, shade off 30 boxes from top left onwards, so you can see how much life you have left (by average life expectancy of course).

How Much More Life Do You Have?

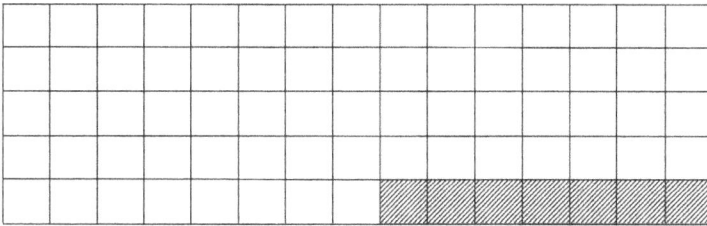

SHADE OFF FROM THE TOP – AS MANY SQUARES AS YOUR AGE

If you're like me, with eight or so million minutes left, what does that feel like to you? How does this alter your thinking about life? How does it cause you to think about your productivity? Does it bring about the concept of a legacy?

Do you have any plans about what you will leave your family or the world in your lifetime? And how much time do you have left to create or build that legacy? While even one million minutes might seem a lot, each minute that passes is a minute that is gone forever and we know how quickly they pass. Chances are by the time you've read this chapter, ten or so of your minutes will have vanished forever. By the end of today another 1,440 minutes will be gone. Eventually like me, your time will be up. You might only be a memory, perhaps remembered for how much you valued your time or what legacy you left while here on earth or perhaps remembered for what you did or didn't do while you were here. Now that we put context to time, it again changes time itself.

When Einstein's lifelong friend Besso's 35 million minutes were up. Einstein wrote a letter to Besso's family, saying "… that although Besso had preceded him in death it was of no consequence, for us physicists believe the separation between past, present, and future is only an illusion, although a convincing one."

Einstein proved that time is relative, not absolute as Newton once claimed. Einstein believed that with the proper technology, such as a very fast rocket ship, the person in the rocket will experience several days while another person on the ground, moving at the speed of the rotation of the earth, simultaneously experiences only a few hours or minutes. The same two people can meet up again, one having experienced days or even years while the other has only experienced minutes. The person in the rocket only needs to travel near to the speed of light to distort time. The faster they travel, the slower their time will pass relative to someone planted firmly on the earth. If they were able to travel at the speed of light, their time would cease completely and they would only exist trapped in timelessness.

If you've ever been in a car or motorbike accident at high speed, you will have experienced Einstein's theory of relativity. I recall being in a high-speed accident on a motorbike. My front wheel slipped out from under me and while the accident took only five or so seconds to conclude, it didn't feel like that at all. While I wasn't travelling anywhere close to the speed of light (officer), I recall every second as if it were minutes. As I mentally recall the accident, it seems as though it lasted at least two minutes.

Conversely, can you recall an entire joyous holiday that

※
Time stays long enough for those who use it.
– Leonardo Da Vinci

lasted days or weeks? My guess is that the holiday felt like it was over in a flash! That is what Einstein called *relativity*. He described it in a simpler way: "Put your hand on a hot stove for a minute, and it seems like an hour. Sit with a pretty girl for an hour, and it seems like a minute. That's relativity." Time is relative to the observer and the value of time is dependent upon what you do with it. Leonardo Da Vinci said, "Time stays long enough for those who use it. "

YOUR TIME IS VALUED BY THE DURATION AND INTENSITY OF YOUR FOCUS

With over seven billion people on the planet today, the next hour will be experienced radically different by almost everyone. It seems that what we believe about time is very different depending upon who we are, what is going on in our life at the time, and how old or young we are. The irony is that older people seem to take their time while they have less of it, while teenagers sometimes act like there's no tomorrow. The issue is not how much time we have or haven't, the issue is what we're focusing on and how long we can hold our focus! So you could say that *your time is valued by the duration and intensity of your focus.*

Wherever you place your focus determines how you experience time. The power of focus is the power of life. If you can focus on a solution then you'll surely nail it. If you focus on the problem, it is likely you'll keep the problem and the problem might even get bigger or worse. When we have problems time seems to drag on forever. Where your focus goes, energy flows, and energy alters time. Get motivated, get energized, get ferociously focused and time will become insignificant. The irony of life is the more passionate and energetic you are, the faster life seems to evaporate.

The Illusion of Time

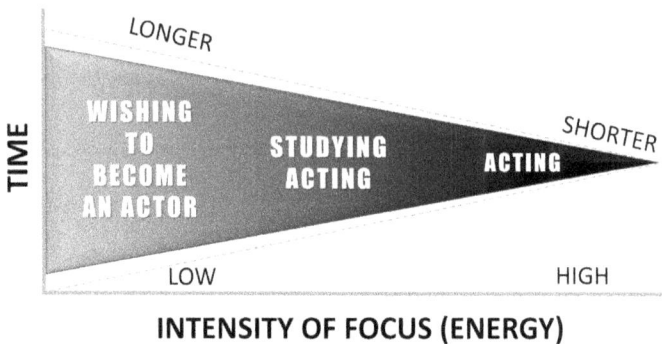

Concentrating our attention upon our mental experience, whether through a thought, a picture in our mind, an insight or an emotional situation or fear, maintains the brain's neural pathways; this holds that state in association with the experience. Over time, paying enough attention to any specific brain connection keeps the relevant circuitry open and dynamically alive. These circuits can then eventually become not just chemical links but stable, physical changes in the brain's structure.

Cognitive scientists have known for 20 years that the brain is capable of significant internal change in response to environmental changes, a dramatic finding when it was first made. We now also know that the brain changes as a function of where an individual puts his or her attention. The power is in the focus.

People who practice a specialty every day literally think differently, through different sets of connections, than do people who don't practice the specialty. In business, professionals in different functions; finance, operations, legal, research and development, marketing, design, and human resources, have physiological differences that prevent them from seeing the world and time in the same way.[3]

This explains why my training company is often called into organisations to help them to work together in a more harmonious way. I recall a media company where the sales team could not work together with the editorial team because both believed they were working for a different cause and were competing to dominate the same media space. However when they worked together, it made everyone's lives easier, the profit increased and the company agreed to give both departments a piece of the financial benefit — in the form of a party at the end of each successful quarter. This was a small investment in time and resources with a big and harmonious upside.

Let's get you focused for a moment. I want you to think about people in society who just plod along and play it safe. Think about what you believe about them. Are they valuable to society? Are they contributing to society or the future? What do you think about them? Now hold that thought while we move on — we'll come back to this later.

PEOPLE WHO HAVE TOO MUCH TIME ON THEIR HANDS CREATE DRAMA

It seems to me that people for whom time drags often create drama to make it feel like time is actually moving. Drama provides them with an actual feeling of significance. For them, it creates the illusion that something's happening in their lives, when nothing really is.

It almost seems that moving slow keeps one safe when it actually keeps one dull and not sharp at all. If we don't take risks with our time, our businesses, we don't add adventure to our lives, we don't create magic then we live dull and boring lives. Like turtles these people metaphorically hide beneath their shell, it's a room in their house. It's a favourite chair and a routine. *Turtles* often make mountains out of molehills; it appears to make their boring lives seem interesting. They typically occupy their lives by appearing clever. This is achieved by criticizing and judging others, and advising the active ones, the risk takers, the entrepreneurs, the legacy makers and creators of what they're doing wrong. *Turtles* get themselves caught up in the little things while their counter parts focus upon the bigger things in life. Turtles can hardly see above their shell.

What do you now think about people in society who just plod along and play it safe? Think about what you believe about them. Are they valuable to society? Are they contributing to society or the future? What do you think about them?

Forgive me, but hopefully I just demonstrated how quickly we are able to form a belief. For the sake of the exercise I painted a segment of our community into a corner by calling them *Turtles* — a reptile known for being timid and slow. This almost gives them the character of a slow moving, fearful reptile just by assigning a name to them and marrying behaviour to the name. Though for some, you may see some truth in it. It's drawing a bridge between one thing and another to make a point — advertising does this all of the time. Politicians do it. Marketers do it. Lawyers do it. Almost everyone you know does it. We use metaphors to sell our beliefs.

IS IT TIME TO WAKE UP?

There is no more time to waste! If you want success, best you be the master of your own metaphors. Start using your time powerfully by telling yourself powerful stories. Note also the stories that others tell you. Become awake to them or you'll fall under their illusions. If you hang around with people who whine and moan all the time about how the world is — soon, your world will be similar. What or who you associate with determines how you carry yourself in the world.

To gain mastery is to be the master of your beliefs and your time. Develop convenient beliefs and focus on what you *do* want, and not on what you *don't* want. Listening to the media can also be a recipe for disastrous beliefs.

To link *Belief #2 — I don't have enough money* and *Belief #3 — I don't have enough time*, can be the perfect recipe for failure. After years of wealth coaching, a powerful distinction I have made on the subject is that people who *value* their *time* will typically make more money. The longer you sustain your focus on wealth, the more wealth you will likely acquire. It seems to me that too many people these days look for the fast buck and as a result seldom succeed. These days I run from anyone who uses the words, *fast* and *money* in the same sentence. I prefer to listen to the advice of stable wealth creators, real wealthy people rather than cashed up cowboys. On writing this, only last week I read that …*gold has lost its lustre* and this week I read *Gold and bank stocks fuel bumper 3.4% rise…!* If I take a short term view, then my view of gold would have changed dramatically from one week to the next. If I acted in the first week I would have utilised the least effective investment strategy and perhaps sold low. The following week I would have bought high. I'm sure you would agree that buying high and selling low is not the best investment strategy. Managing your emotional state is also a key.

Money vs Time

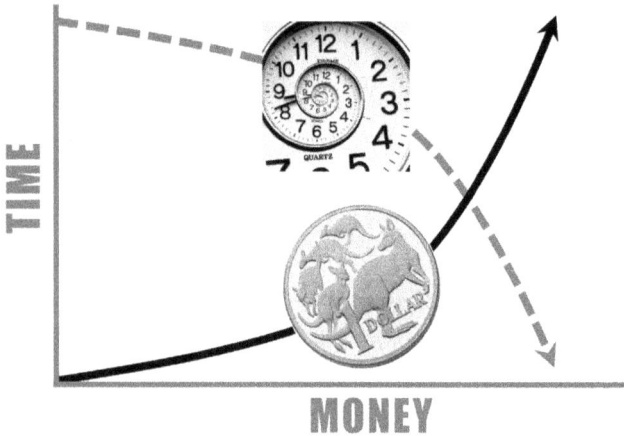

Copyright 2013 – Rik Schnabel

POOR PEOPLE VALUE *MONEY* OVER TIME
RICH PEOPLE VALUE THEIR *TIME* OVER MONEY

Time is a conundrum as is wealth. Most people get these mixed up when aiming to grow their wealth. For example: poor people value money over time. They will give away their days, their months and their years of life for money and perhaps a gold watch. Wealthy people value time over money. They know that their time is precious and well invested, what most people make in a month, they can make in a day, perhaps even minutes.

The fascinating thing I've observed with money is the more you have, the more you value your time. Poor people will ask, "How much do I get paid per hour?" while wealthy people will ask, "Is it worth my time?" or "Is there a better place to invest my time?"

Expand your vision ten or twenty years into the future, instead of just focusing on tomorrow or yesterday. The best time strategy in my mind is to plan for the future and be conscious enough to act in the present. Perhaps you could even have a vision to create a legacy and extend your vision to a thousand years! What would your time look like if you were to build something of value that was to be appreciated for the next thousand years, instead of somewhere in this lifetime? Would you value time differently?

People for whom time moves quickly are usually focused on creating their lives as if every minute counts! While for others who have little or no focus, time will seem to drag. Create a vision and time becomes a well-assigned asset. Create no vision and you will more likely squander time.

GET YOUR FREE FIVE BY FIVE TO THRIVE

Here's a tool that you might find helps you to master your time, I call it my *five by five to Thrive*. At the end of each day, whether I'm working or not, I invest five minutes listing all the things I could do tomorrow — just in bullet points. I have three columns; *Must Do*; *Interested in Doing;* and *What's Bothering Me*. Over breakfast I read through the list and prioritize my list from #1 onwards. After breakfast I start on #1, then move on to #2 and so forth. At the end of the day I start the cycle again. It's amazing how much you can get through and more importantly, it helps you to remove overwhelm.

Overwhelm is simply not listing tasks or doing the things you know you need to do until there is so much to do that you can't even remember what needs to be done. Overwhelm leads to shutdown and ultimately depressed or repressed states and that's not good for anyone. So get going on your *five by five to Thrive* — you can get a copy of it from our website:

http://www.lifebeyondlimits.com.au/free/free-articles/

WE CANNOT MANAGE TIME — WE CAN ONLY MANAGE OURSELVES

Time is the only resource that must be spent and can only be spent at 60 minutes per hour. We truly cannot manage time. We can only manage ourselves in time. Use my *five by five to Thrive* system and you will become the master of your 1,440 minutes each day. Then you will:

1. Reduce stress.
2. Get more time to balance your life.
3. Improve your productivity, and
4. Help you to achieve goals and get what you really, really want in life.

One final thing about improving the value of time, you might find this useful. While the average person may have 595,680 hours available to them, most people will be sleeping for 198,560 of them or for 8,273 days. If you got up just one hour earlier or went to bed one hour later each day, you would have another 24,820 hours available to you. It was never about time; was it? It's more about focus and commitment; isn't it?

So what's really, really important to you? Make it happen in this lifetime by valuing this second and making a decision to start now!

I use hypnotic audio programs while I sleep to create my nighttime University — you can download some here:

http://www.lifebeyondlimits.com.au/shop/nlp-/Itemid-463.html

❊

WHAT ARE FOUR POSSIBLE OUTCOMES THAT COME FROM THE BELIEF *I DON'T HAVE ENOUGH TIME*?

1. We'll probably never start anything of value.
2. We'll get stuck in patterns and the status quo.
3. Don't expect to find inner confidence or courage with this belief.
4. Our reticular activating system (our sorting filter) will ensure we'll squander time.
5. We're probably spending too much time watching the *Time Vampire* (TV) or distracting ourselves by believing we have loads of friends and interacting with them on *social media websites*.

PERHAPS A BETTER BELIEF COULD BE:

I CREATE TIME BY CHOOSING WHERE TO FOCUS MY ENERGY AND MY VISION.

17

BELIEF #6:
I'M NOT ENOUGH

If there was ever a belief that holds the power to stop us in our tracks — this is it. It's typically not just one belief — it's many. It might sound like, "I can't write, I'm not confident, I can't speak up in public, I'm not good enough to be a …, I'm not good enough at …" etc.

Whether it's coaching, training or I'm doing one of my motivational or educational talks — I usually follow a system I designed. I call it *The Success Matrix*. So my number one goal is to get my clients, students and participants to adopt the best *attitude* for what we are about to do. This shifts their emotional state. If you're emotional state is energised or high, it is difficult to feel low or think negatively, so this is always a good place to start.

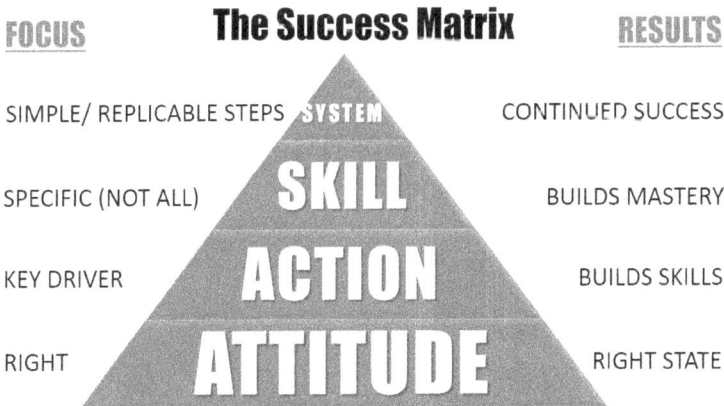

FOCUS	The Success Matrix	RESULTS
SIMPLE/ REPLICABLE STEPS	SYSTEM	CONTINUED SUCCESS
SPECIFIC (NOT ALL)	SKILL	BUILDS MASTERY
KEY DRIVER	ACTION	BUILDS SKILLS
RIGHT	ATTITUDE	RIGHT STATE

Copyright 2013 – Rik Schnabel

My second goal is to have them commit to at least one *action*. Taking action by doing not everything, but just one thing, the one *key driver* that will get them a result. This helps them to build their skill and building skills over time gives them mastery over their craft.

People are not typically masterful at first action, though if they can get a result, it often has them wanting to get another result, and another, and another. This is not a case of growing *all* your skills, just the specific ones that give you the results that you need.

TIME + FOCUS = MASTERY

A common mistake that people make in their businesses and careers, is that they aim to learn *everything* rather than keeping focused on their main game. That's why the world is filled with so many different people, there are others who can provide what we do not have and they love to do the things we do not.

These days, we need to niche our talents, rather than being the all-rounder or a jack-of-all-trades that we used to be. This one mistake had me struggling for success for years and years. The one key driver I needed to master was *communication*. Later I made the distinction to master *transformational* communication and when I did, my career took a quantum leap! Where once upon a time I was rarely paid to speak, at time of printing I now get paid a minimum of $5,500 per hour plus expenses. This is the financial value of this formula: *Time + Focus = Mastery*.

The final step to continued success in any area, is to be able to *systemise* your *actions* in simple and replicable ways — in other words, create a routine that you can commit to and one that will ensure success over time. That's *The Success Matrix*.

Follow it, commit to it and you will find success — I guarantee it. It's a powerful philosophy and one I live by. Though we know that all success starts with a decision…

We make decisions around significant emotional events and these decisions turn into beliefs. I recall a belief I held until I turned 21. I cannot recall the specific decision, though I truly believed that I would not live beyond 21 — don't ask me why or where I got that dumb belief. Can our beliefs be dangerous? This one certainly was.

On reflection I can see that this belief may have led me to many close encounters with death. One of those was a fall from a tree at seven years old where I was speared by a branch that entered my body, right between my liver and my lung. After the operation to remove the splinters and put me back together, the surgeon told me that I was very lucky to be alive. At 17 a 303 bullet ricocheted off a target I was marking at a rifle range. It hit me in the chest. It burned me but it didn't pierce my chest. At 20 I smacked into an open window, it knocked me off my feet and knocked me out. I was told that I had stopped breathing but somehow revived myself. Something brought me back, though I did go to a very interesting place while I was out cold — but that's a whole other book.

I did things I shouldn't do and tried things I shouldn't have, but strangely I survived and after turning 21 my belief came of age too. My belief then shifted to, *I am highly protected*. I still hold that belief today though it has expanded to — *I'm here for a special reason*. Perhaps you are too?

Sometimes we create beliefs from significant emotional events that shift our thinking and sometimes for some unknown reason (to us) we fabricate beliefs. Either way, these beliefs influence our lives, sometimes in every way.

ENOUGH IS ENOUGH!
IT'S TIME FOR A 'F@#K THAT!' DECISION!

I'm not *smart* enough. I'm not *pretty* enough. I'm not *strong* enough. I'm not *creative* enough. I'm not *fun, flexible, and playful* or *brave* enough. Enough is *enough!* Should we hold a belief that we're not enough, this is the very belief that is stopping us from achieving in whichever area we focus this belief.

For instance, if we believe we're not attractive enough, then it's likely that we'll avoid going out socially or connecting to potential love interests and so we will be right. If we believe we're not smart enough, perhaps we'll avoid situations where we'll demonstrate our lack of intelligence and therefore not advance our intelligence and again, we will be right. If we believe we're not strong enough or young enough, then we'll avoid physical activities to maintain or even strengthen our bodies and so we will be right. As a result, our muscles will waste away and we'll confirm our belief over time and degeneration.

My family and I live on the Sapphire Coast of New South Wales, Australia and with its more than usual sunshine, pristine beaches and bushlands, its retirees' heaven. And while it might be quite idyllic, I hear some of the older population's beliefs coming out in their tales of woe and their stories: ...*when I was younger I used to love to go for long walks along the beach. But of course I'm too old now*, I hear them say. While others of the same age and older are running marathons, dragon boat racing, surfing, sea kayaking and power walking the beaches! Could it be our beliefs even age us? I believe they do, but that too is a whole new book!

Just like believing we're *unlucky,* too many of us miss out on opportunities in life because we *believe* we're not enough, it's the essential belief that perpetuates a lack of self-confidence. Whether it's public speaking, taking on a leadership role, or asking someone out on a date, we've made it all up in our heads. Because at some level, we just don't feel equipped to handle the challenges we're faced and so, we consciously avoid opportunities to prove ourselves wrong and improve our situation. So again we're right.

PARENTS, PLEASE FORGIVE ME IN ADVANCE FOR THIS GOLDEN ADVICE

One way to remove this stupid belief — *I'm not enough*, is to make one of the most powerful decisions you can make. I got this from Tony Robbins and have now made this my own — thanks Tony. I now own it and I want you to own it too. Imagine what would happen if you focused on *just one* area of your life, where you knew there was *just one* thing that you could do to kick that belief out of existence — what would it be?

Would you like to get up on a stage? Ask someone out on a date? Propose to your partner? Start your own business? Take that career of yours with both hands and become the best you, you can be? And what would happen if you got yourself so worked up, so juiced, so fuelled in such a powerful state that you were able to shout out, *F@#k That*! And just do it! Do that thing you know you *must* do. Sometimes, that's all you need to break out of the hypnotic coma that's stopping the greater you from bursting out of your skin. If it's a CAN'T, make it a MUST!

Let me share what happens when you have a *F@#k That* moment! You'll read her short story near the end of the book, though if I can share a memory with you to demonstrate the power of changing a belief.

Her name is Lynn, she's a coaching client of mine. Lynn's highly intelligent and a very successful doctor. She was about to do a talk to very large room of very clever business people and she was concerned she couldn't do it, so we focused on this in our coaching session.

Through a series of relatively quick processes, I helped her to shift her beliefs and make a new empowering decision. After doing so, Lynn not only got what she came for by completing a great talk. Today, together with her General Practice and her own coaching business, she now speaks for a living. People still rave about that talk she did! If you've got a challenge before you it's not a reason to stop, it's the very reason to say, *F@#k That!* and charge forward, and grow! Only then can we really see what we're capable of and we'll grow our self-esteem to boot!

Avoiding challenges is what I believe continues to build our beliefs that we're *not enough*. Conversely, this begins to provide sound reasons as to why people do what some would consider to be crazy behaviour such as base jumping, ice waterfall climbing, sky diving, canyoning, swimming with sharks, eating fagu and running with the bulls to name a few.

While these things might seem dangerous to some people, conquering our fears makes everything else seem smaller by comparison. The very act of meeting a dangerous challenge has us taking on the bigger challenges in our lives, our businesses and our careers.

I once had a fear of heights that I created after falling out of the tree I told you about earlier. Yes, it hurt like hell and yes, I broke a lot of ribs and common sense would say that was a fair enough reason to have a fear of heights.

I hated having the phobia so I decided to jump out of a

plane and parachute my way out of my fear. It worked! More so, afterwards I was able to grow my business from a cottage industry into a multi-million dollar business. I ruled over heights and took my business to new heights! It's funny how our limitations can become metaphors that affect all other areas of our lives. Equally our wins become metaphors that have us climb even bigger metaphorical mountains.

YOU CANNOT ESCAPE YOUR LIMITATIONS — YOU MUST FACE THEM

The truth of the matter is we cannot avoid our limitations forever. Life has a way of making sure that we face our limitations in order to get through them and evolve. We may well have avoided our limitations in one area of our life and then, Wham! They show up in another area of our life.

When it is obvious that there is a limitation that we're avoiding, there's a saying that is recited among my peers. It is based on the belief that our challenges are there to show us what we can truly achieve when we choose courage. It goes something like this. *First the Universe will whisper in your ear, then it will tickle you with a feather and if you do not listen then, it will hit you with a train!* How many people stick their heads in the sand until their lives create the opportunity to face their issues, in an unavoidable way? Too many perhaps.

I believe that sometimes our limitations even cause us to get sick. When we avoid moving beyond our limitations, we keep getting opportunities presented to us to learn from our limits, and to rise above them.

If we retain our beliefs that we're *not enough*, the circumstances where we experience our limitations, without moving beyond them brings about stress. The stress hormone releases cortisol into our bodies, causing deterioration in everything from our gums to our heart.

Many highly informed practitioners now believe that stress makes us more susceptible to everything from the common cold to cancer. Stress however is not the real culprit. If we follow the trail of stress we find at the very core of it a debilitating emotion, namely *fear.*

Fear is what stops us from doing so many things in our lives and in this modern age of avoidance, we often see people replacing all they are *not* with a new hormone replacement therapy called, *shopping.* There are others too; *over eating* or addictions such as; *sex; alcohol; drugs* while others prefer avoidance therapies such as *work; TV* and *Facebook®.* It's all in the name of filling a hole we call, *lack.*

All the *I'm not enoughs* in our life are simply the self-esteem hole called *lack.* It is easy to understand what price we pay for lack when we compare it to the great rush of chemicals we get when we move beyond our challenges.

Success is a good feeling, isn't it! So if we're not achieving, how do we get that same rush, those same feelings? Easy! We replace the feelings with actions that give us a similar dose of feel good chemicals.

We can have food high in sugars and fats will do the trick. Shopping will do it. Buying that handbag we've always wanted; that car; boat; watch; those golf clubs; that new outfit; anything that gets us a little excited. All of these fulfilments are of course temporary and are simply paying the price for holding on to fear. Sometimes even alcohol and drugs will fill the hole left from fear and a low self-esteem, though society will pay a larger price for self-induced substitutes.

When we really place a price on any beliefs that say, *I'm not enough* we soon realise we're paying a much higher price than one would think. What is the cost of obesity, poverty, a liver that's packed it in? What about the cost of a heart that's on the way out or even a lung that's blackened and hardly functioning? These are not the problems; the core of the problem is elsewhere.

STAYING SAFE IS LIKE SAYING —
I'M NOT ENOUGH

Some suggest that F.E.A.R is an acronym for "False Evidence Appearing Real" while others believe it stands for "F@#k Everything And Run!" I think it stands for, "Find Energetic Audacity and Rule!" Depending upon what acronym you assign to F.E.A.R determines how you'll respond to it. The part of our mind that is responsible for cataloguing fear is our memory filter. How it works is very simple. If for example, we experienced an emotional event in our lives such as someone jumping out from a dark corner one night and frightening us, our memory filter will store that experience as an event. So the next time a similar event should occur, we will know what to do and we will keep ourselves *safe*. Keeping *safe* is an intellectual way of saying *I'm not enough* — I can't handle it.

Now that we have stored a *fear memory*, in future, anything that is similar to the event that reminds us of the danger will now *trigger* a *fear response*. In essence we are now programmed to *over react* to anything that closely resembles the initial fearful event — even in a metaphorical or symbolic way. For example, one night we're walking along the street, someone rushes past us and we immediately react with a fear response. Soon we have a multitude of triggers such as being startled by a sudden noise or seeing something fall from a shelf.

We can also generate fear more easily, triggered by events that even seem totally unrelated; however they're *like* the fear. For example, an idea that comes out of *left of field* and surprises us, or a person that doesn't appear normal suddenly appears in our path or a new or unfamiliar business idea is presented to us at an *inappropriate* moment. Anything that doesn't meet our expectation might create a fear response. Is this starting to make sense? As a coach, so often the area I'm working with my client, is to remove the initial event that caused the fear in the first instance and miraculously, all present fears diminish.

FIND ENERGETIC AUDACITY AND RULE

Fear is the response when our brain detects a threat; these are due to the *error detection signals* mentioned earlier and reside in a much older part of our brain called the amygdala and the orbital frontal cortex. These parts of our brain are remnants of evolutionary history. They were perhaps highly necessary when we roamed among animals and reptiles and were lower in the food chain.

When these parts of our brain are activated, they draw metabolic energy away from the prefrontal region, which promotes and supports higher intellectual functions. The prefrontal region is particularly well developed in humans, and doesn't exist at all below the higher primates. *Error detection signals* can thus push people to become emotional and to act more impulsively: Animal instincts take over.[1]

This is why fear seldom makes logical sense. It is important to know that if we are to move our *I'm not enough* program and associated beliefs, then we need to realise intellectually, that our oldest part of our brain is doing its job and we need to *consciously* move beyond our *error detection signals* and our fear. Sometimes that just means that we use the first two parts of my "Success Matrix", adjust our *attitude* and take *action* regardless. Unless of course if our life is truly at risk, it will be helpful to *Find Energetic Audacity and Rule!*

Our brain is a highly sophisticated instrument and it seems that we're only just now getting to understand the capacity of its functionality. Our brain is simply working to protect us from any *perceived* and *real* dangers, though it's only the real dangers we need to protect ourselves from. The *perceived* fears or the ones that have not happened yet, they are products of our imagination; they are the fears that we need to neurologically repattern.

WHATEVER YOU FOCUS UPON EXPANDS

The reason that fears become larger in our mind than they really are is due to our focus — *whatever we focus upon expands*. If we focus upon one specific thing, our brain will become more sensitised on that one element or pattern of thinking. It will build an array of sophisticated data that will alert us of the threat, or anything that closely resembles the threat. This also works in other areas too.

If you've ever decided to buy a new car and upon making the decision to buy that car you start to notice they're everywhere — it's due to our focus. So how do we consciously move beyond our fear and learn to ignore the irrelevant *error detection signals?*

One way to move yourself through your fears is to split your mind into two parts. One part of your mind is focused on the task at hand while the other part activates a future memory (that you created earlier) where (in your mind) the task has already been completed successfully and safely. Another method can be found in *Chapter 12, Belief #1 — It's Not Safe to Be Me* and I'll share one more in this chapter.

These are techniques that I believe everyone should learn. In fact if they were taught in schools our country would have a population of more courageous people with good intent. I believe this would help not only our country, but the world as a whole.

Fears are only a problem when they control us or hold us back from achieving our dreams or goals or worse, stopping us functioning effectively day to day. *Perceived* fears destroy adventure, business ideas, and fun, and have us missing out on the many opportunities that come our way. The truth is that *everyone* feels fear at some level, though some focus on the fear while others focus on courage and take action. We all, at times, believe we're not enough. Though how we manage the emotions that arise from those thoughts and feelings is what makes all the difference.

SUCCESS IS MAKING PEACE WITH OUR PAST

Fear is just our brain telling us to proceed with caution, usually because what we're about to do is unfamiliar or perhaps like many artists, we have not as yet mastered it. While confidentiality in my business is vital, I can tell you that many well-known, talented celebrities and super stars that I've coached, often feel like they're going to be found out a fraud or a fake, believing that *they're not enough*.

Even politicians, prime ministers, presidents and world leaders equally experience fear. Though instead of focusing on the fear they learn to focus on doing the best they can at the task at hand. The difference is that they have learned to control and master their emotions or better still, have done the work at the

❋

The doors we open and close each day decide the lives we live.

– Flora Whittemore

unconscious level to shift their programming. Mastering our emotions by making peace with our past are the skills, which in my view, are at the very core and definition of success.

It is true that you can learn to be or do anything, so it is true, you can be *more* than enough! Fear is the only thing that stops us from ever starting to learn and moving to mastery. So the real question this chapter needs to address is *how do you conquer fear?*

HOW DO WE CONQUER FEAR?

The first thing we could do is lower our expectations and live an average and less than ordinary life — but my guess is that's not your preferred solution.

For most, those who have broken through fear typically discover that fear saps their energy to the degree that they become tired or worse, sick. Then they become so sick and tired of being sick and tired until they say, "ENOUGH!!!" They say, "NO MORE!!!" And that's our breakthrough moment! Fear is almost always a state of reluctance or indecision. It's like a desire is present, yet we're frozen in time and fail to take action. Fear does not dissolve or shift in any way until we *make a real decision to move forward*.

I've found that while my clients may agree with my ideas and advice, my biggest job is to focus them on removing their fear. Otherwise fear does all the talking and as a result, they'll get no result. Nothing will improve until they make a *decision* to take action. Success requires us to commit to the *decision* to succeed, so that we'll take the action necessary. So typically most of my work in the beginning is getting my clients to commit to getting the results they came for and helping them to shift their unconscious programming and make new and empowering decisions.

If we want to stay stuck in our fears, it's easy. Here's how. Don't change a thing. Don't enhance our vision; tell ourselves the same convincing, limiting story; hold onto the same gut wrenching fear and don't change our strategy. This will guarantee that our fear remains intact and we don't have to do a thing differently. Though if we want to move beyond our fear, here's how.

Removing fear in a way that helps us to move beyond debilitation and into motivation can be achieved perhaps not always easily, though always through a new strategy, persistence and discipline. But the first step is a real, full body, empowering emotional and definite, decisive decision. A decision that is emotionally charged by a F@#K THAT! I'M NOT DOING THAT AGAIN! I'M DOING THIS!!! type of decision! Until we make a real, emotionally engaged decision to move forward — even if it's just to find a way how or to find answers, that's the very first thing to do. Without a real whole body commitment, there is no commitment.

While I'm not endorsing that we swear at every given opportunity, it's just that sometimes we need that level of guttural power to shift a fear. While the profanity might not be our cup of tea, try making a massive life shifting decision that moves you beyond fear without it.

So once we've made our new empowering, emotional *decision*, what we now need is a *compelling reason* to move beyond our fear. A real and personal benefit that we get as a result of moving through our fear. It *must* hold significant value for us personally. While I'm all for decisions to heal people, save people and save the planet, rarely is there enough personal gain and momentum for a person to move forward. I call these the *noble reason*, though if we were to create a *compelling reason* to move forward, I'd be searching for the *real reason*, not the *noble reason*. Real reasons are what you get personally — the *real* reason you want to do something, not the reason that sounds good or seems *noble*.

Back in 2012, my family and I made a life shifting decision to move from the city of Melbourne to the seaside for a sea change. While there was some fear involved in making the decision, the benefits of living by a beautiful ocean, with fresh unpolluted sea air and the opportunity to walk beaches, surf, kayak, fish and enjoy the sunshine was certainly compelling. So then it got to decision time for us. Did we want what the seaside lifestyle offered or not. The decision was easy, the move was not — but that didn't stop us.

We moved not only our whole family we moved our businesses too. It involved enrolling our girls into a new school, buying another house and a whole new way of living and doing business. We could have said that moving to the seaside would improve our thinking and give us more time to create better products and programs for our clients and students, but while that would be true, it was a *noble* reason it was not compelling enough because the gain did not have a personal value attached to it. The kayaking, surfing, beach walks and the great and healthy lifestyle for my family and I certainly had enough compelling and personal gain from making the decision. The real decision though had more to do with our health.

I recall one evening talking to our sound engineer and good friend Warren French. Now Warren moonlights as a police officer and he told me one evening that in his early training he had to go to a morgue to view a cadaver. The coroner conducting the training opened up the chest cavity of the body to reveal a blackened lung. Warren said that he and his buddies, in unison, all said, "Smoker!" The Coroner replied, "No. City dweller." That story removed any remaining fear of moving to live among fresh seaside air. All I could think about were my lungs, my wife's lungs and what really did it for me is the little lungs of my two gorgeous girls. Once we got that, the decision was easy.

The Belief Shift Process

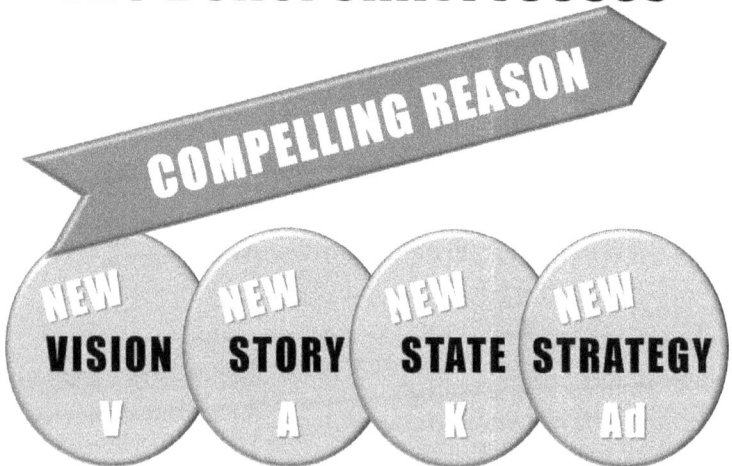

COMPELLING REASON

| NEW VISION | NEW STORY | NEW STATE | NEW STRATEGY |
| V | A | K | Ad |

Copyright 2013 – Rik Schnabel

If we make a new decision, we need to create a *New Vision*, create a whole *New Story* determine a *New Emotional State* that will help us to generate the energy we need to take action and create a *New Strategy* so that we have a process to follow. This process is what we call, "Neurological Reprograming" and it works because we're training our mind in a complete and holistic way and in a way that our mind adapts and easily learns.

For our mind to create a new pattern, it needs compelling pictures (V or visuals), sounds (A or auditory), feelings (K or kinesthetic) and finally a clear strategy (Ad or Auditory Digital) to move through that old and withered fear. I call it, "VAKAd-ding" our future. Vaccuming away all our limitations and adding resources in their place.

Perhaps it's time to start *VAKAd-ding* your new life? You're more than enough! Thinking you're not enough is a LIE! You can always improve your skills. You can always be more and your whole life has already been witness to that. You were once a child who couldn't do much, you now can do more. You were once less and now you are more, even if you have backslid from time to time, you have the skills to get up again — it's just a decision! Intellectually, perhaps even energetically and resourcefully you can do a whole lot more today than you could half your lifetime ago. Remember, we are still running off some old patterns that were installed when we were children, we just have to make some small adjustments to those patterns and shift some of those limiting beliefs.

❋

WHAT ARE FOUR POSSIBLE OUTCOMES
THAT COME FROM THE BELIEF *I'M NOT ENOUGH?*

1. We'll avoid almost everything.
2. We'll typically hide our fear by judging others and perhaps even being overly critical.
3. We'll program our reticular activating system (RAS, our sorting filter) and find all the areas in which we're "not enough."
4. We'll likely eat more, shop more, perhaps even take drugs or drink alcohol to make up for all we think we are not.

PERHAPS A BETTER BELIEF COULD BE:

I'M EVERYTHING I NEED TO BE TO TAKE MY NEXT STEP. THE MOMENT I DO, I'M ALREADY MORE!

18

BELIEF #7:
IT'S GENETIC

When we believe the reason underlying our issues or afflictions stem from our genetics, we are insinuating that our circumstances cannot be changed. Perhaps this is just an excuse to *be* no more or to *do* no more than our family. Therefore our beliefs will ensure that we do no more than follow in our parent's footsteps or perhaps even lag behind. This is a hugely inconvenient belief used conveniently to do — nothing.

I'm sure we will have heard this belief or something similar coming out of the mouths of our friends or our relatives. *It's genetic* is an excuse that is typically given as a reason that one cannot do something or has an annoying habit that cannot be broken or perhaps it's even a *curse*?

We may have heard that same belief in a judging way, such as — *You're just like your father* (or *mother*) or *Rotten fruit doesn't fall far from the tree*, it is a belief that typically suggests like *Birds of feather flock together*, that we cannot become more than our parents or with whom we associate. They are LIES that if we keep telling them we'll believe them and so never have to be more than who we currently are. Let me expose you to some history that defies genetic limitations and in as such, the belief in question.

While it might be hard to believe, Albert Einstein's parents were academically speaking, very average people and yet genetically created a genius son. After giving birth to Albert, his mother Pauline thought that he was deformed due to the size of his head. His mother thought he was odd, so her beliefs had her sorting for oddities to prove her belief. Because of Albert's slow rate of speech, Pauline thought that he was backward and perhaps had a mental illness. It turns out that Albert Einstein defied his genetics and had significantly more glial cells in the region of the brain that is responsible for synthesizing information.

Another example of perhaps genetic or character differences is found in Vincent Damon Furnier or you might know him by his stage name, *Alice Cooper*. He was the first star of *Shock Rock* and at his alcoholic peak it was rumoured that he was consuming up to two cases of *Budweiser*® and a bottle of whiskey a day.

Alice Cooper was known as the 70s *Anti-Christ* though his father Ether Furnier was a tee totalling layman priest in the Church of Jesus Christ. Alice is nothing like his mother or his father. Just for the record though, he did eventually master sobriety. Alice at first struggled with identity. Was he his stage persona or the man at home? So he also mastered transformation. Alice was eventually able to move from one identity to another; his identity as the performer to his off-stage persona.

I believe that *anyone* has the potential to become *anything* as long as they're willing to let go of their former *identity* by altering their neurological associations and identities. It starts with a decision, then a *compelling reason* followed by a new vision, a new story, a new state and whole new strategy and we will then commence the process of a belief shift.

Many of the richest people in our history, didn't associate

with wealthy people nor were born into wealth, yet they became wealthy. Just as numerous celebrated individuals were not born into fame. So we know that the character, assets and skills that it takes to become famous or wealthy can defy our genetics and even our upbringing. There are just too many examples to say otherwise. Wealth and fame among other results of a belief, are a learned *skill*, the results are rarely genetic — though some people have of course inherited their wealth. This was not the case of the fourth richest man in the world with a net worth of $53.5 billion according to Forbes. Warren Buffet's father was a stockbroker and became a Congressman — he wasn't rich. Warren Buffet's parents never appeared anywhere on Forbes rich list. Carlos Slim, currently the richest man in the world with a net worth of $73 billion — his parents never appeared anywhere on that list either.

Beliefs often sound like excuses. While these excuses might sound intelligent or akin to scientific murmurings, they provide us with nothing but an easy choice to never improve our lot in life. When we maintain a belief, such as *it runs in my family, its genetic*, we're actually making a decision not to change and for some, they can wear their limitation like a badge of honour or as part of their personality or their identity. It's like giving up. Now I'm guessing that because you've made it this far into the book, that you don't associate with the identity of a *quitter* and you're more than likely going to follow through with anything that you set your mind to do. It stands to reason; how we do one thing is often how we do everything. Congratulations! You've got what it takes!

THE *UNCONSCIOUS* IS NOT THE *SUB*CONSCIOUS

So let us get beyond genetics and understand the mind a little better, because there's two parts to the mind, namely the *conscious* mind and the *unconscious*. The unconscious, used to be called the *subconscious* until scientists with bigger microscopes and bigger brains realised that they were being controlled by the *subconscious*. *Sub* means *under* as in *under conscious* control, but the unconscious isn't under the control of the conscious at all, it's the other way around. *Un* means *not*, so the unconscious is not the conscious. The *unconscious* as it is now more intelligently known, controls most of what we do. So if we're going to create lasting change or transform in a complete way, we must commence at the level of the unconscious — we want to get to the control room of our lives.

Together, the two aspects of our minds are a truly phenomenal mechanism. The conscious mind is the *self*, the voice of our own thoughts. Consciously, we can create great visions and make plans for a prosperous future filled with love, health, happiness and financial splendour. However the unconscious is actually running the show. If we asked who is commanding and steering the ship, the answer is the unconscious. So if that's true, how is the unconscious going to manage our affairs let alone create a future filled with love, health, happiness and financial splendour? Precisely the way it was programmed is the answer.

WHAT WE DON'T PAY ATTENTION TO WE PAY WITH PAIN

Sometimes, the unconscious seems to be directing our behaviours into the complete opposite direction of our dreams and our desires, particularly when we are not paying attention. When we are not conscious of what is happening within us and around us. This is typically where most of our problems are perpetuated. *What we don't pay attention to we pay with pain.*

So why would our own unconscious work against us? The contrary behaviour is answered simply. Most of our fundamental behaviours are not even ours. They were copied and programmed, without question from observing other people and most often our parents as discussed earlier. If you're not a parent already, you'll laugh when you hear your mum or dad coming out of your mouth as you address your children. We're often stunned, as we become parents, to realise that we have modelled mum or dad or both, the people who programmed our unconscious. These are not *genetic* behaviours; these are *learned* behaviours and subsequent beliefs that have been acquired from other people. So the good news is this — those limiting beliefs and behaviours can be unlearned.

Prior to discovering and mastering the science and art of psychological repatterning I so wanted to change but had no idea how. The very first step I discovered was making a decision to change and the second step was to believe that it was at least possible. Had I believed only in my genetics and not believed I could change, I wouldn't have searched and thus wouldn't have found my transformational tools. The moment I did, I discovered many tools and processes that make neurological change possible. So how did we get programmed to think like we do?

MORRIS MASSEY'S PERIODS OF DEVELOPMENT

From the moment we are born until around age seven, we find ourselves in what sociologist, Morris Massey, termed the *Imprint Period*. This is when many of our beliefs and our values were formed. Up to the age of seven, we are like sponges, absorbing our world around us and accepting most of what we experience as the only truth, especially when it comes from our rulers and authority figures who seem to know so much, namely our parents. We are taught to listen to our parents and listen and watch we do. During this period we are often confused about how the world works and sometimes our blind beliefs formed during this time can lead to trauma and other deep issues later in life. Here we also learn a sense of right and wrong — programming our *orbital frontal cortex* with *error detection signals* and this is also aided with a concept we've come to know as, *good* and *bad*. There's *good* behaviour and *bad* behaviour and we're quickly reminded by our parents or carers when we get it wrong.

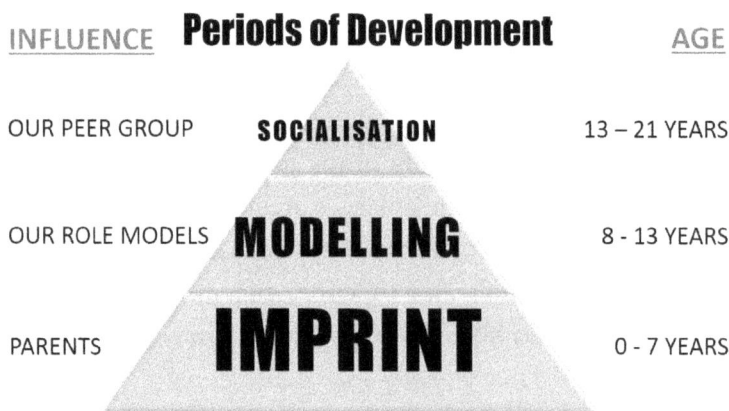

INFLUENCE	**Periods of Development**	AGE
OUR PEER GROUP	**SOCIALISATION**	13 – 21 YEARS
OUR ROLE MODELS	**MODELLING**	8 - 13 YEARS
PARENTS	**IMPRINT**	0 - 7 YEARS

Copyright 2013 – Rik Schnabel

From the ages of eight to 13, we move into the *Modelling Period*. Here we *copy* people, usually the people we aspire to become, role models and significant people such as; rock stars; pop stars; movie stars; business leaders; heroes and unfortunately for some;

villains. Rather than blind acceptance, we are now trying on *things* like we would clothes, to see how we feel in them.

THE POWER OF THE THREE MS

The next phase runs from around 13 to 21 and is called, the *Socialisation Period*. This is where we will try out the personality we created in our modelling in our social world — to see if our behaviour is accepted. Depending upon the level of acceptance or non-acceptance, we will either abandon our personality or retain it. During this period we seek the approval of our peers and are highly influenced by their opinions. We will adjust our behaviour to gain acceptance into social cliques, groups, gangs and clusters as socialisation moves up our values hierarchy.

Our values may make a major shift from *clever* to *cool* for example, meaning we'll value our social standing more than our academic achievements. As we develop as individuals we move away from our parents' way of thinking and start looking for ways to transcend our earlier programming. Naturally we turn to people who seem more like us or groups whom we wish to be more alike. Other key influences at these ages include "The Three Ms:" Media, Movies and Music. We will gravitate to the programs, movies and music that mimic the values of our peer groups. So what influence do *The Three Ms* have upon our societies' psyche?

The 3 Key Influencers of the Modelling Period

MEDIA

MOVIES

MUSIC

Copyright 2014 – Rik Schnabel

Start watching what teenagers wear, their brand alliances and mimicry and you'll soon see the power and influence of *The Three Ms*. Watch particularly the impact that TV has on people in the *Socialisation Period* — you will be amazed at how influential *The Three Ms* really are. This provides a massive clue to parents; how they can help to positively influence their teenage children. *The Three Ms* are the key. The movies, music and media that parents choose to allow into their homes will not only influence their children's' neurology, but their entire family.

Advertising as a medium is massively influential — particularly when the creative directors and writers truly understand the psychology of their market. Picture yourself watching your favourite movie on TV. The movie pauses to reveal a healthy, cool, good looking, tall and muscular guy holding a can of drink. Slowly he moves it to his mouth as from behind him appears the most gorgeous, sexy and seductive looking woman you've ever seen. She brings her mouth to his to share his can of drink. Just one viewing and should the advertising agency have gotten the mix right, the viewer will have already created an association between the drink, the talent in the commercial and themselves.

Back in the 90s advertisers knew that they had to make at least three impressions or three viewings of an advertisement to commence the process of influencing our buying habits. These days we're being exposed to 25,000 to 30,000 advertising messages a day so advertisers are competing against each other more than ever to get our attention. Though our concern should not be exclusive to adults, as we now know how vulnerable children are to advertising messages. These are messing with their beliefs and installing new ones.

An American study conducted back in 2004, concerned with the rising rate of obesity in children concluded that television was a major influence in this trend, "We estimate that children ages two to eleven saw about 25,600 television advertisements, 17 percent more than in 1977. Children saw approximately 5,500 food ads in 2004, 22 percent of all ads viewed."[1]

What's even more disturbing is the percentage of overweight children in the United States is growing at an alarming rate, with one out of three kids now considered overweight or obese. Many kids are spending less time exercising and more time in front of the TV, computer, or video-game console. And today's busy families have fewer free moments to prepare nutritious, home-cooked meals. From fast food to electronics, quick and easy is the reality for many people.[2]

The problem while not as grave as the US, in 2007–08, one-quarter (25%) of all Australian children, or around 600,000 children aged five to 17 years, were overweight or obese, up four percentage points from 1995 (21%).[3]

What are those commercials selling and what beliefs are food advertisers installing into our children's minds? After all I have come to understand about how our brains work — there is cause for concern and reasons to become consciously aware. What I am about to share with you, television commercial users and their advertising agencies understand all too well.

Advertisers know that our minds are expert in identifying and creating patterns. More so, we give these patterns names as we're *meaning making machines*. Let me elaborate. When we create associations between one thing and another, we create a "Neurological Bridge." Simply, it means that one thing leads to the association of another. It's as simple as singing, "Humpty Dumpty sat on a wall, Humpty Dumpty had a...." and our minds finish the line of the rhyme with the words "great fall." It's the power of repetition and association. For example; our kids see their favourite cartoon character eating a particular food and saying, "Yummy" or better still a made up word like, "Yunchie!" Our mind bridges the good feelings we have every time we see our favourite cartoon character exclaiming *Yunchie!* The child now associates the advertising's pictures, sounds, words and feeling good with the food. The association has cemented.

There is also a good reason that at the end of most commercials, we will be shown what the product looks like packaged. Now all we have to do is see the packaged food on the shelves of the supermarket, with the *Yunchie!* cartoon and our children instantly want to replicate the good feeling and so they ask/shout/scream/yell at mum to buy the food so they can feel good. Advertising uses this process in subtle and often overt ways, though very symbolic methods to influence our initial purchase and to turn that purchase into a habit. There's an intentional psychology in the choice of colour used in advertisements, the typeface, the characters and actors they choose. If we're not consciously aware, we will fall under the advertisers' spell.

To give you a sense of how this works. Just for a moment, let's play a game. I'm going to expose you to some logos and logotypes that represent companies. I want you to express the first sound or sounds that come out of your mouth when you see them below. Don't think about this at all, just intuitively and automatically express the first sound that comes out of your mouth as you see the images below — are you ready?

What sounds come out of your mouth when you see? —

What sounds come out of your mouth when you see? —

What sounds come out of your mouth when you see? —

What sound comes out of your mouth when you see? —

Mercedes-Benz

When you think of *Apple* ® what associations do you have with that brand? What about *Microsoft* ®, or *Coke* ® *or Mercedes-Benz* ®? Whatever you think of them know now that they've worked very hard to get those associations into your mind, or they've failed. You be the judge.

Advertising creates these associations with clothing labels, sunglasses, shoes, cars, watches, cosmetics, healthcare products, food and anything else that must be sold to keep the production lines moving. Advertisers have been selling you, waving that carrot at you or brandishing that stick, using your *Version 1.0* and *2.0* beliefs about how the world works to persuade you to buy. It is another good reason to upgrade to *Version 5.0*.

Some advertisers motivate us to buy by using aspirational themes while others use fear, guilt and, every emotion that will stir us to buy. Though advertisers aren't the only ones using our *Version 1.0* and *2.0 beliefs* to program and install in us new beliefs. Politicians and governments do as well, though retailers tend to do it best.

Now as I point this out to you, you might be saying to yourself, *I know this*. I'm sure you do. Others do too. But why is it that we fall under the spell of our own beliefs and while in a shopping centre, millions of people the world over, get into what appears to be a trance, buying things they don't need from people they don't know? Have you ever wondered about that? It's because our beliefs have been programmed and they're not in your conscious mind, they're somewhere else. They're in your unconscious and now that you know all you know about beliefs — it's time to change them at the unconscious level.

YOUR PAST DOES NOT EQUAL YOUR FUTURE

Your unconscious is where we need to do the work if we wish to make a changes stick. If we are serious about transforming our lives then we must focus our attention on the unconscious.

Over the years I have watched people wanting to be wealthier, healthier and happier only to see them improve their skills, their knowledge but not their plight. The unconscious is the biggest impediment to realising success *and* it is our greatest liberator. Our limitations are almost always programmed deep into our unconscious. These unconscious limitations not only influence our behaviour, they can also play a major role in determining our physiology and health. In my clinical work, I have witnessed illnesses and conditions vanish, following helping a client to change their beliefs around their illness. I have seen people get well, get wealthy and happy by consciously making a real decision to change their beliefs and so their lives.

In 2011, Australian newspapers featured a dear friend who was a client that not only changed his beliefs; he dramatically changed his financial life. In an article entitled, "Millionaire Club – Wealth Creation Tips That Worked." The article goes on to say, "Rohan Simmons, 40, works in a gritty field, running the Melbourne plastering firm *South City Plaster*. Simmons's yearly turnover is $3.5 million. His success is embedded in his adherence to a range of rituals. For a start, Simmons has been seeing a business coach weekly for the past six-and-a-half years. The coaching sessions have taught him to set short-term and long-term goals. He looks up to five years ahead and ensures every step he takes keys into his company's vision, he says. Another of his productive habits is attending neuro linguistic programming (NLP) seminars run by the training and coaching group *Life Beyond Limits*, devoted to overcoming stifling beliefs. According to the *Life Beyond Limits* website, every excuse for lacking wealth is a "finite belief" that can be changed. [4]

Rohan did not originate from wealthy genes, great coaching helped him to change his beliefs and realise his talents, and as a result he became wealthy. Your family, your genetics are not your road map. *Your past does not equal your future.* In fact your genetics are an illusion and the beliefs that hold the illusion in place are a LIE! You can grow beyond your parents, you can do more than your siblings, and you are not your genetics. You are currently the summation of your beliefs, though your new decisions can change them! It's time to move to the next chapter and start making the changes that will get you what you want from your career or your life. It's time to go beyond your genes! It's time to live a *life beyond limits*!

❋

WHAT ARE FOUR POSSIBLE OUTCOMES THAT COME FROM THE BELIEF *IT RUNS IN MY FAMILY, IT'S GENETIC?*

1. We will model our family traits believing they are ours too.
2. This belief stops us from breaking genealogical patterns.
3. If our parents succumb to a serious physical illness, we'll likely follow our beliefs and so create our fate.
4. Don't expect to sound intelligent with this belief; it's an excuse and the world is waking up to it and will be on to us (eventually, if not today).

PERHAPS A BETTER BELIEF COULD BE:

MY THINKING CREATES MY LIFE. IF I AM NOT SATISFIED WITH MY LIFE, I CAN ALWAYS CHANGE MY THINKING.

19

IMAGINATION CHANGES YOUR BELIEFS

In first grade, I was six years old and I even loved the mere announcement that we were about to do art. Though even at six, I was led to believe that art was foolhardy and would never be of any use as an adult. Why would a child own an adult belief such as this one? Much later in life, I realised this belief wasn't only mine.

The belief that *art was foolhardy* came from my parents, their peers and was accepted by much of society at the time. It was utter BS — a *Belief System*, it was utter rubbish. It won't take much for you to recite many of the worlds rich and famous who are — you guessed it — artists! The value of art isn't in art alone, it is in the mindset and the skills that created it, it is all about developing our imagination and later in my life I enjoyed a prosperous career using mine.

Use your imagination, master your thinking and *you* will no longer be subject to being swayed by the minor emotional disturbances in life. You will no longer be led by other people's ideas of what your life should be, must be, and has to be. *You* will determine the course of *your* life. At the beginning of all dreams

✿

Imagination is more important than knowledge.

– Albert Einstein

you'll find a sandman called "imagination".

When Albert Einstein, the man with the abundance of glial cells said, "Imagination is more important than knowledge," it got me thinking. Why would a man who was highly respected for his *intellect* and his *knowledge* say that? Through my training and research, I quickly discovered that the very reason business leaders, visionaries and *all* successful people use their imagination to accomplish their dreams is because it works! It takes us beyond our logical problems and the thinking that created them.

Your imagination is the lens that you choose to look through; it colours or dulls your focus. Sharpen your lens, your focus and sharpen your life! Blur the lines and we lose our definition. Keep imagining what you choose to believe in your mind, until you can start to actually believe it is possible. This is just one way to install a new empowering belief into your unconscious. That's the slow way, though I'm about to teach you the fast way.

Imagination is certainly more powerful than intellect and logic; in fact, imagination is sometimes the only tool we have to pull us out of a rut. Think about it. If you don't know how to solve a problem, you've got no idea within your logical mind — what are you going to use? How about starting with your imagination? Create a solution from the air — that's precisely where solutions can be found.

Some of my greatest insights were learned and practiced in sales. It taught me how to use these insights at the coalface and my financial world ballooned as a result. Here's how I did it.

CREATE AN *OPTIMUM OPUS*

Moments before my sales presentations, I sat quietly in my car and in my mind I imagined my ideal desired outcome. Mentally I created an *optimum opus* — an ideal conversation — a literary piece of genius, I made it all up in my mind. I dreamed up the ideal conversation of the meeting that was about to take place, hearing the conversation moving toward our mutual success. At the same time, I visualised it. I allowed myself to see the meeting in my mind's eye. Until I could *feel* in my body the elation from a highly positive meeting — in essence, I created a *success state*. Seeing is believing and feeling is experiencing. This process pre-programs your unconscious mind so that your conscious mind will do everything it can to emulate it.[1]

It's like you're rehearsing for a play. It's not real, life is an illusion, albeit a convincing one, it's all just a game and we are the creators and producers of our lives.

If something *feels* real, your unconscious mind will come to believe it *is* real. When I began to feel what I imagined, I felt a sense of calm, a sense of success. I then knew I was ready for my meeting. The process adjusted my beliefs; it aligned them with good intentions and actions. My unconscious was then programmed. During my meetings, I felt relaxed, successful and confident. What I thought was really amazing, was when the conversations I imagined in my head, actualised in reality.

Try it for yourself. Imagine a desirable outcome *prior to* the outcome and notice what happens to you along the way. Perhaps you could try this in a situation that is not normally ideal. Let's say every time you have dinner with a particular person it ends in an argument. Prior to the dinner, sit yourself down in a quiet place and rehearse the dinner in your mind in an optimum way. Maybe you see yourself and this person actually hitting it off — really getting along, even genuinely laughing? Try it and let me know what happens. One of my missions in life is to move people to conscious awareness so that they are back in control of their lives and living their ideal outcomes. If you can be inspired to do so you can post your thoughts and results by posting them to our *Facebook* ® page:

https://www.facebook.com/InfinityBelief — and help and inspire others to do so too.

The point of this short chapter is to prepare you to use your imagination. You will come to learn that it is one your most valuable assets. Now let's create a strong foundation, and prepare to change those beliefs…

20

YOUR BELIEF CHANGE PREPLAY

To truly change a limiting belief, it is important that two things are present. One: we must *want* to shift the belief. If we are not fully invested in removing that old belief, then we will consciously or unconsciously sabotage our efforts. In fact, I've experienced students and clients almost wanting to argue with you, providing you with reasons to keep their old problems — yes it sounds crazy, but it's true. As Richard Bach said, "If you argue for your limitations you get to keep them."

Two: the second thing we need to explore is a *reason* to shift the limiting belief. We pay a price for every limiting belief. If the cost to us is substantial, we will develop a compelling reason to do the work. Once we have identified the specific limiting belief and the price we're paying to hold onto it, then we're more likely to do what's necessary to shift it, particularly if the price were paying is higher than the cost to shift it.

So, for the final preparations to help you to shift some of those limiting beliefs, I've prepared this chapter to enhance the power of your focus and make the process easy.

Below I have included a *Dharma Wheel* — otherwise known as the "Wheel of Life." In coaching we will use it to help our clients to find out where they are stuck or which area requires some coaching work. So let's start you here.

While there are many aspects to your life, I've chosen

eight common areas to focus upon. This will help you to determine where to focus your energy.

STEP ONE — WHAT AREA OF YOUR LIFE NEEDS YOUR ATTENTION?

The Wheel of Life

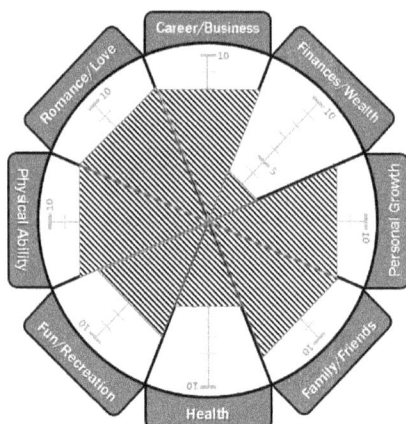

MARK WHERE YOU'RE AT OUT OF 10 AND SHADE THAT AREA -

In the illustrative example of a completed *Wheel of Life*, you will see eight areas of a person's life has been scored from zero to ten (ten being fulfilled, zero unfulfilled). In this example, we can see that this wheel seems fairly balanced, except for "Health" and particularly the area of "Finances/Wealth." After completing your *Wheel of Life,* we can gain an idea as to where to focus our attention.

To start working on your *Wheel,* flick over to the blank *Wheel of Life* and simply and without too much thought draw a line across the area, anywhere from zero to ten and shade that area. For example; if you're *Career* or *Business* is not where you would like it to be then it's definitely not a ten — what number is it?

So go ahead and mark that part of *The Wheel of Life* and do the same for each slice of life. You're *Wheel* might look something like the example, or it might look completely different. If the example *Wheel* was yours, I would be focusing in the area of *Finances and Wealth* or perhaps even in the *Health* area of your life.

Once you have determined the area of your life that you wish to focus upon we can move to step two. Perhaps its an area that you have neglected or you are doing everything you can, though you are getting nowhere or perhaps it's just that something's missing.

So let's start by completing your *Wheel of Life*. Simply and without too much thought draw a line across every area in your *Wheel of Life*, anywhere from zero to ten and shade that area…

The Wheel of Life

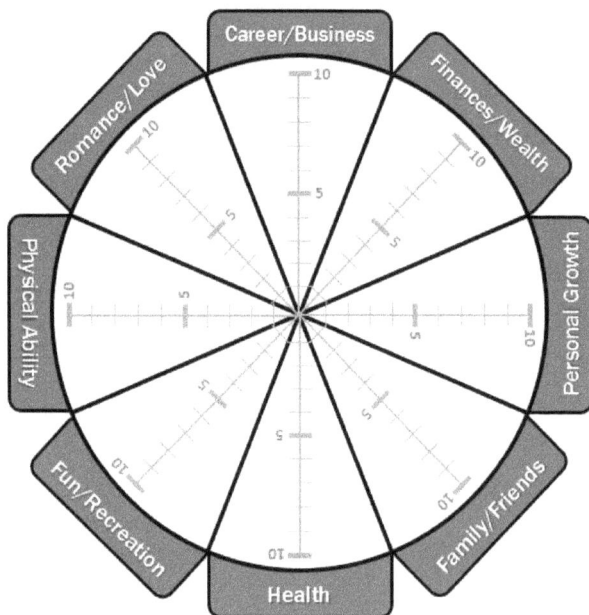

Career/Business

Romance/Love

Finances/Wealth

Physical Ability

Personal Growth

Fun/Recreation

Family/Friends

Health

MARK WHERE YOU'RE AT OUT OF 10 AND SHADE THAT AREA -

Which area of your life are we focusing on? ....
....

STEP TWO — IDENTIFYING THE PROBLEM

Here's the next step. It starts with a question to help you to reveal the problem and then the belief underlying the problem. Are you ready?

How is this (area of your life) a problem for you, specifically? Be as focused as possible, for example if the area that you're focusing on is *Health* then why is *Health* specifically a problem for you? The answer could be — *I'm not eating healthy,* though I would aim to be more specific. You could ask yourself — *What am I not eating that I could be* or *what am I consuming that I shouldn't*? So if the answer is now, *I'm eating too much fried food and not enough whole foods* — then we're ready for *Step Three.* Though it is sometimes better to go even deeper and you can do that by continually asking yourself one question.

Keep asking yourself — *how is that a problem*? And no matter what answer you get, keep asking — *how is that a problem* or ask, how *specifically* is that a problem for you? And you'll start moving to the very core of the problem.

How *specifically* is this a problem for you? ....
....
....
....
....
....

STEP THREE — WHAT IS THE ULTIMATE PRICE THAT YOU'RE PAYING?

If we don't know the price we're paying for a problem to exist, then typically most people will play the ostrich game of problem solving — that is, they'll just stick their head in the sand and pretend the problem doesn't exist, until it becomes unbearable. So to ensure that we don't do that, let's put a price on our problem. By the way, it doesn't have to be too accurate, guesses are all we're looking for here and there won't always be a monetary price — sometimes not getting what we want from life or losing what we once had is simply, *priceless*.

For every problem there is a price that we're paying. Be it a financial cost or a cost to our career or business, our relationships, our health, our fun or recreation or social costs — there is always a price. For example: if too many of our meals are in the fast food category and you know the ones I'm talking about here, then the price or the costs could look like this...

1. FINANCIAL COSTS

☒ Fast food instead of fresh vegetables: *$1,825 per year (extra $5 per meal x 365 days)*

☒ Potential heart attack: *$50,000 per year loss of income (unless you're insured)*

☒ Potential heart attack: *$25,000 out of pocket expenses (unless you're insured)*

2. CAREER AND BUSINESS COSTS

☒ Loss of promotion due to low energy and poor attitude −: *$30,000 per year loss of income*

☒ Just won't feel like that vital Manager anymore: *Priceless = you can't put a price on this*

3. RELATIONSHIP COSTS

☒ I don't look or feel like the terrific and vital partner I used to be: *priceless*

☒ My partner has lost interest as I look less desirable, possible divorce: *Loss of self-esteem and assets due to divorce*

4. PHYSICAL & HEALTH COSTS

☒ Fearful of playing sport with my kids, just in case it I have a heart attack: *Priceless*

☒ I'm scared of exercising as I put on more weight and lose energy: *Priceless*

5. FUN AND RECREATION COSTS

☒ Fear of exerting self at family activities outdoors; life will get boring: *Priceless*

☒ Shift from energetic and vital to timid about life: *Priceless*

6. SOCIAL COSTS

☒ Don't have the energy to keep up with my friends: *Priceless*

☒ Feeling like lesser of a vital and functional person among network: *Priceless*

STEP THREE — WHAT IS THE ULTIMATE PRICE THAT YOU'RE PAYING?

So are you ready to get real? Add the price that you are paying for the problem in all six areas.

1. FINANCIAL COSTS & THE PRICE YOU ARE PAYING?

☒ ....

$ ....……

☒ ....

$ ....……..

☒ ....

$ ....……..

2. **CAREER AND BUSINESS COSTS & THE PRICE YOU ARE PAYING?**

    ☒...

    $...

    ☒...

    $...

    ☒...

    $...

3. **RELATIONSHIP COSTS & THE PRICE YOU ARE PAYING?**

    ☒...

    $...

    ☒...

    $...

    ☒...

    $...

4. PHYSICAL HEALTH COSTS & THE PRICE YOU
    ARE PAYING?

☒...

$..

☒...

$..

☒...

$..

5. FUN AND RECREATION COSTS & THE PRICE
    YOU ARE PAYING?

☒...

$..

☒...

$..

☒...

$..

6. SOCIAL COSTS & THE PRICE YOU ARE PAYING?

☒…………………………………………

$………………………………...............…

☒…………………………………………

$………………………………...............…

☒…………………………………………

$………………………………...............…

I bet this is a pretty expensive problem to have. Now it's time to discover the belief and shift it.

STEP FOUR — WHAT IS THE BELIEF?

Now that we have an idea of what the problem is and the price that we're paying to keep it, it's time to ask ourselves the vital question — What is the belief that we're holding that's causing the problem? Let me give you some examples.

If as in the example: I'm eating too much fried food and not enough whole foods.

And we ask: How is that a problem for you?

We get an answer such as: If I keep doing this I'll have a heart attack.

Then the very belief may be: I believe that I will have a heart attack.

Though I would go deeper by asking again: How is that a

problem for you? And we might get this answer…I believe I can't stop eating fried-food or I'm addicted to fried food.

Neither of these are helpful beliefs. I would start by shifting any one of these beliefs, as doing do will put you back in charge of your life. It is also much more likely to change the unhealthy behaviour. By the way, changing the beliefs: I believe I can't stop eating fried-food or I'm addicted to fried food is better than — I believe fried food causes heart attacks as this latter belief doesn't change the unhealthy behaviour.

So it's time to search for your limiting beliefs — are you ready? The question is simple and it starts with the words — I believe….

What beliefs are: causing your problem(s) to exist?

Answer: I believe ....
....
....
....

Ask — *How is that a problem for you* or ask — *Why do you believe that?* This will help you to get to the core of the problematic belief.

Phew! You must be feeling better already now that that's out of the way. So the following chapters will show you three ways to change your beliefs. Enjoy some great belief changing…

21

THE BODY BELIEF CHANGE

Before I teach you the first belief change method, remember beliefs are concepts or ideas created in our imagination. They'll often sound like opinions. While calling beliefs "illusions" may be trite, for some, we know that two people can experience the same event, yet create very different beliefs as a result. Once we have created a new belief, we store it in our unconscious. We do not have to think of the belief consciously anymore — we'll automatically adjust our patterns, our habits to conform to our new belief. So how are they stored in our unconscious? I thought you'd never ask ;)

Beliefs are stored in our brain within the unconscious, and you may be surprised to learn that our bodies store beliefs as well. There is an interrelationship between our minds and our bodies that is more than physical. A clue is found when asked what one truly believes, you will often witness a person placing their hand on their heart. It's no surprise therefore that many of our truest truths are stored in our heart. *"The things you believe in your heart, as opposed to your head, are the things you live by. It's hard to even spot them, let alone explain them; they are so much a core part of you."*[1]

There are three parts to our brain; the "primitive brain" that deals with self-preservation and aggression; the "intermediate brain" or the "limbic system" that processes our emotions and the "rational brain" otherwise known as the "neo-cortex" that rationalises tasks. Our obsession with the mind and the brain, in which we believe thought is influenced and processed, will easily miss two other significant breakthroughs in brain research that suggests that there are two other brains located in our bodies; namely the "heart brain" and the "enteric brain" otherwise known as the "gut brain."

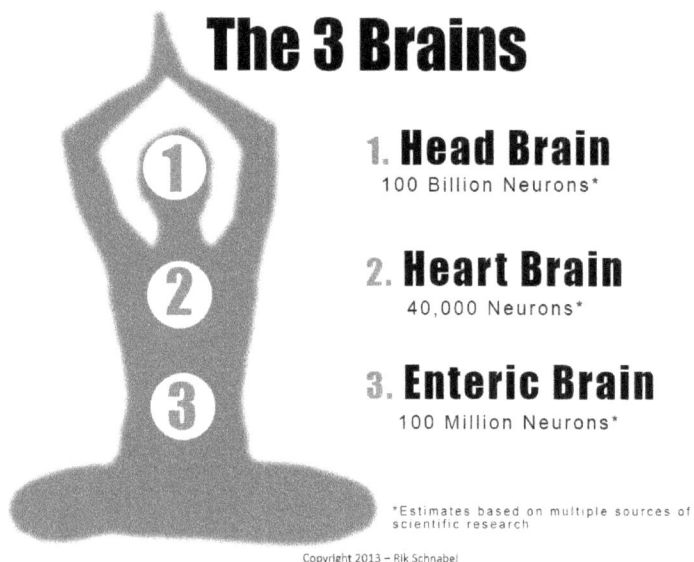

The 3 Brains

1. **Head Brain**
100 Billion Neurons*

2. **Heart Brain**
40,000 Neurons*

3. **Enteric Brain**
100 Million Neurons*

*Estimates based on multiple sources of scientific research

Copyright 2013 – Rik Schnabel

YOUR ENTERIC BRAIN AFFECTS YOUR MOODS AND YOUR THOUGHTS

As Olympians go for the gold, even the steeliest is likely to experience that familiar feeling of "butterflies" in the stomach. Underlying this sensation is an often-overlooked network of neurons lining our guts that is so extensive some scientists have nicknamed it our "second brain."

A deeper understanding of this mass of neural tissue, filled with important neurotransmitters, is revealing that it does much more than merely handle digestion or inflict the occasional nervous pang. The little brain in our innards, in connection with the big one in our skulls, partly determines our mental state and plays key roles in certain diseases throughout the body.

Michael Gershon, chairman of the Department of Anatomy and Cell Biology at New York–Presbyterian Hospital/Columbia University Medical Center, an expert in the nascent field of neurogastroenterology and author of the 1998 book, "The Second Brain" (HarperCollins).

Technically known as the enteric nervous system, the second brain consists of sheaths of neurons embedded in the walls of the long tube of our gut, or alimentary canal, which measures about nine metres (9.84 yards) end to end from the esophagus to the anus. According to Gershon, the second brain contains some 100 million neurons, more than in either the spinal cord or the peripheral nervous system.

This multitude of neurons in the enteric nervous system enables us to "feel" the inner world of our gut and its contents. Much of this neural firepower comes to bear in the elaborate daily grind of digestion. Breaking down food, absorbing nutrients, and expelling of waste requires chemical processing, mechanical mixing and rhythmic muscle contractions that move everything on down the line.

Thus equipped with its own reflexes and senses, the second brain can control gut behaviour independently of the brain, Gershon says. We likely evolved this intricate web of nerves to perform digestion and excretion "on site," rather than remotely from our brains through the middleman of the spinal cord. "The brain in the head doesn't need to get its hands dirty with the messy business of digestion, which is delegated to the brain in the gut," Gershon says. He and other researchers explain, however, that the second brain's complexity likely cannot be interpreted through this process alone.

"The system is way too complicated to have evolved only to make sure things move out of your colon," says Emeran Mayer, professor of physiology, psychiatry and biobehavioral sciences at the David Geffen School of Medicine at the University of California, Los Angeles (U.C.L.A.). For example, scientists were shocked to learn that about 90 percent of the fibres in the primary visceral nerve, the vagus, carry information from the gut to the brain and not the other way around. "Some of that info is decidedly unpleasant," Gershon says.

The second brain informs our state of mind in other more obscure ways, as well. "A big part of our emotions are probably influenced by the nerves in our gut," Mayer says. Butterflies in the stomach—signalling in the gut as part of our physiological stress response, Gershon says—is but one example. Although gastrointestinal (GI) turmoil can sour one's moods, everyday emotional well-being may rely on messages from the brain below to the brain above.[2]

YOUR HEART BRAIN STORES MANY OF YOUR CORE BELIEFS

A transplant patient developed an insatiable craving for junk food after receiving a new heart from a teenager with a taste for fatty snacks. David Waters is the latest example of an extraordinary phenomenon which sees some transplant recipients take on the characteristics of the donor. Before being given the heart of 18-year-old Kaden Delaney, who was left brain dead after a car crash, Mr Waters, 24, had 'no desire at all' for *Burger Rings®*, ring-shaped hamburger-flavoured crisps.

It was two years before he found out why the cravings had started suddenly after his operation. Kaden's family tracked him down to see who had benefited from their son's heart, and they began exchanging emails. A curious Mr Waters then asked: "Did Kaden like Burger Rings? That's all I seemed to want to eat after my surgery." He was astonished to hear that Kaden ate them daily.

The case in Australia adds weight to a theory that the brain is not the only organ to store memories or personality traits. Scientists say there are at least 70 documented cases of transplant patients having personality changes which reflect the characteristics of their donor.

Other astonishing examples include the case of American Sonny Graham, who received the heart of Terry Cottle, who had shot himself in the head. After the transplant in 1995 Mr Graham met Mr Cottle's widow Cheryl, falling in love and marrying her. Twelve years later Mr Graham picked up a gun and shot himself in the throat, leaving Cheryl a widow for the second time grieving for husbands who had shared a heart.

In another example, an eight-year-old girl received the heart of a murdered ten-year-old and began having terrifying dreams about a man murdering her donor. Until then, the murderer had not been caught, but recollections from the girl's dream were so precise that police were able to track down the killer and he was convicted. [3]

If there is a connection between speech-dominated communication and locating aspects of consciousness in the chest, will we continue to act as if knowledge originates in the brain or will the notion of a deeper wisdom emanating from somewhere in the chest (the heart) gain ascendancy? An individual can have a heart, take heart, be heartless, show heart, and be in the heart of things. Our language betrays deeper beliefs about the heart. We speak of our core beliefs or principles, *cor*, from the Latin for *heart*. When we want to truly understand a topic, we seek to get to the heart of the matter. Throughout our culture, the heart is portrayed as the site of emotions and of perceptions that correspond to the true beliefs of an individual. When Janis Joplin (Berns & Ragovoy, 1967) sang, "take another little piece of my heart," she was not discussing by-pass surgery. [4]

The heart is one of the most important organs of the human body. Life starts when it starts beating (21 days after conception) and ends when it stops (clinical death). The heart has nearly two billion muscle cells and 40,000 neurons. The heart's neurons are very few in number compared to those in the brain (100 billion) or gut (100 million). Nevertheless these neurons transmit heart signals and its condition to the brain.

The heart-mind interaction takes place both by electrical signals (via the vagus and the spinal cord nerves) and through chemicals (heart is an endocrine gland also). Recent studies have shown that the heart sends signals to the brain that are not only understood by it but also obeyed. Scientists have discovered neural pathways and mechanisms whereby input from the heart to the brain inhibits or facilitates the brain's electrical activity — just like what the gut brain is capable of doing. Thus both gut and heart mind help in overall thought process.

Recently scientists have also discovered that the heart is involved in the processing and decoding of "intuitive information." Tests done on the subjects showed that the heart appeared to receive the intuitive information before the brain.

This could be the basis of saying, "Follow you heart and you will never go wrong." [5]

CHANGE HOW YOUR BRAIN STORES
A BELIEF AND YOU CHANGE THE BELIEF

The ways in which we can install and equally remove a belief is by undoing the very fabric that keeps them real. That fabric is stored in our *head brain*, our *heart brain* and in our *gut brain*. The very fabric I'm speaking of is what we call "submodalities" and these are what hold our beliefs in place — neurologically speaking.

Submodalities are our interpretation of the chemicals that make up our thoughts and feelings and we can interrupt them and reprogram our thinking. *Submodalities* however are how we interrupt and shift our beliefs and we do this by changing the qualities of the modalities, namely Pictures (Vision), Sounds (Auditory), Feelings (Kinesthetic) and Auditory Digital (the Words we use that describe our experience). These are the building blocks of our experiences. I have been using this process now for over ten years and have worked successfully with thousands of people to help them change their beliefs and so their lives.

Because beliefs are essentially illusions of our own creation, we have created ideas around our experiences and these have representations that make up pictures, sounds, feelings and we can describe them in words either out loud or in our heads. Therefore we can now easily and simply dismantle our beliefs. However, to do so, we require a process.

I'm going to show you three ways to change your beliefs. You can use all of them or just one them — your favourite perhaps. Eventually like me, you will find a favourite and choose to use that technique. So here is technique number one, *The Body Belief Change.*

TRUST THE FIRST PICTURE THAT JUMPS INTO YOUR MIND

Firstly, these processes will require you to create a picture in your mind. The key to success is to allow the *very first* picture that jumps into your mind when you consider the belief — even if the picture bears no relationship to the belief that you're considering. Sometimes it makes no sense at all — remember our beliefs are held in the unconscious and this is an unconscious process — it's not meant to make sense, it's not conscious.

Finally, some people find it challenging to see pictures in their mind when closing their eyes, while others can see pictures easily, even without closing their eyes. It's okay either way. If you cannot see pictures in your mind, you will get a sense of the picture — even though you cannot see it visually — you see it with your mind. It's like you can describe it in detail, but cannot see it at all.

All you have to do is just trust your unconscious and have faith in yourself through each step of the process. At the beginning and end of each process, you will measure or *calibrate* the belief and that will tell you if you've succeeded or not. And if you haven't succeeded, just do the process again — or move on to the next one.

Now in preparation, make sure that the belief you are about to change is what I call, "ecological." That simply means that changing the belief will not harm you, others or the planet as a whole. Equally, understand that there is no point in changing a belief that isn't a problem for you or an issue in your life. So the first step is to answer honestly; is it *really* a problem and if so, is it ecological to change it? If the Answer to both questions is: *yes*, it's time to change the belief — wouldn't you agree? Let's get stuck into changing those limiting beliefs! So what belief do you want to change first?

THE BELIEF I'M GOING TO CHANGE IS?

I believe ....
....

✳

THE BODY BELIEF CHANGE —
THE PROCESS

STEP 1: CALIBRATE THE BELIEF.

Now we need to measure the extent of the *truth* of the belief. If we don't measure it, how will we know if it has changed? So the key is that we want an *unconscious* answer. In other words, the first answer that comes to you. In a moment, not now, quickly answer this next question without thinking; otherwise your answer will be manipulated consciously. Are you ready to answer the following question?

Question: On a scale of zero to ten, ten being totally "TRUE" what number comes up when you verbalise your belief? Now circle the number on the scale below...

Calibrate Your Belief

0	1	2	3	4	5	6	7	8	9	10

LIE   Copyright 2013 – Rik Schnabel   TRUE

STEP 2: UNCOVER THE NEUROLOGICAL VISUAL AND KINESTHETIC SUBMODALITIES OF THE BELIEF.

Now it's time to change the belief. Every belief will be represented in our neurology by a picture (V) and a feeling (K), among other modalities. Though we will just focus on these two in this process. Going through the process sometimes feels like you're making it up and that's okay. Are you ready?

A. What is the very first **Picture** (V) that springs to mind as you think of your limiting belief? Verbalise your limiting belief and notice the very picture or idea that springs to mind. Close your eyes if it's easier. We'll call this the, *First Picture*. Describe your *First Picture* (briefly): ....
....
....
....

B. Now close your eyes and recreate the **First Picture** (V) and notice the very first place that you become aware of a feeling in your body, as you think of this belief? We'll now call this the, **First Feeling** (K).

C. Now while still seeing the **First Picture** in your minds-eye, use your imagination and move the **First Picture** over the area you first felt in your body, the *First Feeling*.

D. Now again using your imagination; imagine moving both the *First Picture* and the *First Feeling* down one leg (any one), until it moves out of your heel and out of your body altogether. Take your time doing this. Remember, this is not a logical process — just use your imagination. When Einstein said, "Imagination is more important than knowledge!" Understand that you're moving into an amazing realm now — you can adjust your entire life!

E. Finally, create a new empowering belief (that might be the opposite of the limiting belief) and when you think of your empowering belief, allow the first picture that springs to mind to move into your heart. If the empowering belief doesn't start in your heart, move it there by using your imagination. Again it's often better to close your eyes and let your imagination do the work.

STEP 3: RE-CALLIBRATE THE OLD BELIEF.

Now we need to again measure the truth of the old belief so we know that it has changed. It only has to move one or two points to know that the belief has shifted. Again, the key is that we want an unconscious answer. We want to be able to quickly answer this question without thinking; otherwise our answer will be manipulated consciously. Are you ready, answer the question below?

Question: On a scale of zero to ten, zero being a total "LIE" what number now comes up when you verbalise your old belief? Now circle the number on the scale below...

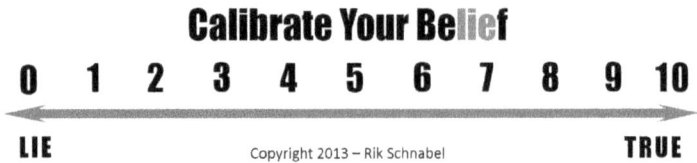

Calibrate Your Belief

| 0 | 1 | 2 | 3 | 4 | 5 | 6 | 7 | 8 | 9 | 10 |

LIE   Copyright 2013 – Rik Schnabel   **TRUE**

STEP 4:

Now if you've done this correctly, you should have made a shift along the scale away from your original number, closer to zero. If you haven't, simply repeat the process, though this time move a bit faster through the process. Once you get the hang of this process, you can do it much more quickly by just shifting the picture around your body.

When for example you re-calibrate an old belief and you move from ten to five, that's a 50 percent shift! Though aim to get your belief to around three or lower.

22

THE VISUAL BELIEF CHANGE

For those who prefer a more visual process, I've designed this simple technique. Because I'm more kinesthetic, I personally favour the first one, though this is just as effective. So here is technique number two, *The Visual Belief Change*.

THE BELIEF I'M GOING TO CHANGE IS?

I believe ....

....

THE VISUAL BELIEF CHANGE — THE PROCESS

STEP 1: CALIBRATE THE BELIEF.

Let's start by measuring the extent of the *truth* of the belief. Again, quickly answer this next question without thinking. Are you ready to answer the following question?

Question: On a scale of zero to ten, *ten* being a total "TRUE" what number comes up when you verbalise your belief? Now circle the number on the scale below...

Calibrate Your Belief

0	1	2	3	4	5	6	7	8	9	10

LIE   Copyright 2013 – Rik Schnabel   TRUE

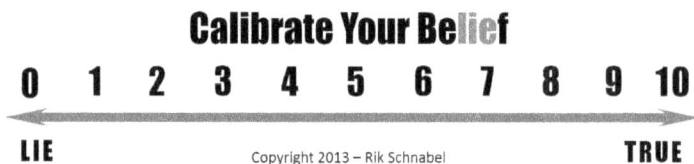

STEP 2: WHAT IS THE FIRST PICTURE THAT COMES UP?

Now it's time to change the belief. Every belief will be represented in our neurology by a picture (V), among other modalities. Though we will just focus on the pictures. Going through the process sometimes feels like you're making it up and that's okay. Are you ready?

A. What is the very first **Picture** (V) that springs to mind as you think of your limiting belief? Close your eyes if it's easier. We'll call this the *First Picture*.

B. Now close your eyes and recreate the ***First Picture*** and notice the details or the submodalities of the *First Picture*. *For example, is it* Colour or Black and White? Is it Bright or Dark? Is it like a Movie or a Photo? Note the size of the picture and how close or far away it is from you. Are you in the picture or are you not in the picture? Is it focused or not focused? And finally, is it three-dimensional or is it flat?

C. Now while still seeing the ***First Picture*** in your mind's-eye, use your imagination and change as many of the qualities you noticed in the ***First Picture*** to their opposite. For example; if the picture is black and white, change it to colour; if it's A4 in size, make it smaller or bigger, anything but A4; if you're in the picture, remove you from the picture, etc... I'm sure you get the idea. You're not changing what's in the picture *per se*; you're only changing the qualities of the picture.

D. Finally, create a new empowering belief (that might be the opposite of the limiting belief) and note the first picture that springs to mind. Now simply change the qualities of this picture, to all the qualities of the ***First Picture***. In other words, if the ***First Picture*** was colour and the new picture of the empowering belief is colour, then change nothing there. But if the ***First Picture*** is a movie and the new picture is a still photo, then change it to become a movie like the ***First Picture***. So all you're doing is changing the new picture that represents the empowering belief to all the qualities of the ***First Picture***.

STEP 3: RE-CALLIBRATE THE OLD BELIEF.

Question: On a scale of zero to ten, zero being a total "LIE" what number now comes up when you verbalise your old belief? Now circle the number on the scale below...

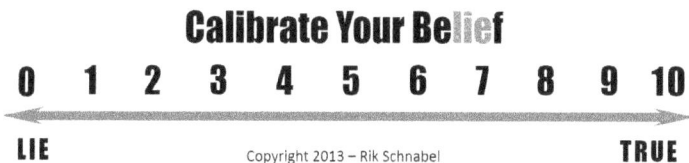

Calibrate Your Belief

0	1	2	3	4	5	6	7	8	9	10

LIE   TRUE

Copyright 2013 – Rik Schnabel

STEP 4:

Now if you've done this correctly, you should have made a shift along the scale away from your original number, closer to zero. If you haven't, simply repeat the process, though this time move a bit faster through the process. Once you get the hang of this process, you can do it much more quickly by just changing the submodalities of the picture.

23

THE FIVE STEP BELIEF CHANGE

Here is an ideal belief change technique that comes directly from our *CALM Level I* program. It's perfect for those people who enjoy a complete process, a more scientific and methodical approach. Though it takes a little more practice, patience and effort to master than the first two techniques. You can do this yourself, though it is easier to have someone take you through the process while your eyes are closed.

To help with your understanding of this process I've decided to focus this example on something that *most* people want more of; that being *money*. You can of course use this same process to change *any* of your limiting beliefs. Let's get into shifting those limiting beliefs for good! So here is technique number three, *The Five Step Belief Change*.

THE BELIEF I'M GOING TO CHANGE IS?

I believe ....
....

THE FIVE STEP BELIEF CHANGE — THE PROCESS

STEP 1: CALIBRATE THE BELIEF.

Let's start by calibrating the belief by measuring the extent of the *truth* of the belief. If we don't measure it, how will we know if it has changed? So the key is that we want an *unconscious* answer. In other words, quickly answer this next question without thinking; otherwise your answer will be manipulated consciously. Here's your question to get the ball rolling, are you ready?

Question: On a scale of zero to ten, ten being a totally "TRUE," what's the first number that springs to mind when you verbalise your belief? Now circle the number on the scale below...

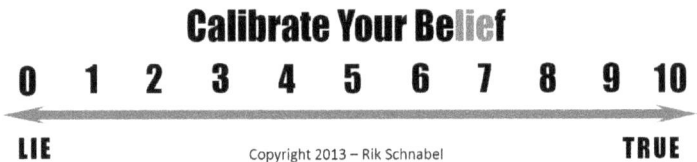

Calibrate Your Belief

0 1 2 3 4 5 6 7 8 9 10

LIE   Copyright 2013 – Rik Schnabel   TRUE

STEP 2: UNCOVER THE NEUROLOGICAL SUBMODALITIES OF THE BELIEF.

Now it's time to change the belief. Every belief will be represented in our neurology with pictures (Visual), sounds (Auditory), feelings (Kinesthetic) and we'll be able to verbalise our thoughts or feelings around the belief in a sentence (Auditory Digital). What do you

say in your head when you think of your belief? Write it down
below:..

....

So in essence every belief has a Visual (V), Auditory (A),
Kinesthetic (K) and Auditory Digital (Ad) representation.
We already know the Auditory Digital, that is, we know the
sentence, so now we need to map out the rest. The process
sometimes feels like you're making it up and that's okay. It's
usually easier to read the question and close your eyes to get
your first responses to these following three questions below
(A, B and C)...

A. What is the first **Picture** (V) that comes to mind as you
    think of this belief? Close your eyes and then open them to
    answer the following questions.

Is the ☑ picture:

☐ Colour or   ☐ Black and White?

☐ Bright or   ☐ Dark?

☐ Moving or   ☐ Still?

☐ What is the size of the picture.....................................?

☐ How close or far away is it...?

☐ Are you in the picture or ☐ Are you not in the picture?

☐ Is it focused or ☐ Is it not focused

                    ☐ or is the focus changing?

☐ Is it three-dimensional or ☐ Is it flat?

Describe the picture...

....

B. What are the first **Sounds** (A) that come to mind as you think of this belief? Close your eyes and then open them to answer the following questions. If there are no obvious sounds coming to consciousness then skip this step. If there is…

Is the ☑ sound:
- ☐ Loud or ☐ Soft?
- ☐ Fast or ☐ Slow?
- ☐ High pitched or ☐ Low pitched?
- ☐ Clear or ☐ Muffled?
- ☐ Moving toward you or ☐ Away from you or ☐ Across you?

Describe the sound..

....

C. When you have the Picture in your mind's eye, you will also have a relationship to that picture in your body. It will be represented with a feeling. Notice where you first become aware or where you feel it in your body. What are the first **Feelings** (K) that you felt in your body as you think of this belief? Close your eyes and then open them to answer the following questions.

Where in your body is the feeling:...................?
What is the shape of the feeling:...................?
What is the size of the feeling:...................?

What does the feeling weigh:....................................?

Is the ☑ feeling:
☐ Hot or ☐ Warm or ☐ Cold?
☐ Is the feeling moving in a particular way
☐ And if it is moving, is it moving clockwise or
 anti-clockwise or, is it ☐ Still?

Describe it:..
....

STEP 3: CHANGE THE BELIEF.

Now that you've mapped out what I call the *neurological submodalities* of the belief, it's time to change them and so the belief will vanish. How do you do that? Simple.

Recreate in your mind's eye, the **First Picture** that came up when you thought about your belief — For example: *I can't earn more money!* and look back at the *neurological submodalities* of that belief and change the elements (or submodalities) of the picture, sounds and feelings to the opposite of what you noted. The key is to make the picture change its elements, but not the picture's itself.

For instance, if the picture is black and white make it colour. If the picture is bright make it dark. If the picture is a movie, make it stop moving and become a still. If the picture's sound is loud, make it quiet. If when you look at the picture you feel a feeling in your stomach, move the feeling to the top of your head or down to your toes, anywhere but in your stomach. So go ahead and do that now.

STEP 4: RE-CALIBRATE THE BELIEF.

Now we need to again measure the truth of the old belief so we know that it has changed? Again, the key is that we want an unconscious answer. We want to be able to quickly answer this question without thinking; otherwise our answer will be manipulated consciously. Are you ready?

Question: On a scale of zero to ten, zero being a total "LIE" what number now comes up when you verbalise your old belief, for example: "*I can't earn any more money!*" Now circle the number on the scale below...

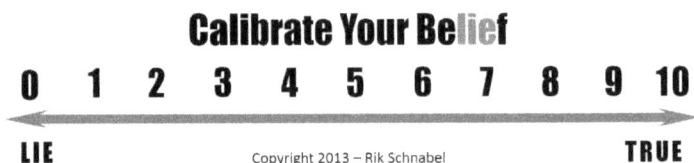

Calibrate Your Belief

0 1 2 3 4 5 6 7 8 9 10

LIE   Copyright 2013 – Rik Schnabel   **TRUE**

STEP 5: TURBO CHARGE YOUR NEW BELIEF.

Now if you've done this correctly, you should have made a shift along the scale away from your original number and closer to zero. If you haven't, simply repeat the process, though this time be sure to change the submodalities of the picture, the sounds and the feelings — and move faster through the process.

Once you get the hang of this process, you can do it while you're walking! By just changing the submodalities (the qualities) of the picture as soon as a limiting belief springs to mind, as just changing the picture's qualities will usually change the sounds and feelings automatically and so it will equally shift the belief.

The final step is instead of the old belief, for example: "*I can't earn more money*" determine a new belief that will move you forward in this area and one that you can now believe, such as;

- *I can learn new ways to make more money* or
- *I don't need more money, I can change my spending habits* or
- *I will find someone who can show me ways to make more money.* Or simply
- *I can create ways to make more money.*

Once you've changed an old belief, it's time to install a new belief, though I like to *Turbo-Charge* them so I don't only believe them, they also empower me! Are you ready?

24

TURBO CHARGE
YOUR NEW BELIEFS

In order for our beliefs to resonate with us both consciously and unconsciously, it is important that we have created enough references for them to move from imagined to real. This process will help you to do that.

Once you've worked out what beliefs need changing and you've gone ahead and changed them, it's now time to ensure that they've got the fuel to drive your behaviour. The answer is to *Turbo Charge Your New Beliefs* and here's how you do it.

Now that you have gotten rid of that old ridiculous belief, for example: *I can't earn more money* and replaced it with an empowering belief, such as: *I can create ways to make more money* it's time to create a *compelling reason* to do so.

If you created ways to make more money; how much money would you like to make per year, per day, per contract, per product, per service? Let's make this up as it is important to define it so it has personal meaning to you. So if you made (say) an extra $30,000 per year you would...

1. Pay all your credit card bills (say) $10,000
2. Go on a seven day holiday to the Caribbean (say) $5,000
3. Place $15,000 in an investment account.

Is that compelling enough for you to take action? Yes or No? If the answer is *No* — then what would *you* have to do to take massive action? What goal is attractive enough for you to do what is necessary? What if you invested the full $30,000 to pamper yourself? Or is $30,000 not a big enough incentive? Once you're certain that your goal is compelling enough, here are the final steps to installing your new belief...

The Belief Shift Process

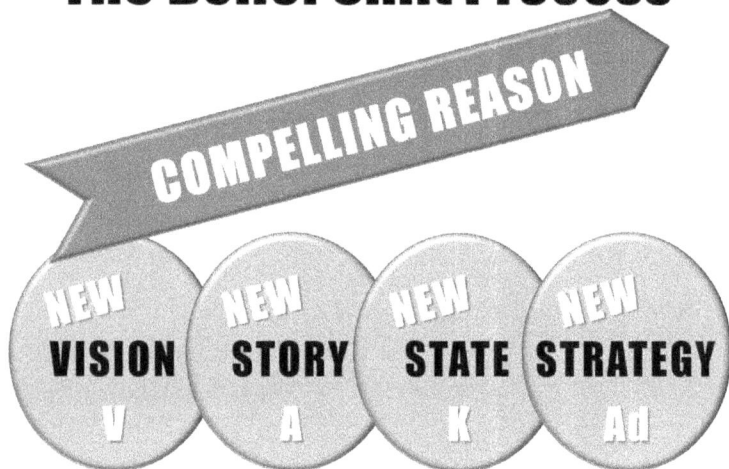

COMPELLING REASON

NEW VISION V   **NEW STORY** A   **NEW STATE** K   **NEW STRATEGY** Ad

Copyright 2013 – Rik Schnabel

STEP 1: What is your **Compelling Reason**(s) for you to take massive action? Write them here: ....
....
....
....
....
....
....

STEP 2: When you consider your new belief, what would you like your **New Vision *look*** like? Describe it here: ....
....
....
....
....
....
....

STEP 3: When you consider your new belief, what would you like your **New Story** to *sound* like? Write it here: ....
....
....
....
....
....

STEP 4: When you consider your new belief, what does your **New State** *feel* like? Describe it here: ....
....
....
....
....
....
....

STEP 5: When you consider your new belief, what is your **New Strategy**? In other words, what are the *action steps*? Write the steps down first, and then sequence them in order here: ....
....

....
....
....
....
....

STEP 6: Now close your eyes and run your new belief through your mind using your imagination. See yourself gaining all the imagined results of this new belief and allow yourself to feel the great energy of gaining the benefits of this new belief. Run it through your mind three times.

The Belief Shift Process helps you to install the new belief in a compelling way into your neurology. If you've followed the steps well, you will have installed it deeply into your unconscious, so much of what you need to do to establish the new belief has already been done.

To ensure that you fulfil your goals means you'll have to take the necessary steps, though it should be much easier with the new belief intact. So take action now because you're not going to achieve your goals by just sitting on the coach watching TV. So what is the very first step you need to take now?

My very first step to embrace my new belief is ....
....
....
....
....
....
....
....

Now it's time to do it.

25

HOW TO UPGRADE TO *VERSION 5.0*

If you feel like you can fully express yourself and speak your mind then chances are you have upgraded your thinking to *Version 5.0*. If you believe that you're lucky and regardless of what happens to you or others around you, you realise that everything is not *good* or *bad*, but just another lesson to add to your personal evolution — then chances are you've upgraded to *Version 5.0*.

If you believe that you can grow beyond your family's limitations and you know you're more than enough to do so, then chances are you can make as much money as you like and still have time for you. Then you've definitely upgraded to *Version 5.0*.

Though if time or money are not your friends and even some of your friends are not your friends then here is what to do next now that you've read the entire contents of this book.

Now if you don't know what you want from your career or your life then you won't have much of a career *or* life other than the one you have now. Goals are important because they give us a focus and the journey to the goal teaches us to be more resourceful, inventive, curious and resilient. So your next step is simple.

Step 1: Set a goal — what do you want now?

Step 2: What beliefs get in the way of taking the next step toward your goal? Dissolve that belief and every other belief that gets in your way.

Step 3: What beliefs do you need in order to realise your goal? Install them, *Turbo Charge* them and you will take your *life beyond limits*.

Step 4: If you would like some personal assistance and would like to work with us at *Life Beyond Limits* — here are four links to get you started…

1. **Get a Coach** — visit: http://www.lifebeyondlimits.com.au/our-nlp-coaches.html
2. **Learn how to become a Life Coach** — http://www.lifebeyondlimits.com.au/nlp-training/life-coach-training.html
3. **Learn Neuro-Linguistic Programming (NLP)** — http://www.lifebeyondlimits.com.au/nlp-training/nlp-practitioner/
4. **Join us in our Career And Life Mastery Training (CALM)** — http://www.lifebeyondlimits.com.au/calm-i.html
5. **Download any Life Beyond Limits audio products** — http://www.DigitalWisdom.eu
6. **Gain access to any of our free products** — http://www.lifebeyondlimits.com.au/free/free-articles/

25

CLOSING THOUGHTS

I hope that my work in writing this book has allowed you to understand your beliefs at a much deeper level. I hope too that you have become conscious of some of your beliefs that have been getting in the way of your desired achievements, and you now have the tools and insights to change them.

Beliefs are not real while they certainly seem real. It's just that we've made them so. Our beliefs are so important in determining our next thoughts and so our future, though so few people invest anything like the time that you have invested in understanding them. So for that reason you must congratulate yourself — you even got to the end of the book — well almost, there's just a few pages more. Perhaps now could be time to share this book with the people you care for most.

I have gained so much knowledge and learned so many transformational tools over the years and one of my beliefs is that I'm here to give this life everything I've got. To give *you* everything I've got. Sometimes I find myself wishing to share all my knowledge in just one book. Thank you to my Editors who kept reminding me of this. I will give you even more in my next array of books.

Thank you from the bottom of my heart for choosing to read this book. It heartens me so to know that a new idea, a technique or a conceptual understanding may have helped you in some way — well actually, you've helped yourself. If you would like to drop me a line I would certainly enjoy that and I can be reached via: rik.schnabel@lifebeyondlimits.com.au I get hundreds of emails every day and it might take me awhile to get to your email, but I assure you, I read and answer every one of them personally.

I know how much this knowledge changed my life and the lives of all those who I have taught. If you would like to join me and learn more about what is possible for you — visit our website via: www.LifeBeyondLimits.com.au and check out two popular areas of the site, namely the "Events" tab and the "Free" tab — I promise we'll keep adding loads of resources for you there.

If you would like to learn so much more about how to take your career and your life to the next level, I've included a short snippet from our *Career and Life Mastery* (CALM) program in the following pages and hope to see you there sometime soon.

Finally, I would love to leave you with *Three Eternal Truths* that evolve you and your spirit. Know these and know they are true.

You are always loved.

You are always safe, and

You can do no wrong.

Warmest Wishes and Blessings

Rik Schnabel
Life Beyond Limits Pty Ltd

26

CLAIM YOUR FREE TICKETS TO *BREAKTHROUGH*

GET FREE TICKETS TO BREAKTHROUGH BEYOND LIMITS — VALUE $297 EACH!

DISCOVER HOW TO CREATE A PERSONAL BREAKTHROUGH IN YOUR CAREER OR YOUR LIFE!

Imagine two transformational days with Rik Schnabel, focusing on removing the psychological blocks and barriers that stand between you and your success. Welcome to *Breakthrough Beyond Limits*! There is something special that happens when you are in the presence of Rik Schnabel — something almost magical and simply by using the web link below, you can come as our guest, completely free of charge! What's more, you can use this link as many times as you like and bring as many of your friends and family as you wish. By buying this book, you save

$297 per person and you can bring anyone with you — FREE!

This is *Life Beyond Limits* service to the wider community — it's our way of giving back. For more information and to claim your free tickets, visit: http://www.lifebeyondlimits.com.au/Breakthrough — Remember to use "**Coupon Code**" 8888 and you can come as our guest — FREE!

WHAT HAPPENS WHEN YOU CHANGE YOUR BELIEFS?

After practicing the principles of this book, here is what some of Rik Schnabel's clients and students from his *Career and Life Mastery* programs (CALM) enjoyed…

At first my new beliefs expanded my paradigm of what is possible. Then they shifted my thinking and helped me to double my income!

—Vlad Platil, Sales Executive, Melbourne, Australia.

After experiencing a stroke I was really struggling. Rik's CALM training helped me to start believing in myself again and find my life's purpose

— Nikki Mennel, Entrepreneur and director of
CheekyChimpSmoothies.com, Brunswick, Australia.

I now realise how my beliefs were creating immense blocks in my life and I am having a ball smashing through those blocks, WOW! My world is continually transforming since my Career and Life Mastery Level 1 and II Training with Rik and Life Beyond Limits. I am constantly sifting and finding gold nuggets throughout the whole journey. Rik's way of experiential teaching is absolutely priceless, a holistic learning experience which has impacted me to the core.

— Nina Shayan, Counsellor/Life Coach,
Glen Waverley, Australia.

I was asked to speak to 500 people at a finance forum for a major public organisation about balancing their life and work. I did not believe I could do this. After one coaching session with Rik, I not only spoke with confidence, but also my talk was so successful that people still mention it years later!!! This was my turning point and since then I have spoken in front of thousands and lives have been changed as a result. Thanks Rik for planting the seeds of belief so deeply that they have grown and flourished and many others have and will continue to benefit as a result.

— Dr Lynn Scoles, GP and Executive Coach, Melbourne, Australia.

Engulfed by the dark clouds of debt and misery, spiralling down, captured and bound by the restraints of a limiting belief, blinding me to any possible way out, I attended one of Rik's CALM training sessions and BANG! A light-bulb moment of realisation and the magic of a belief change has given the sun permission to shine and the winds of change have blown those dark clouds away. Life is awesome!!!

— Rhonda E Abraham, Remedial Massage Therapist and NLP Practitioner, Cranbourne, Australia.

Rik is brilliant at inspiring people to be their best by believing in themselves, as well as explaining the science behind beliefs for the sceptics.

— Pat Macwhirter, Veterinarian, Notting Hill, Australia.

The best thing I did for myself was join Rik and the Life Beyond Limits CALM program. Rik is an amazing trainer who delivers from the heart. His passion and integrity sets the course apart from all others. Rik creates a magical, powerful and empowering series of experiences that took me to a whole different level. The light bulb moments that triggered throughout opened my eyes to my unlimited potential. My only regret is that I didn't learn the power of Life Beyond Limits as a teen!

— Jenny Trad, NLP Trainer, Melbourne, Australia.

Just do it!! If you want to know what to do with your life, find your passion or purpose, Life Beyond Limits will encourage these out of you. Absolutely fantastic!

— Luanne Simmons, Director of Goddess on Purpose, Pearcedale, Australia.

Rik is all heart. He is a passionate writer, coach and change agent. His ability to see beyond what is evident is incredibly empowering. I now have a new career that I love and for the first time, my business is growing and I'm being financially rewarded, WOW!

— Jill Hosken General & Funeral Celebrant, Melbourne, Australia.

Rik Schnabel is the most passionate and charismatic person I know whose very presence demands action!

— Heather Kaesler, Adelaide, South Australia.

I listen to Rik's Hypnotic CDs three to four times a week — they're like magic every time. I relax, I learn and I usually discover something new about myself!

— Michelle Anthony Reiche, Business Owner, Hampton, Australia.

I had depression for six years, under psychiatric care and medicated for four of those years. In one session with Rik I overcame depression! I couldn't believe it was possible, now I do.

— Michael, Sales Executive, Melbourne, Australia.

I now know without a shadow of doubt that there is this great creative process that helps us to manifest; it's all here and now. Thanks a million, no, actually thanks two million!

— Steven Kolakowski, Melbourne, Australia.

NOTES

❋

CHAPTER 1: ARE YOUR BELIEFS YOURS?

1. Leading Personality. 2013, *Get Out of the Box,* http://leadingpersonality. wordpress.com/tag/fleas-in-a-jar-experiment/

❋

CHAPTER 2: THE EVOLUTION OF BELIEFS

1. U.S. Patent and Trademark Office, Electronic Information Products Division — PTMT, Alexandria, Virginia U.S.A, *US Patent Activity Calendar Years 1790 to the Present,* http://www.uspto.gov/web/offices/ac/ido/oeip/taf/h_counts.htm

2. Nick Collins, Science Correspondent at Telegraph 2012 UK, *Nature vs nurture: outcomes depends on where you live,* http://www.telegraph.co.uk/science/ science-news/9326819/Nature-vs-nurture-outcome-depends-on-where-you-live.html

3. Deborah Carr, professor of sociology at Rutgers University, *Most Americans Don't Care About Living Near Family,* http://www.marketwatch.com/story/ most-americans-dont-want-to-live-near-relatives-2013-08-26

4. *Judith Graham, Extension human development specialist. Revised by Leslie A. Forstadt, Ph.D. Child and Family Development Specialist, Children and Brain Development: What We Know About How Children Learn,* http://umaine.edu/ publications/4356e/

5. PBS, *Life in Roman Times,* http://www.pbs.org/empires/romans/empire/life. html

6. Various Authors of The Secret Shropshire Project, *Nineteenth Century Crime and Punishment,* http://www.secretshropshire.org.uk/Content/Learn/Crime/

7. *Author Unknown, Protests in the 1960's, http://www.lessonsite.com/ArchivePages/ HistoryOfTheWorld/Lesson31/Protests60s.htm*

8.   *Wikipedia, Bed In, http://en.wikipedia.org/wiki/Bed-In*

9.   *John F. Kennedy, Inaugural Addresses of the President of the United States*, Friday, January 20, 1961, *http://www.bartleby.com/124/pres56.html*

10.   Julie Bort, *How Many Websites Are There?* 9 March 2012, http://www.businessinsider.com.au/how-many-web-sites-are-are-there-2012-3

11.   Jim and Audri Lanford, Internet Scambusters™ USA. *10 Tips to help you avoid fake anti-virus software scams: Internet Scambusters #232,*, http://www.scambusters.org/fakeantivirus.html

12.   World Health Organisation, *Depression* Fact sheet N°369, October 2012, http://www.who.int/mediacentre/factsheets/fs369/en/

❇

CHAPTER 3: WAKING UP FROM A TRANCE

1.   Time. Health and Family, *Healthy Foods That Really Aren't— Nutritionists Weigh In*, Alexandra Sifferlin, April 19, 2012, http://healthland.time.com/2012/04/24/healthy-foods-that-really-arent-nutritionists-weigh-in/slide/light-yogurt/

❇

CHAPTER 4: THE INVISIBLE BELIEFS THAT GUIDE YOU

1.   Free Press, *Rupert Murdoch Scandal*, http://www.freepress.net/rupert-murdoch-scandal

2.   Yahoo Voices, *Why Jaws is Considered to Be the Most Influential Movie of All Time*, Larry Poupard, June 5, 2007, http://voices.yahoo.com/why-jaws-considered-most-influential-372597.html

3.   Graham Chapman, The Five Love Languages, (Strand Publishing, Australia 2000).

❇

CHAPTER 5: THE CARROT AND THE STICK DOESN'T WORK

1.   Daniel Pink, *Drive* (Canongate Books Ltd, Great Britain, 2010)

2.   Mark Lepper, David Green and Robert Nisbett, Undermining Children's Intrinsic Interest with Extrinsic Rewards: A Test of the Over Justification Hypothesis, Journal of Personality and Social Psychology 28, no. 1 (1973): 129-37

❋

CHAPTER 6: IS YOUR LIFE AN ACCIDENT?

1.   Rik Schnabel, *The Secrets of Creating a Life Beyond Limits*, (Brolga Publishing Pty Ltd, Australia, first printed in 2005)

❋

CHAPTER 8: WHAT ARE BELIEFS *REALLY*?

1.   Bud Bilanich, *50 Famous People Who Failed At Their First Attempt At Career Success*, http://www.budbilanich.com/50-famous-people-who-failed-at-their-first-attempt-at-career-success/

2.   Martin Kojc, *The Manual of Life*, (Self-Published)

3.   Rik Schnabel, *The Secrets of Creating a Life Beyond Limits*, (Brolga Publishing Pty Ltd, Australia, first printed in 2005)

4.   John Davidson, The Secrets of the Creative Vacuum — Man and the Energy Dance, (New Age Books, March 2009)

❋

CHAPTER 10: WHO'S DRIVING YOUR BUS?

1.   Louise Hay and Cheryl Richardson, *You Can Create An Exceptional Life,* (Hay House, Inc. Carlsbad, California USA, 2011)

※

CHAPTER 10: WHY YOUR BRAIN OBEYS YOUR BELIEFS?

1. Albert A. Abbot, *Flatland — A Romance of Many Dimensions,* (Dover Publications, Inc. Mineola, New York USA, 1992)

※

CHAPTER 12: BELIEF #1 — IT'S NOT SAFE TO BE ME

1. Brian Tracy, *Fight or Flight: Overcoming Your Fears.* (Brain Tracy's Blog October 2011 — Brian Tracy International California, USA), http://www.briantracy.com/blog/personal-success/fight-or-flight-overcoming-your-fears/

2. Brendan L. Smith, *The case against spanking. Physical discipline is slowly declining as some studies reveal lasting harms for children.* April 2012, Vol 43, No. 4 Print Version: page 60 (American Psychological Association, Washington USA), http://www.apa.org/monitor/2012/04/spanking.aspx

3. Jan Hunt, *Ten Reasons Not to Hit Your Kids. 2002,* (EPOCH Worldwide, London UK), http://www.naturalchild.org/jan_hunt/tenreasons.html

4. Tom Johnson, *The Sexual Dangers of Spanking Children. 2002,* (Alamo, California USA), http://nospank.net/sdsc.pdf

5. Rik Schnabel and Life Beyond Limits Pty Ltd, *Career And Life Mastery (C.A.L.M) NLP Practitioner and Life Coach Training, 2013,* (Melbourne, Victoria Australia), http://www.lifebeyondlimits.com.au/calm-i.html

6. Ben Benjamin, PhD and Ruth Werner, LMT, *The Primacy of Human Touch,* http://www.benbenjamin.net/pdfs/Issue2.pdf

※

CHAPTER 13: BELIEF #2 — I'M NOT LUCKY

1. Jeff Hadden, *Your Secret Underwear* — (INC, USA 2012), http://www.inc.com/jeff-haden/the-performance-boost-found-in-your-underwear.html

2. Richard Wiseman, *How to Get Lucky: Scientific proof that you make your own breaks* — (Readers Digest), http://www.rd.com/advice/how-to-get-lucky/#ixzz2i9LL6pWs

CHAPTER 14: BELIEF #3 — IT'S EITHER GOOD OR BAD

1. David Rock and Jeffrey Schwartz, *The Neuroscience of Leadership*, http://www.strategy-business.com/article/06207

2. Derek Lin, *Tao Te Ching: Tao and Virtue Classic (*www.Taoism.net and *Tao Te Ching: Annotated & Explained*, published by SkyLight Paths in 2006), http://www.taoism.net/ttc/complete.htm

3. Louise Hay and Cheryl Richardson, *You Can Create An Exceptional Life,* (Hay House, Inc. Carlsbad, California USA, 2011)

4. Rik Schnabel, *The Secrets of Creating a Life Beyond Limits*, (Brolga Publishing Pty Ltd, Australia, first printed in 2005)

❈

CHAPTER 15: BELIEF #4 — I DON'T HAVE ENOUGH MONEY

1. World Food Programme, *Hunger Statistics 2013* , http://www.wfp.org/hunger/stats

2. The Centre for Global Prosperity, The Hudson Institute, *The Index of Global Philanthropy and Remittances 2013* , http://www.hudson.org/files/documents/2013IndexofGlobalPhilanthropyandRemittances.pdf

❈

CHAPTER 16: BELIEF #5 — I DON'T HAVE ENOUGH TIME

1. David Rock and Jeffrey Schwartz, *The Neuroscience of Leadership*, http://www.strategy-business.com/article/06207

2. Wikipedia 2011, *List of Countries by Life Expectancy*, http://en.wikipedia.org/wiki/List_of_countries_by_life_expectancy

3. David Rock and Jeffrey Schwartz, *The Neuroscience of Leadership*, http://www.strategy-business.com/article/06207

❈

CHAPTER 17: BELIEF #6 — I'M NOT ENOUGH

1. David Rock and Jeffrey Schwartz, *The Neuroscience of Leadership*, http://www.strategy-business.com/article/06207

✻

CHAPTER 18: BELIEF #7 — IT RUNS IN MY FAMILY, IT'S GENETIC

1. Debra J. Holt, Pauline M. Ippolito, Debra M. Desrochers, Christopher R. Kelley, *Children's Exposure to TV Advertising in 1977 and 2004, Information for the Obesity Debate* (Federal Trade Commission Bureau of Economic Statistics, June 2007 USA), http://www.ftc.gov/os/2007/06/cabecolor.pdf

2. Mary L. Gavin, MD, *Overweight and Obesity* (Kids Health 2012 USA), http://kidshealth.org/parent/general/body/overweight_obesity.html

3. *Overweight and Obesity* (Australian Bureau of Statistics 2009 Australia) Mary L. Gavin, MD, *Children Who Are Overweight or Obese* (Kids Health 2012 USA), http://www.ausstats.abs.gov.au/ausstats/subscriber.nsf/LookupAttach/4102.0Publication24.09.093/$File/41020_Childhoodobesity.pdf

4. *Millionaire Club – Wealth Creation Tips That Work* (The Sydney Morning Herald 2011 Australia) David Wilson, http://www.lifebeyondlimits.com.au/blog/millionarie-club-wealth-creation-tips-that-work.html

✻

CHAPTER 19: IMAGINATION WILL CHANGE YOUR BELIEFS

1. Rik Schnabel, *The Secrets of Creating a Life Beyond Limits*, (Brolga Publishing Pty Ltd, Australia, first printed in 2005)

✻

CHAPTER 21: THE BODY BELIEF CHANGE

1. Dr Harriet Braiker, *The Disease to Please*, (McGraw-Hill Books, New York, USA, 2001), http://unhealthyrelationships.wordpress.com/verbal-abuse/heart-beliefs/

2. Adam Hadhazy, *Think Twice: How the Gut's "Second Brain" Influences Mood and Well-Being,* (Scientific American, USA, Febrary 12, 2010), http://www.scientificamerican.com/article.cfm?id=gut-second-brain

3. Richard Sheers, *Do hearts have memories? Transplant patient gets craving for food eaten by organ donor*, (The Daily Mail, UK, 23 December 2009), http://www.dailymail.co.uk/news/article-1237998/Heart-transplant-patient-gets-craving-food-eaten-organ-donor.html

4. Robert K. Blechman, *The Heart of the Matter: An Exploration of the Persistence of Core Beliefs*, (St Georges University, New York, USA, 2005), http://www.media-ecology.org/publications/MEA_proceedings/v6/Blechman.pdf

5. Anil K Rajvanshi, *The 3 Minds of the Body; Brain, Heart and Gut*, (Nimbkar Agricultural Research Institute (NARI), India May 2011), http://www.nariphaltan.org/gut.pdf

LIFE BEYOND LIMITS
TRAINING PROGRAMS

❋

CAREER AND LIFE MASTERY LEVEL I

NLP PRACTITIONER AND
LIFE COACH CERTIFICATE TRAINING

Most people enrol in this program because they want to learn how to unleash their true potential by improving their thought patterns and get more from their lives. Some quickly realise the power of these tools and insights and create a second income by starting a new career as a *Life Coach* or *Neuro Linguistic Programming Practitioner* and *Hypnotherapist*.

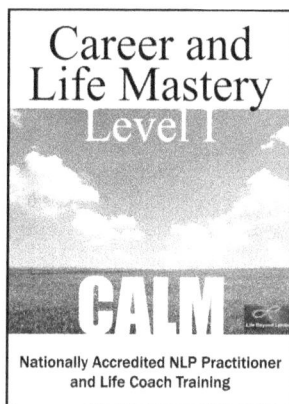

Career and
Life Mastery
Level I

CALM

Nationally Accredited NLP Practitioner
and Life Coach Training

If accelerating your career, improving your relationships, health and wealth are important to you — this program delivers. You will learn how to dramatically improve your thinking using the most revolutionary psychological tools available today. You will discover how your mind *really* works and gain quick, practical tools that hold the power to turn your life around, without drugs and without pain. If you're not creating the career or the life that you want now, commit to learning Neuro-Linguistic Programming and the exclusive tools at *Career and Life Mastery Level I* (CALM I).

This program is a nationally accredited program and includes three certifications as a Life Coach, an NLP Practitioner and an Ericksonian Hypnotherapist. For more information visit: http://www.lifebeyondlimits.com.au/calm-i.html_

✻

CAREER AND LIFE MASTERY LEVEL II

NLP MASTER PRACTITIONER & LIFE COACH CERTIFICATE TRAINING

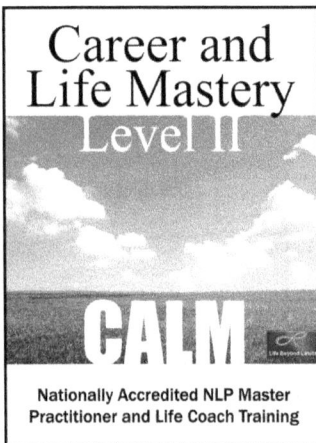

Career and Life Mastery Level II

CALM

Nationally Accredited NLP Master Practitioner and Life Coach Training

This is Part II of our CALM program. It's called "Masters" because our participants truly learn how to *master* every area of their lives.

In this program you will discover how your beliefs cluster into values that become the invisible rudders of your life. You will learn how to uncover the values that are creating the life you are currently living and then change them — this will completely transform your career and your life! This training delivers within you a feeling of power and a sense of calm and peace.

On completion of this course, you will discover why leaders, managers, life coaches, teachers and those with a big vision highly value the insights, the tools and personal shifts they gain from *Career And Life Mastery Level II — Master Practitioner Training*.

This program is a nationally accredited program and includes three certifications as a Master Life Coach, a Master NLP Practitioner and a Master Ericksonian Hypnotherapist. For more information visit: http://www.lifebeyondlimits.com. au/nlp-training/nlp-masters/

�֎

SPEAKING WITH CONFIDENCE

NLP PRESENTERS CERTIFICATE TRAINING (PART I OF TRAINERS TRAINING)

Confident, powerful and effective presenting is more than just stagecraft and PowerPoint slide design. When you apply Rik Schnabel's unique approach to best practice, you'll literally watch your audiences make life-changing shifts before your eyes. You'll shift too as you remove the fear of being yourself in front of an audience and discover the art of confidence. You can take what you'll learn into your social interactions, business presentations and sales calls. Everyone will

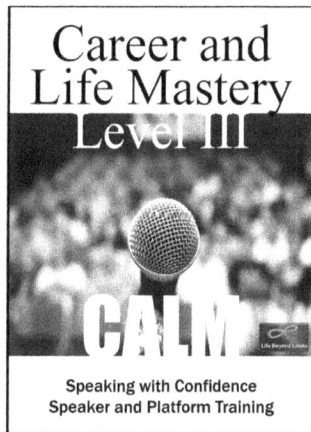

Career and Life Mastery Level III

CALM

Speaking with Confidence
Speaker and Platform Training

massively benefit from this confidence-building program.

This training forms part one of our NLP Trainers' Training and so therefore expect a high level of speaker insights that even most professional speakers don't know. You'll discover; how to put together a talk in a tenth of the time it normally takes; learn to memorise your talk; follow our 'expertise pattern' to launch your speaking, training or coaching career; discover how to transform your story into a six or seven figure income; and turn your *fear* into *fabulous*;

Whether you're a professional or you have never been on a stage — this course will take you to a whole new level of speaker mastery. For more information visit: http://www.lifebeyondlimits.com.au/nlp-training/nlp-presenters/

❋

TRAINERS TRAINING

NLP TRAINERS CERTIFICATE TRAINING
(PART II OF TRAINERS TRAINING)

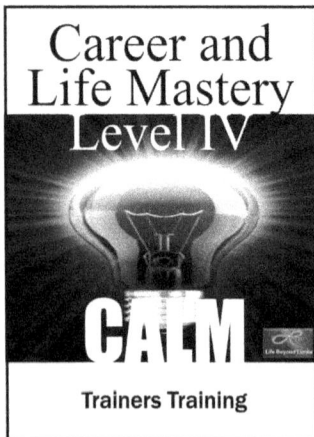

Our vision is to train and coach leaders to step up to the world stage and help others to reach their highest potential.

If you have a passion burning inside you and you love taking people beyond their limits, then let us help you to do that. You will use our systems, our templates, our formulas for success to deliver your message into the hearts and minds of others. You will become part of what we believe is the biggest transformation in the history of the world — the age of truth — the world's upgrade to Conscious Awareness — *Version 5.0* thinking.

This training, coupled with *Level III — Speaking with Confidence* is a nationally accredited *NLP Trainers Training*. On completing this course you will be able to generate a prosperous lifestyle doing what you love. We'll show you how.

For more information visit: http://www.lifebeyondlimits. com.au/nlp-training/nlp-trainers/

✳

GET WHAT YOU WANT, BY WORKING WITH ONE OF OUR COACHES

ENJOY A ONE ON ONE, PERSONAL BREAKTHROUGH IN YOUR CAREER OR YOUR LIFE!

If you could only get out of your current thinking and start thinking *beyond your limits* — imagine what you could achieve?

One of the best ways to accomplish success is to work one on one with a personal or business coach. *Life Beyond Limits* have a variety of highly trained, professional coaches to help you get beyond your paradigms and more so, they're

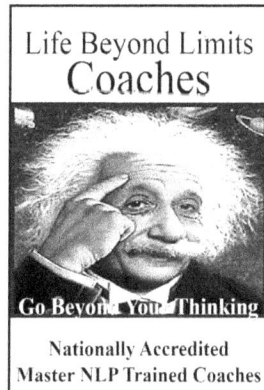

Life Beyond Limits
Coaches

Go Beyond Your Thinking

Nationally Accredited
Master NLP Trained Coaches

all NLP trained to Masters level. Plus they've worked with a large selection of people with all sorts of challenges — and it's amazing how by using NLP, you can get to the very core of your problems, in what might take a genius months — it takes our coaches less than a quarter of the time!

If you've never worked with a coach before, we provide a free half hour chat with one of our coaches to find out how we can help and to get comfortable with your coach — before you invest a cent. You'll soon discover that making this decision was the best thing you've ever done!

To find out more and check out our coaches, visit: http://www.lifebeyondlimits.com.au/our-nlp-coaches.html

ABOUT THE AUTHOR

✳

RIK SCHNABEL is a respected authority in behavioural change. He's Australia's #1 Brain Untrainer and is one of the most passionate people you'll meet in self-development. He believes we're over thinking our problems and by untraining our brain will uncover our solutions. He's an entertaining heart-led speaker and enchants audiences around the world.

He's an internationally recognised and nationally accredited Life Coach Trainer and a Trainer of Neuro-Linguistic Programming (NLP) and Neurological Repatterning™. He is also an NLP Master Practitioner, Master Hypnotherapist and Master Results Coach.

He loves surfing and being a father of two spirited daughters, and is married to Rebecca, a highly clairvoyant and Intuitive Coach who is equally respected for her powerful work.

His previous book, *The Secrets of Creating a Life Beyond Limits* enthralled audiences with his profound insights into the metaphysical and the psychological world of wealth, yet included simple principles that govern success. One reviewer exclaimed it's the *Reader's Digest* of Self-Development with its comprehensive approach to transformation.

Prior to working in the field of personal and professional development, Rik was a highly successful Marketing Manager for News Limited and a respected Creative Director in Advertising. He was also the founder of Whozu Advertising & Marketing, and Schnabel & Knights Advertising and an XL Results Foundation Member who helped Entrepreneurs from around the world to connect with each other.

You can connect with Rik via:

rik.schnabel@lifebeyondlimits.com.au

DIGITAL WISDOM
CHANGE YOUR THINKING WHILE YOU SLEEP!

We spend a third of our life asleep. For the average person, that equates to 198,560 hours of opportunity lost over a lifetime! Wouldn't it be great if you could put that time to use? New research suggests you can. According to *Science News*, the brain is not passive while you sleep. It's quite active. New information can ease into your mind and you can benefit while sleeping. A recent study, published in *Nature Neuroscience*, demonstrates that we can learn new information while we sleep and with no conscious knowledge of it.

Through *Digital Wisdom*, you can download *Life Beyond Limits* full range of hypnotic audios that help you to reprogram your thinking in powerful ways and to have you become more resourceful. The aim of *Digital Wisdom* is to become the Internet's Number 1 Resource Centre for people looking to improve their lives. They have made the site incredibly easy to navigate so anyone can easily find what they're looking for.

To find out more and download any of our audio programs, visit: http://www.digitalwisdom.eu

THE POWER OF BELIEFS
RIK SCHNABEL

		Qty
ISBN 9781922175434		
RRP	AU$24.99	.....
Postage within Australia	AU$5.00	.....
	TOTAL* $_____	
	* All prices include GST	

Name:...

Address: ....

....

Phone:..

Email: ....

Payment: ❏ Money Order ❏ Cheque ❏ MasterCard ❏ Visa

Cardholders Name:...

Credit Card Number: ....

Signature:..

Expiry Date: ....

Allow 7 days for delivery.

Payment to: Marzocco Consultancy (ABN 14 067 257 390)
PO Box 12544
A'Beckett Street, Melbourne, 8006
Victoria, Australia
admin@brolgapublishing.com.au

Be Published

Publish through a successful publisher.
Brolga Publishing is represented through:
• **National** book trade distribution, including sales,
marketing & distribution through Dennis Jones and
Associates Australia.
• **International** book trade distribution to
    • The United Kingdom
    • North America
    • Sales representation in South East Asia
• **Worldwide e-Book distribution**

For details and inquiries, contact:
Brolga Publishing Pty Ltd
PO Box 12544
A'Beckett St VIC 8006

Phone: 0414 608 494
markzocchi@brolgapublishing.com.au
ABN: 46 063 962 443
(Email for a catalogue request)

* 9 7 8 1 9 2 2 1 7 5 4 3 4 *